MUSIC
AN APPRECIATION

W9-BIN-944

ALSO BY ROGER KAMIEN

Music: An Appreciation, Fourth Edition

This highly acclaimed, comprehensive introductory textbook provides forty-two listening outlines and profiles on sixty-two composers; gives detailed discussions of music and musicians in society; has separate parts on the Middle Ages, the Renaissance, jazz, rock, and nonwestern music; and includes technical appendixes, a bibliography, and a chronology. It is generously illustrated with color plates and black-and-white photographs.

Music: An Appreciation is accompanied by an eight-record set, an eight-cassette set, and a two-record instructor's set; a *Study Guide and Student Workbook*; an *Instructor's Manual*; and a *Test File* and *Computerized Test Generator*.

BRIEF
EDITION

Roger Kamien

Zubin Mehta Chair in Musicology,
The Hebrew University of Jerusalem

Professor Emeritus:
Queens College of the City University of New York

McGraw-Hill Publishing Company

New York   St. Louis   San Francisco   Auckland   Bogotá
Caracas   Hamburg   Lisbon   London   Madrid   Mexico   Milan
Montreal   New Delhi   Oklahoma City   Paris   San Juan
São Paulo   Singapore   Sydney   Tokyo   Toronto

This book was set in Palatino by York Graphic Services, Inc.
The editors were Lesley Denton, Marian D. Provenzano, and Susan Gamer;
the designer was Joan E. O'Connor;
the production supervisor was Salvador Gonzales.
The photo editors were Elsa Peterson and Inge King.
The permissions editor was Elsa Peterson.
Arcata Graphics/Halliday was printer and binder.

Cover Credit: The Red Orchestra by Raoul Dufy.
Courtesy of Mrs. Charlotte Bergman in agreement
with the Israel Museum, Jerusalem.

MUSIC: AN APPRECIATION

Copyright © 1990, 1988, 1984, 1980, 1976 by McGraw-Hill, Inc.
All rights reserved. Printed in the United States of America.
Except as permitted under the United States Copyright Act of 1976,
no part of this publication may be reproduced or distributed in
any form or by any means, or stored in a data base or retrieval
system, without the prior written permission of the publisher.

4567890 HDHD 99876543210

ISBN 0-07-033568-0

Acknowledgments appear on pages 329–330; copyrights are
included on this page by reference.

Library of Congress Cataloging-in-Publication Data

Kamien, Roger.
  Music, an appreciation.

  Includes index.
  1. Music appreciation.   I. Title.
MT6.K22M9   1990   781.1'7   89-8068
ISBN 0-07-033568-0

For Anita, David, Joshua, and Adina

CONTENTS

LISTENING OUTLINES LISTED BY COMPOSER

PREFACE

Music: An Appreciation—Brief Edition is intended for introductory college courses lasting from eight to fifteen weeks. My goal has been to write a book that is concise yet clear, accurate, and engaging, useful both for study and in the classroom.

This text provides an approach to perceptive listening and an introduction to musical elements, forms, and stylistic periods. Its discussions of composers' lives, individual styles, and representative works aim not merely to impart facts but to stimulate readers' curiosity and enthusiasm and heighten their love of music. Many listening outlines are included, to help students concentrate more easily on the musical compositions discussed; and many of these compositions are available on the two-cassette package accompanying the text.

The Brief Edition is a condensation of *Music: An Appreciation*, Fourth Edition (it is about 350 pages shorter), and retains the general organization and the special features that have been so popular with readers.

HOW THE BRIEF EDITION IS ORGANIZED

Part I of the Brief Edition examines the elements of music both in general terms and with reference to attractive, brief illustrative pieces. Notation is used sparingly here—usually in connection with familiar tunes that allow students to begin by analyzing music they have known since childhood.

Parts II through VI deal with periods of music history from the Middle Ages and Renaissance through the present. Jazz and rock are considered within Part VI, The Twentieth Century; nonwestern musical instruments are discussed in Part I, Elements. Each of Parts II through VI opens with a section providing background material and a stylistic overview of the period. Then, in the sections that follow, forms, trends, and representative composers and works are discussed.

Through exposure to a variety of compositions, students are encouraged to develop their listening skills. And the color plates and black-and-white photographs help readers relate music to its cultural context.

A Glossary, a Chronology, and a guide to the accompanying recordings are provided at the end of the book.

KEY FEATURES

Listening Outlines

A distinctive feature of *Music: An Appreciation* is the use of "listening outlines" to be followed while the compositions are heard. A listening outline focuses attention on musical events as they unfold and is easy to follow because it describes what students can readily hear. These outlines are useful for outside listening assignments as well as for classroom work. (A list of listening outlines is given on pages xvii–xviii.)

Opera Texts

The study of opera is aided in this book by excerpts from librettos; these appear with brief marginal notes that indicate the relationship between words and music and help readers follow the drama.

Flexibility

The Brief Version takes a chronological approach but can be adapted easily to individual teaching methods. Each stylistic period is subdivided into short, relatively independent sections that can be studied in any order; some could even be omitted.

Music examples—and notation—can also be treated flexibly. Basic notation is described in Part I, and music examples are given throughout, providing visual aids for those who want them. But the discussions of compositions require no knowledge of music notation; students may prefer simply to read the text and skip the details of notation.

Readability

Clarity of expression has been a chief goal. This is a book that students can feel comfortable with. They will recognize that it was written for them by a musician who loves music and who wants to convey its essentials without creating confusion or boredom.

The biographical sketches and descriptions of composers' individual styles attempt to give the flavor of each composer's personality and music, using anecdotes and quotations to enliven the discussion. Musical terms are defined simply and appear in **bold italic** type, and these terms and their definitions appear in the Glossary.

SUPPLEMENTARY MATERIALS

1. *Recordings*: As mentioned above, the Brief Edition is accompanied by two cassettes (180 minutes in all) that include complete compositions or movements representing many of the works discussed in the text. So that the cassettes can be easily used with the text, marginal notes in the text refer the reader to the appropriate side and band.

    Accompanying *Music: An Appreciation*, Fourth Edition, are an eight-record/cassette package and a two-record instructor's set, which may also be used to accompany the Brief Edition. These include all but one of the compositions discussed in the Brief Edition and are also keyed to the Brief Edition through marginal notes, as described above.

2. *Study Guide and Student Workbook*: The Study Guide/Workbook, developed by Professor Raoul Camus to interact with the text, provides students with exercises, reviews, self-tests, and other materials.

3. *Instructor's Manual/Test Bank*: This manual, also by Professor Camus, follows the organization of the text and provides objectives, suggested classroom activities, listening experiences, questions, discussion topics, student essays, and exams. The test file contains multiple-choice, completion, true-false, and matching questions.

4. *Computerized Test Generator*: For Apple and IBM computers, Microexaminer contains all questions found in the test bank within the Instructor's Manual.

ACKNOWLEDGMENTS

I am grateful to the academic reviewers of the Brief Edition: James Anthony, Towson State University; Raoul Camus, Queensborough Community College; Steven C. Edwards, Franklin and Marshall College; Sharon Girard, San Francisco State University; Kenneth Keeling, University of Rhode Island; Leo Kreter, California State University, Fullerton; Jerome Laszloffy, University of Connecticut, Storrs; Patricia Root, Washington State University, Pullman; Joseph A. Salvatore, York College of Pennsylvania; Richard C. Sang, Queens College, CUNY; and Mary Alice Spencer, South Dakota State University.

In addition, of course, the contribution of the reviewers of *Music: An Appreciation*, Fourth Edition, continues to be felt in the Brief Edition—as does the generous help I received from colleagues in the music department of Queens College.

I am also grateful to my editors at McGraw-Hill: Phillip A. Butcher, Lesley Denton, Cynthia Ward, Marion Provenzano, and Susan Gamer; the designer, Joan O'Connor; and the production supervisor, Salvador Gonzales. My deep thanks go to Susan Gamer for her invaluable help in abridging the text, and to Phillip Butcher for initiating the project.

My gratitude, also, to Raoul Camus for the fine *Study Guide and Student Workbook* and the *Instructor's Manual* which accompany the text.

Finally, as with all the editions of *Music: An Appreciation*, the advice and encouragement of my wife, Anita Kamien, have helped to shape this new Brief Edition.

Roger Kamien

MUSIC
AN APPRECIATION

ELEMENTS

All the musical elements come together when people play or sing.

[1] SOUND: PITCH, DYNAMICS, AND TONE COLOR

Sounds bombard our ears every day—the squeaks and honks of traffic, a child's laugh, a dog's bark, the patter of rain. Through them we learn what's going on; we need them to communicate. By listening to speech, cries, and laughter, we learn what others think and feel. Silence—an absence of sound—also communicates. When we hear no sounds of traffic in the street, we assume that no cars are passing. When someone doesn't answer a question or breaks off in the middle of a sentence, we quickly notice and draw conclusions.

What is sound? What causes it, and how do we hear it? *Sound* begins with the vibration of an object, such as a table that is pounded or a string that is plucked. The vibrations are transmitted to our ears by a *medium*—usually air—and our eardrums start vibrating too. As a result, *impulses*, or signals, are sent to the brain, where they are selected, organized, and interpreted.

Music is part of the world of sound, an art based on the organization of sounds in time. We distinguish music from other sounds by recognizing the four main properties of musical sounds: *pitch* (highness or lowness); *dynamics* (loudness or softness); *tone color* (quality); and *duration, or rhythm* (time). We'll look now at pitch, dynamics, and tone color; duration is discussed in Section 3, "Rhythm."

PITCH: HIGHNESS OR LOWNESS OF SOUND

Pitch is the relative highness or lowness that we hear in a sound. When you sing the beginning of *The Star-Spangled Banner*, for example, the pitch on *see* is higher than the pitch on *say*:

see,
•

Oh,   you
•   •

•   can
•

say!
•

The pitch of a sound is determined by the *frequency* of its vibrations—

that is, their speed, which is measured in cycles per second. The faster the vibrations, the higher the pitch; the slower the vibrations, the lower the pitch. All other things being equal, smaller objects vibrate faster and have higher pitches: thus plucking a short string produces a higher pitch than plucking a long string.

In music, a sound that has a definite pitch is called a **tone**. It has a specific frequency, such as 440 cycles per second. The vibrations of a tone are regular and reach the ear at equal time intervals. But noiselike sounds (the squeal of brakes or the clash of cymbals) have an indefinite pitch and are produced by irregular vibrations.

Two tones will sound different when they have different pitches. The "distance" in pitch between any two tones is called an **interval**. When tones are separated by the interval called an **octave**, they sound very much alike. Sing the opening of *The Star-Spangled Banner* again. Notice that the tone you produce on *see* sounds like your tone on *say*, even though it's higher. An octave lies between them. The vibration frequency of the *say* tone is exactly half that of the *see* tone. If the *say* tone were 440 cycles per second, the *see* tone—an octave higher—would be 880 cycles per second. A tone an octave lower than the *say* tone would be half of 440, or 220 cycles per second. When sounded at the same time, two tones an octave apart blend so well that they seem almost to merge into one tone.

The octave is important in music. It is the interval between the first and last tones of the familiar scale:

$$do \quad re \quad mi \quad fa \quad sol \quad la \quad ti \quad do$$

If you sing this, starting with the low *do* and ending on the high *do* which "duplicates" it, you will fill the octave with seven different pitches, rather than sliding up like a siren. This group of seven tones (they are produced by the white keys of a piano) was the basis of western music for centuries. Eventually, five more pitches were added (the black keys on the piano), making twelve tones in all, each of which is "duplicated" in higher and lower octaves. (In nonwestern music, the octave may be divided into a different number of tones.)

The distance between the lowest and highest tones that a voice or an instrument can produce is called its **pitch range** or simply its **range**. The range of an average untrained voice is about 1½ octaves; a piano's range is over 7 octaves.

The organization of pitch is a composer's first resource. In Sections 5 and 6, where melody and harmony are explored, we will look at how pitch is organized. For now, we'll simply observe that composers can create a special mood in their music by using very low or very high pitches. For example, low pitches can intensify the sadness of a funeral march; high pitches

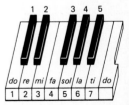

Seven different tones are produced by the white keys of the piano.

can make a dance sound lighter. And a steady rise in pitch often increases musical tension.

Though most music we know is based on definite rather than indefinite pitches, noiselike sounds—such as those made by a bass drum or by cymbals—figure strongly in the rhythmic aspects of music. In parts of Africa, the indefinite pitches of drums are very important. And with recent developments in electronic music, indefinite pitches have come to play a vital role in western music as well.

DYNAMICS

Degrees of loudness or softness in music are called *dynamics*—our second property of sound. Loudness is related to the *amplitude*, or width, of the vibration that produces a sound. When instruments are played more loudly or more softly, or when there is a change in how many instruments are heard, a dynamic change—which can be sudden or gradual—results. A performer can emphasize a tone by playing it more loudly than the tones around it; this is called a *dynamic accent*.

Skillful, subtle changes of dynamics add spirit and mood to performances; they may be written into the music, but often they are unwritten and are inspired by the performer's feelings. Today, the technology of musical instruments has greatly increased the range of dynamics.

When notating music, composers have traditionally used Italian words, and their abbreviations, to indicate dynamics. The most common terms are:

✷ Know meaning ✷

Term	Abbreviation	✷Meaning✷
pianissimo	*pp*	very soft
piano	*p*	soft
mezzo piano	*mp*	moderately soft
mezzo forte	*mf*	moderately loud
forte	*f*	loud
fortissimo	*ff*	very loud

For extremes of softness and loudness, composers use *ppp* or *pppp* and *fff* or *ffff*. The following notations indicate gradual changes in dynamics:

Symbol	Term	Meaning
>	decrescendo (decresc.) *or* diminuendo (dim.)	gradually softer
<	crescendo (cresc.)	gradually louder

Like many elements in music, dynamic indications are not absolute: a tone has a dynamic level—is soft or loud—in relation to other tones around it.

TONE COLOR

We can tell a trumpet from a flute even when they are playing the same tone at the same dynamic level. The quality that distinguishes them—our third property of sound—is called **tone color** or **timbre** (pronounced *tam'-ber*). Tone color is described by words like *bright, dark, brilliant, mellow,* and *rich*.

Changes in tone color create variety and contrast: for example, the same melody will have different expressive effects when it is played by one instrument and then another, or a new tone color may be used to highlight a new melody. Tone color also contributes to continuity; it is easier to recognize the return of a melody if the same instruments play it each time. And specific instruments can reinforce a melody's emotional impact—in fact, composers often invent melodies for particular instruments.

A practically unlimited variety of tone colors is available to composers: instruments (see Section 2) can be combined in various ways, and modern electronic techniques now allow composers to invent entirely new colors.

LISTENING OUTLINES AND THE PROPERTIES OF SOUND

To understand the properties of musical sound, we must *listen for them*. In this book, listening outlines—which should be read *as you are listening to the music*—will help focus your attention on musical events as they unfold.

Each item in a listening outline describes some musical sound, such as dynamics, prominent instruments, pitch, or mood (but remember that indications of mood are subjective). Before you listen to a piece of music, glance over the entire outline; then, as you listen to each item, look ahead to see what's next.

Every listening outline is preceded by a description of the music's main features. Instrumentation, approximate duration, and recording notes (where important) are also given.

Here are our first two listening outlines.

LOHENGRIN, PRELUDE TO ACT III,
BY RICHARD WAGNER

Wagner makes wide and brilliant use of dynamic contrasts in the Prelude to Act III of *Lohengrin* to set the scene for the wedding of the opera's hero and heroine. The prelude opens with a feeling of exultation—great energy is conveyed by the massive sound of the full orchestra. Later, the music

Side C, band 2
[*8-record/cassette set:*
Side 11, band 3]

suddenly becomes calm and gentle as we hear fewer instruments, playing softly. This is followed by another sudden contrast when Wagner again employs the full orchestra.

Listening Outline To be read while music is heard

LOHENGRIN, PRELUDE TO ACT III (1848),
BY RICHARD WAGNER (1813–1883)*

3 flutes, 3 oboes, 3 clarinets, 3 bassoons, 4 French horns, 3 trumpets, 3 trombones, bass tuba, timpani, triangle, cymbals, tambourine, 1st violins, 2d violins, violas, cellos, double basses

(About 3½ minutes)

1. *a.* Full orchestra, very loud *(ff)*, main melody in violins, cymbal crashes.
   b. Brass melody, pulsating accompaniment in strings.
   c. Full orchestra, main melody in violins, cymbal crashes.
2. Soft *(p)*, contrasting oboe melody. Melody repeated by flute. Clarinet and violins continue.
3. *a.* Full orchestra, very loud *(ff)*, main melody in violins, cymbal crashes.
   b. Brass melody, pulsating accompaniment in strings.
   c. Cymbals. Becomes softer (decrescendo). Becomes very loud, brass proclamation at end.

HOTTER THAN THAT, BY LOUIS ARMSTRONG AND HIS HOT FIVE

Side D, band 6
[*8-record/cassette set:*
Side 15, band 8]

A succession of different tone colors contributes to the variety within *Hotter Than That,* for jazz band. After an introduction played by the full band, we hear solos by the trumpet, clarinet, voice, guitar, and trombone. Louis Armstrong performs as both trumpeter and vocalist. His singing is like his trumpet playing in sound and style. Instead of lyrics he sings nonsense syllables like *dat-a bat-a dip-da.* In one section, the guitarist, Lonnie Johnson, imitates the melodic phrases sung by Armstrong, whose voice takes on a guitarlike twang.

Unlike the preceding composition by Wagner, this music was improvised by the performers. Their point of departure was the tune *Hotter Than That,* by Lillian Hardin Armstrong, the band's pianist.

Within item 2 of the listening outline, the trumpet is momentarily heard alone, without its accompaniment of piano and guitar. This unaccompanied solo should not be mistaken for the entrance of the clarinet (item 3), which sounds like a high-pitched whine.

*With concert ending.

Listening Outline   To be read while music is heard

HOTTER THAN THAT (1927),
BY LOUIS ARMSTRONG (1900–1971) AND HIS HOT FIVE

Voice, clarinet, trumpet, trombone, piano, banjo, guitar

(About 3 minutes)

1. All instruments, trumpet predominates.
2. Trumpet accompanied by piano and guitar. Trumpet briefly alone, piano and guitar rejoin.
3. Clarinet, high-pitched whine, piano and guitar accompany.
4. Voice, guitar accompaniment.
5. Voice imitated by guitar. Piano leads into
6. *a.* Muted trombone accompanied by piano and guitar.
   b. Trumpet, all instruments join. Guitar, trumpet, guitar at end.

PERFORMING MEDIA: VOICES AND INSTRUMENTS

ELEMENTS

2

VOICES

Throughout history, singing has been the most widespread and familiar way of making music. Singers seem always to have had a magnetic appeal, and the exchange between singer and audience contains a bit of magic—something direct and spellbinding. The singer becomes an instrument with a unique ability to fuse words and musical tones.

For many reasons, it is difficult to sing well. In singing we use wider ranges of pitch and volume than in speaking, and we hold vowel sounds longer. Singing demands a greater supply and control of breath. Air from the lungs is controlled by the lower abdominal muscles and the diaphragm. The air makes the vocal cords vibrate, and the singer's lungs, throat, mouth, and nose come into play to produce the desired sound. The pitch of the tone varies with the tension of the vocal cords; the tighter they are, the higher the pitch.

The range of a singer's voice depends on both physical makeup and training. Professional singers can command 2 octaves or even more, whereas an untrained voice is usually limited to about 1½ octaves. Men's vocal cords are longer and thicker than women's, and this difference produces a lower range. The classification of voice ranges for women and men follows, arranged from highest to lowest; the four basic voice ranges are soprano, alto, tenor, and bass:

Women	*Men*
soprano	tenor
mezzo-soprano	baritone
alto (or contralto)	bass

Methods and styles of singing vary from culture to culture, and even within a culture: for instance, in the west, classical, popular, jazz, folk, and rock music are all sung differently.

Until the late 1600s, most of the music of western culture was vocal. Since then, instrumental music has rivaled vocal music in importance; but composers have continued to write vocal works—both solo and choral—with and without instrumental accompaniment (which can range from a single guitar or piano to an entire orchestra).

MUSICAL INSTRUMENTS

An instrument may be defined as any mechanism—other than the voice—that produces musical sounds. Western instruments are usually classified in six broad categories: *string* (such as guitar and violin); *woodwind* (flute, clarinet); *brass* (trumpet, trombone); *percussion* (bass drum, cymbals); *keyboard* (organ, piano); and *electronic* (synthesizer).

Compositions are written for solo instruments and combinations of two or more instruments up to orchestras with over 100 musicians. A group may include instruments of only one category (say, strings) or several. Modern symphony orchestras have string, woodwind, brass, percussion, and sometimes keyboard instruments (see the illustration); bands consist mainly of brass, woodwind, and percussion instruments.

An instrument is often made in different sizes that produce different ranges. For instance, there are soprano, alto, tenor, baritone, and bass saxophones. A single instrument's tone color may vary according to the *register*—the part of its total range—in which it is played. A clarinet, for example, sounds dark and rich in its low register but brilliant and piercing in its high register. Most instruments have a wider range than the voice: many command 3 or 4 octaves, and some have 6 or 7. Instruments also produce tones more rapidly than the voice. When writing for a specific instrument, a composer must consider its range, its dynamics, and how fast it produces tones.

(Photo by Marianne Barcellona)

Above: The New York Philharmonic orchestra.

*Below: Typical seating plan for a large orchestra (about 100 instrumentalists),
showing the distribution of instruments and the podium where the conductor stands.*

Woodwinds	Brass	Strings	Percussion
3 flutes, 1 piccolo	4 trumpets	18 first violins	4 timpani (1 player),
3 oboes, 1 English horn	6 French horns	16 second violins	bass drum, snare
3 clarinets, 1 bass clarinet	4 trombones	12 violas	drum, cymbals,
3 bassoons, 1 contrabassoon	1 tuba	10 cellos	triangle, xylophone,
		8 double basses	celesta, glockenspiel,
1 piano			etc. (2 to 4 players)
2 harps			

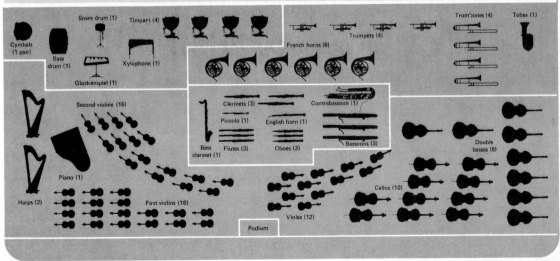

9

People around the world use musical instruments that vary greatly in construction and tone color, and instruments have had many functions at different times and in different cultures. They may provide entertainment; they may accompany song, dance, ritual, and drama; they have sometimes been considered sacred or thought to have magic powers; they have been used for communication; and they have even been status symbols.

Instruments' popularity rises and falls with changing musical tastes and requirements. Today, only a fraction of all known instruments are used; but interest in music of earlier times has led to the resurrection of instruments like the harpsichord (an ancestor of the piano) and the recorder (a relative of the flute). In fact, modern musicians are flexible and far-ranging in their choice of instruments: some classical and rock composers are using nonwestern instruments, and some jazz musicians are turning to classical instruments while classical composers are using instruments associated with jazz.

String Instruments

The *violin, viola, cello* (*violoncello*), and *double bass* (*bass fiddle,* or simply *bass*) form the symphony orchestra's string section. They differ in size, range, and tone color: the violin is smallest and has the highest range; the double bass is largest and has the lowest range. For symphonic music they are usually played with a *bow*—a slightly curved stick strung with horsehair (see the illustration)—but they may also be plucked. Here it will be helpful to consider the strings' construction and tone production; the violin can represent the entire family.

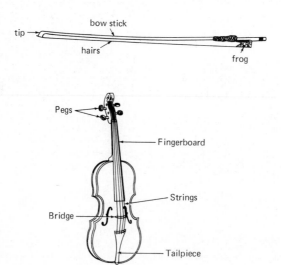

Violin and bow.

The violin consists of a hollow wooden *body* supporting four gut or wire strings which stretch, under tension, from a *tailpiece* at one end and over a *bridge* (which holds them away from the *fingerboard*) to the other end, where they are wound around wooden *pegs*. Each string is tuned to a different pitch by turning its peg to make it tighter or looser (the greater the tension, the higher the pitch). The musician makes a string vibrate by bowing it with the right hand (the speed and pressure of the bow stroke control dynamics and tone color), or by plucking it. The body amplifies and colors the tone. Pitch is controlled by pressing the strings against the fingerboard with the fingers of the left hand to vary the length of the vibrating portion (this is called **stopping** a string); thus each string can produce a range of pitches.

(Eric Kroll/Taurus)

(Martha Stewart/Picture Cube)

The violin (above) is often used as a solo instrument. In the orchestra, the violins are divided into first and second violins, with the former frequently playing the main melody. The violinist shown here is Pinchas Zukerman.

(Erika Stone)

Although eighteenth-century composers generally used the cello (above) in its bass and baritone registers, composers later exploited its upper registers as well.

The body of the viola (left) is about 2 inches longer than that of the violin, and thus the viola's range is somewhat lower. Its tone color is darker, thicker, and a little less brilliant than the violin's.

(Deborah Feingold)

(Randy Matusow)

(Erika Stone)

The double bass, or bass (above), has a very heavy tone and is less agile than other string instruments. It is often heard with the cello, but an octave lower.

The harp (right, top)—with forty-seven strings stretched on a triangular frame—has a wide range of 6½ octaves. The harpist plucks the strings with the fingers of both hands.

The guitar (right) has six strings, which are plucked with the fingers of the right hand. Frets on the fingerboard mark the places where the strings are stopped (pressed) with the fingers of the left hand.

12

How the string instruments are played—what performance techniques are used—determines which of many possible musical effects they produce. Plucking the string, for example, has already been mentioned; this is called *pizzicato*. *Double-stopping* is bowing two strings at once to sound two notes simultaneously; three notes (a *triple stop*) or four notes (a *quadruple stop*) can be sounded almost—but not quite—together by rotating the bow rapidly across three or all four strings. *Vibrato* is a throbbing tone produced by rocking the finger which is stopping a string so that the pitch fluctuates slightly; *tremolo* is rapidly repeated tones created by quick up-and-down strokes of the bow. *Harmonics* are very high-pitched tones produced by lightly touching certain points on the string. The musician can also muffle the tone by fitting a *mute* (a clamp) onto the bridge.

Some string instruments are always plucked rather than bowed. The most important are the *harp* (the only plucked string instrument usually in the symphony orchestra) and the *guitar*.

Woodwind Instruments

The woodwind instruments are so named because they produce vibrations of air within a tube that was traditionally made of wood (although piccolos and flutes are now made of metal). They have little holes along their length that are opened or closed by the fingers or by pads controlled by a key mechanism; this varies the pitch by changing the length of the vibrating air column. Following are the woodwinds of the symphony orchestra, listed from highest (piccolo) to lowest (contrabassoon) in range; the brackets indicate closely related instruments, with the asterisk marking the more important one of each pair:

{ piccolo
{ flute*

{ oboe*
{ English horn

{ clarinet*
{ bass clarinet

{ bassoon*
{ contrabassoon

Woodwind instruments are great individualists and differ more in tone color than the strings do. Their unique sounds result largely from the way vibrations are produced. The flute and piccolo are played by blowing across the edge of the mouth hole (the *recorder*, a relative of the flute, has a "whistle" mouthpiece); but the rest of the woodwinds have a *reed*—a thin piece of cane that is set vibrating by a stream of air. In *single-reed woodwinds* (such as the clarinets), the reed is fastened over a hole in the mouth-

(Costa Manos/Magnum)

(© John Bova/Photo Researchers)

(Clemens Kalischer)

(Clemens Kalischer)

The oboe (above) has a nasal, intense, expressive tone. Because the oboe's pitch is difficult to adjust, the entire orchestra is tuned to its A.

The flute (top right) has a high range and is extremely agile, capable of producing rapid successions of tones. Its tone is full and velvety in the low register and bright and sparkling in the top.

The piccolo (top left)—whose name is short for flauto piccolo, or "small flute"—is half the size of the flute and plays an octave higher. The piccolo's high register is shrill and whistlelike.

The recorder (left), like the flute and piccolo, has no reed. The recorder's tone resembles a flute's but is softer and gentler. Its five main sizes are sopranino, soprano, alto, tenor, and bass.

14

(Randy Matusow)

(Gurtman & Murtha)

(Randy Matusow)

(Waring Abbott)

The English horn (top left) is neither English nor a horn, but simply a low, or alto, oboe.

The clarinet (top right) can produce tones very rapidly and has a wide range of dynamics and tone color. The clarinetist shown here is Richard Stolzman.

The bass clarinet (bottom left) is larger than the clarinet and has a much lower range.

The tone of the bassoon (bottom right) is deeply nasal.

15

(Lisa Limer)

The contrabassoon can produce the lowest pitch in the orchestra.

(David Aronson/Stock, Boston)

The saxophone has a single-reed mouthpiece like a clarinet's, but its tube is made of brass. Its tone is rich, husky, and speechlike.

piece and vibrates when the player blows into the instrument; in ***double-reed woodwinds*** (oboe, English horn, bassoon, and contrabassoon), two pieces of cane are held between the player's lips. Tone colors also differ greatly among the various registers of each woodwind instrument. In general, low registers tend to be breathy and thick and top registers more penetrating.

The woodwinds (unlike the strings) can produce only one note at a time. In symphonic music, they are frequently given melodic solos.

Brass Instruments

From high register to low, the main instruments of the symphony orchestra's brass section are the *trumpet, French horn* (sometimes called simply a *horn*), *trombone,* and *tuba.* Other brass instruments, such as the *cornet, baritone horn, euphonium,* and *bass,* are used mainly in concert and marching bands.

16

(Darryl Pitt/Retna)

(Franck/Magnum)

(© Freda Leinwand/Monkmeyer)

(Marilyn M. Pfaltz/Taurus)

The French horn (above) has a tone that is less brassy, more mellow, and more rounded than the trumpet's.

The trumpet (left, top) sounds brilliant, brassy, and penetrating. The trumpeter shown here is Wynton Marsalis.

The thick, heavy tone of the tuba (left, middle) is used to add weight to the lowest orchestral register.

The trombone (left, bottom) has a tone that combines the trumpet's brilliance with the French horn's mellowness.

17

The brasses are played by blowing into a cup- or funnel-shaped mouthpiece. The vibrations come from the musician's lips and are amplified and colored in a coiled tube that is flared at the end to form a *bell*. Pitch is regulated both by varying lip tension and by using *slides* and *valves* to change the length of the tube (the longer the tube, the lower the pitch); the trombone uses a slide which is pulled in or pushed out, and the trumpet, French horn, and tuba have three or four valves to divert air through various lengths of tubing. (Valves came into use about 1850, making these instruments much more flexible and allowing them to produce many more tones.) Brass players can also alter tone by inserting a **mute**—a hollow, funnel-shaped piece of wood or plastic—into the bell.

Brasses are powerful instruments, often used at climaxes and for bold and heroic statements; but they cannot play as rapidly as most of the strings or woodwinds and serve less often as soloists.

Percussion Instruments

Most percussion instruments of the orchestra are struck by hand, with sticks, or with hammers, though some are shaken or rubbed. Percussion instruments of *definite pitch* produce tones; those of *indefinite pitch* produce noiselike sounds.

Definite Pitch	*Indefinite Pitch*
timpani (kettledrums)	side drum (snare drum)
glockenspiel	bass drum
xylophone	tambourine
celesta	triangle
chimes	cymbals
	gong (tam-tam)

In percussion instruments, vibrations are set up by stretched membranes (like the calfskin of the kettledrum) or by plates or bars (metal, wooden, etc.). Extremely loud sounds can be made by some percussion instruments, but percussion sounds die away quickly. In a symphony orchestra, one percussionist may play several different instruments.

Percussion instruments have long been used to emphasize rhythm and heighten climaxes. But until about 1900, they played a far less important role in western music than strings, woodwinds, and brasses. In this century, composers have been more willing to use the special colors of the percussion group. Yet western musicians barely approach the incredibly varied use of percussion found in Africa and Asia.

(Ludwig Industries)

(Randy Matusow)

(Randy Matusow)

The timpani, or kettledrums (top), are the only orchestral drums of definite pitch. A calfskin head is stretched over a copper, hemispherical shell. The pitch of the timpani is changed by varying the tension of the head. Screws around the shell's rim are tightened or loosened by hand or by a foot pedal. One percussionist generally plays two to four timpani, each tuned to a different pitch.

The metal bars of the glockenspiel (orchestral bells; middle) are struck with two hammers to produce a tone that is bright and silvery.

The xylophone (bottom) consists of a set of wooden bars which are struck with two hard hammers to produce a dry, wooden tone.

(Clemens Kalischer)

(Cynthia Copple)

(Lisa Limer)

The celesta (above left) looks like a small upright piano, but its sounding mechanism is like a glockenspiel's. Metal bars are struck by hammers that are controlled by a keyboard. The celesta's tone is tinkling and graceful.

Chimes (above right) are a set of metal tubes hung from a frame. They are struck with a hammer and sound like church bells.

The dry rattling sound of the side drum, or snare drum (left), is produced by the vibration of snares—strings, which are tightly stretched against the bottom head. The side drum is often used in marches.

The bass drum (opposite page, top left)—the largest of the orchestral drums—is almost 3 feet in diameter.

The tambourine (opposite, top right) is often used to create Spanish or gypsy effects. The player shakes it or strikes its head with the knuckles.

The triangle (opposite, bottom left) is struck with a metal beater and makes a tinkling, bell-like sound.

Cymbals (opposite, middle right) are round brass plates. They are usually struck together with a sliding motion, and their sound penetrates like a sharp crash.

When struck by a bass drum's stick with a soft head, the gong, or tam-tam (opposite, bottom right), produces long-lasting sounds that can seem solemn, mysterious, or frightening.

(Cynthia Copple)

(Randy Matusow)

(Randy Matusow)

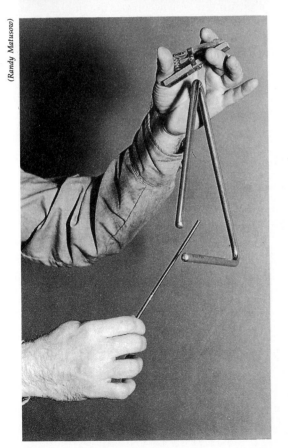

(Erika Stone)

(Randy Matusow)

Keyboard Instruments

The piano, harpsichord, organ, and accordion are the best-known keyboard instruments. Though quite different from each other, they all have a keyboard which allows several tones to be played at once quickly and easily.

The *piano* was invented around 1700 and mechanically perfected by the 1850s. It produces sound through vibrating strings held under tension by an iron frame: striking a key causes a felt-covered hammer to hit a string (the harder the pianist strikes the key, the louder the sound); releasing the key causes a felt damper to come down on the string and end the tone. Pianos have two or three pedals; the *damper pedal* lets the pianist sustain a tone even after releasing the key, the *una corda pedal* (or *soft pedal*) veils the sound, and the *sostenuto* pedal (which not all pianos have) sustains some tones but not others.

Pianos are exceptionally versatile; the eighty-eight keys span more than 7 octaves, the dynamic range is very broad, and the pianist can play many notes at once, including a melody and its accompaniment. Today, the piano is very popular as a solo instrument, for accompaniments, and in ensembles, including the symphony orchestra.

The *harpsichord* was important from about 1500 to 1775, when it was gradually replaced by the piano, and has been revived in the twentieth century for performance of early music and in some new works. It has strings that are plucked by small wedges called *plectra*, controlled by one or two keyboards.

The *pipe organ* was most prominent from 1600 to 1750 (when it was

(AP/Wide World)

The piano is exceptionally versatile. One of the world's best-known pianists is Vladimir Horowitz.

(Annalese Poorman/Indiana University News Bureau)

The harpsichord (above) has plucked strings controlled by one or two keyboards. The harpsichordist shown here is Elisabeth Wright.

(University of New Mexico)

A pipe organ (left) has many sets of pipes, controlled from several keyboards. Shown here is Wesley Selby, organist, University of New Mexico.

known as the "king of instruments") but is still in wide use today, particularly in religious services. It has a very wide range of pitch, dynamics, and tone color. There are several keyboards (including a pedal keyboard) that control valves from which air is blown across or through openings in the pipes; different sets of pipes—each with a particular tone color—are brought into play by pulling knobs called *stops*; dynamics are changed by adding or reducing the number of pipes, moving from one keyboard to another, or opening and closing shutters around some of the pipes.

The *accordion* has free steel reeds that are controlled by a treble keyboard with piano keys (played by the right hand) and a bass keyboard with buttons (played by the left hand). The reeds are caused to vibrate by air from a bellows.

Electronic Instruments

Electronic instruments produce or amplify sound electronically; they were invented as early as 1904 but have had a significant impact only since 1950. The electric piano, organ, and guitar—often used in popular music—are played much like traditional instruments; but other electronic instruments are used by composers to produce sounds on audiotape. The three tools for composing electronic music are the tape studio, the synthesizer, and the computer.

In the *tape studio* (which was widely used in the 1950s), the raw material is recorded sounds of definite and indefinite pitch which may be electronic or from "real life"—flutes, engines, bird calls, etc. The composer manipulates these in various ways: by speeding them up or slowing them down, altering their pitch and duration, giving them echoes, filtering them to change tone color, and cutting and splicing the tape to play them in any desired order. Rhythm can be fully controlled, since the duration of a sound depends only on the length of a tape segment. But the process of splicing and rerecording is laborious and time-consuming, and so many composers of the 1960s turned to synthesizers.

Synthesizers are systems of electronic components which generate, modify, and control sound. They can generate a practically limitless variety of musical sounds and noises. Although they vary in size and capacity, most can be "played" by means of a keyboard. The composer has complete control over pitch, dynamics, tone color, and duration. In addition to their use in studios, they appear in live concerts.

Computers are the most recent tool. Since the vibrating waves which produce any sound can be represented by a series of numbers, a computer can be programmed to accept precise musical specifications fed into it by a composer. The computer then changes these specifications into numbers that represent the final sounds. Later, the numbers are passed through a converter so that the sounds can be heard or recorded. The small computers developed in the 1970s and 1980s allow composers to hear their programmed music instantly.

Today's electronic music studios contain a wide variety of equipment which enables composers to exploit the entire spectrum of sound as never before, but the quality of the music still depends on the imagination and organizing power of the human mind.

Nonwestern Instruments

Nonwestern instruments produce a tremendous wealth of sounds and come in a wide variety of sizes, shapes, and materials. Scholars usually group these instruments into the following basic categories, based on what actually generates the sound:

1. *Membranophones* are instruments—basically, drums—whose sound generator is a stretched skin or other membrane.

(John Moss/Black Star)

Drums are extremely important in the culture of sub-Saharan Africa, where music is closely linked with dancing. While moving, a dancer often sings or plays an instrument.

(Fusako Yoshida)

Fusako Yoshida plays the koto, a plucked chordophone whose importance in traditional Japanese music is comparable to that of the piano in western music.

2. **Chordophones** are instruments—such as harps—whose sound generator is a stretched string.
3. **Aerophones** are instruments—such as flutes and trumpets—whose sound generator is a column of air.
4. **Idiophones** are instruments—such as bells, gongs, scrapers, rattles, and xylophones—whose own material is the sound generator (no tension is applied).

The musical style of a culture is among the important factors influencing its choice of instruments. For example, chordophones (strings) are prominent in Islamic and Indian classical music, whose highly ornamented melodies require instruments with great flexibility of pitch. Idiophones and membranophones (such as bells, rattles, and drums) are features in sub-Saharan Africa, where rhythm is strongly emphasized and music is closely linked with dancing.

A culture's use of instruments is also influenced by its geography and raw materials. Bronze idiophones are especially prominent in southeast Asia, where metallurgy developed around 5,000 years ago. Indonesian orchestras (gamelans) contain up to eighty instruments, including many bronze gongs, chimes, and xylophones. Instruments made of animal skins and horns are common in parts of sub-Saharan Africa, where these materials are easily found. Among the Aniocha Ibos of Nigeria, for example, drums are made of animal skins, and aerophones (winds) made from elephant tusks are used by members of the royal family and some chiefs. Where raw materials are scarce, as in the deserts of Australia, instruments may be few in number.

Along with musical style and geography, religious beliefs may influence the choice of materials. In Tibet, for example, trumpets and drums are made from the bones and skulls of criminals in order to appease demons. Instruments often have symbolic associations and are linked with specific gods and goddesses. They may be shaped like birds, animals, or fish.

RHYTHM $\left[\begin{array}{c} \text{ELEMENTS} \\ \textbf{3} \end{array}\right]$

Rhythm is basic to life. We see it in the cycle of day and night, the four seasons, the rise and fall of tides. More personally, we find it in our heartbeats, and we feel it when we breathe and walk. The essence of rhythm is a recurring pattern of tension and release, of expectation and fulfillment. This rhythmic alteration seems to pervade the flow of time. Time, as we live it, has fantastic diversity; each hour has 60 minutes, but how different one hour may seem from another!

Rhythm forms the lifeblood of music, too. In its widest sense, *rhythm* is the ordered flow of music through time. How musical elements change in time, and their rate of change, has to do with rhythm, which is our fourth property of sound. Rhythm has several interrelated aspects which we'll consider one at a time: beat, meter, accent and syncopation, and tempo.

BEAT

When you clap your hands or tap your foot to music, you are responding to its beat. *Beat* is a regular, recurrent pulsation that divides music into

Beats

Time

Beats can be shown as a succession of marks on a time line.

equal units of time. Beats can be represented by marks on a time line (see the illustration above). In music, such beats occur as often as every ¼ second or as seldom as every 1½ seconds. Sometimes the beat is powerful and easy to feel, as in marches or rock music. Or it may be barely noticeable, suggesting floating or aimlessness.

The pulse of music is communicated in different ways. Sometimes the beat is explicitly pounded out—by a bass drum in a marching band, for instance. At other times it is sensed rather than actually heard.

Sing the beginning of *America* up to the words *Land where my fathers died*:

My	coun-	try,	'tis		of	thee,	Sweet	land	of	lib-		er-	ty,
I	I	I	I	I	I	I	I	I	I	I	I	I	I
Of	thee	I	sing.				Land	(etc.)					
I	I	I	I	I	I	I							

Each of the marks represents a beat. Did you notice that you automatically held *sing* for 3 beats? You *sensed* the beat because you were aware of it and expected it to continue.

Beats form the background against which the composer places notes of varying length, and they are the basic unit of time by which all notes are measured. Notes last a fraction of a beat, or an entire beat, or more than a beat. In the example from *America*, the syllables, or notes, range from ½ beat for *of* to 3 beats for *sing*.

Combinations of different note lengths create rhythm. Earlier, **rhythm** was defined as the ordered flow of music through time; more specifically, it can be defined as the particular arrangement of note lengths in a piece of music, and it is an essential feature of a melody's "personality." Indeed, we might recognize *America* merely by clapping out its rhythm without actually singing the tones. The *beat* of *America* is an even, regular pulsation. But its *rhythm* flows freely, sometimes matching the beat, sometimes not.

METER

In music, some beats feel stronger or more stressed—more emphasized—than others, and we find repeated patterns of a strong beat plus one or more weaker beats. The organization of beats into regular groups is called *meter*. A group containing a fixed number of beats is called a *measure*. The first, or stressed, beat of the measure is called the *downbeat*. There are several types of meter, based on the number of beats in a measure.

When a measure has 2 beats, it is in *duple meter;* we count 1–2, 1–2, etc., as in the following example (vertical lines indicate the measures):

Ma- ry	had a	lit- tle	lamb,	lit- tle	lamb,	lit- tle	lamb,
1	2	| **1**	2	| **1**	2	| **1**	2 |

A pattern of 3 beats to the measure is *triple meter;* we count 1–2–3, 1–2–3, etc. *America* is in triple meter:

My	coun- try,	'tis	of thee,
1	2 3	**1**	2 3

Sweet land	of	lib-	er- ty,
1	2 3	**1**	2 3

Of	thee I	sing.	
1	2 3	**1**	2 3

Quadruple meter has 4 beats to the measure. As usual, the downbeat is strongest, but there is another, slighter stress on the third beat; we count 1–2–3–4, 1–2–3–4, etc. In the following example, the first word is on the *upbeat*, an unaccented pulse preceding the downbeat:

Mine eyes have seen the glo- ry	of the	com- ing of the Lord;	He is
| **1** 2 3	4	| **1** 2 3	4 |

Sextuple meter has 6 rather quick beats to the measure. The downbeat is strongest, but the fourth beat also has a stress; we count 1–2–3–4–5–6. Actually, the measure is subdivided into two 3-beat groups, 1–2–3/4–5–6, so that sextuple meter is a combination of duple and triple meter. For example:

Oh, give me a	home	where the buf-	fa- lo	roam,	where the
| **1** 2 3	4 5	6	| **1** 2 3	4 5	6 |

Quintuple meter (5 beats to the measure) and *septuple meter* (7 beats to the measure) also combine duple and triple meter. In quintuple meter, for example, the measure is subdivided into 2- and 3-beat groups: 1–2–3/4–5 or 1–2/3–4–5. These meters occur frequently in twentieth-century music but only occasionally in earlier music.

Accent and Syncopation

An important aspect of rhythm is how individual notes are stressed. One obvious way to emphasize a note is by giving it a dynamic *accent*, that is, by playing it more loudly than the notes around it. A note can also be emphasized by being held longer or being higher in pitch than nearby notes.

When an accented note comes where we would normally *not* expect it, the effect is known as **syncopation**. A syncopation occurs when an "off-beat" note is accented (that is, when the stress comes *between* beats). In the following example, syncopation occurs on the accented *my*, which comes between beats 1 and 2:

Give	**my**	re-	gards	to		Broad-		way		
1		2	3	4	|1		2	3	4	|

A syncopation also occurs when a weak beat is accented (as in 1–**2**–3–4 and 1–2–3–**4**). It creates rhythmic excitement and is one of the most characteristic features of jazz.

TEMPO

Tempo—the speed of the beat—is the basic pace of the music. We associate fast tempos with energy, drive, and excitement, and slow tempos with solemnity, lyricism, or calmness.

A *tempo indication* is usually given at the beginning of a piece. As with dynamics, the terms that show tempo are in Italian:

Term	Meaning
largo	very slow, broad
grave	very slow, solemn
adagio	slow
andante	moderately slow, a walking pace
moderato	moderate
allegretto	moderately fast
allegro	fast
vivace	lively
presto	very fast
prestissimo	as fast as possible

Tempo indications are often made more specific by the use of qualifiers, such as *molto* (*much*) and *non troppo* (*not too much*): thus *allegro molto* means *very fast* and *allegro non troppo* means *not too fast*. The same tempo is not always used throughout a piece. A gradual speeding up may be indicated by *accelerando* (*becoming faster*), and a gradual slowing down by *ritardando* (*becoming slower*).

All these terms (again, like dynamics) are relative and approximate; different performers interpret them differently, and there is no one "right" tempo for a piece. This is true even though, since about 1816, composers have been able to indicate tempo by means of a metronome setting. A **metronome** is a device which ticks or flashes a light at any desired musical speed, and a metronome setting indicates the exact number of beats per minute.

MUSIC NOTATION ⎡ ELEMENTS **4** ⎤

We use written words to express our thoughts and communicate with others when we can't be with them. In music, ideas are also written down, or *notated*, so that performers can play pieces unknown to them. **Notation** is a system of writing music so that specific pitches and rhythms can be communicated. It is explained here—very briefly—primarily to help you recognize rising and falling melodic lines and long and short notes so that you can follow the music examples in this book. (You will find it helpful to review the material on pitch and rhythm in Sections 1 and 3.)

NOTATING PITCH

With music notation, we can indicate exact pitches by the upward or downward placement of symbols—called *notes*—on a *staff*. A **note** is an oval. (Its duration is indicated by whether it is black or white or has a *stem* and *flags*, as will be explained later, under "Notating Rhythm.") A **staff** (plural, *staves*) is a set of five horizontal lines. Notes are positioned either on the lines of the staff or between them, in the spaces; the higher a note is placed on the staff, the higher its pitch:

If a pitch falls above or below the range indicated by the staff, short, horizontal **ledger lines** are used:

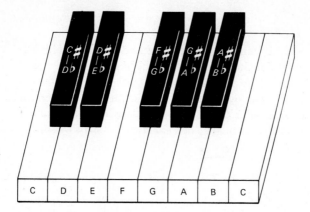

The twelve pitches of the octave and their positions on the piano keyboard.

Seven of the twelve pitches (tones) that fill the octave in western music are named after the first seven letters of the alphabet: A, B, C, D, E, F, G. This sequence is repeated over and over to represent the "same" tones in higher and lower octaves, and it corresponds to the white keys of the piano. The other five tones of the octave correspond to the black keys of the piano and are indicated by one of the same seven letters plus a *sharp sign* (♯) or a *flat sign* (♭) (see the illustration above). Thus the pitch between C and D may be called C sharp (C♯; higher than C) or D flat (D♭; lower than D). A *natural sign* (♮) is used to cancel a previous sharp or flat sign.

A *clef* is placed at the beginning of the staff to show the pitch of each line and space. The two most common clefs are the *treble clef,* used for relatively high ranges (such as those played by a pianist's right hand), and the *bass clef,* used for relatively low ranges (played by the pianist's left hand):

Treble clef   Bass clef

Keyboard music calls for a wide range of pitches to be played by both hands; for such music, the *grand staff*—a combination of the treble and bass staves—is used. The illustration (top of opposite page) shows how the notes on the grand staff are related to the piano keyboard. Note that the C nearest to the middle of the keyboard is called *middle C.*

NOTATING RHYTHM

Music notation does not indicate the exact duration of tones; instead, it shows how long one tone lasts in relation to others in the same piece. A single note on the staff lasts longer or shorter depending on how it looks—on whether it is white or black and has a *stem* or *flags.*

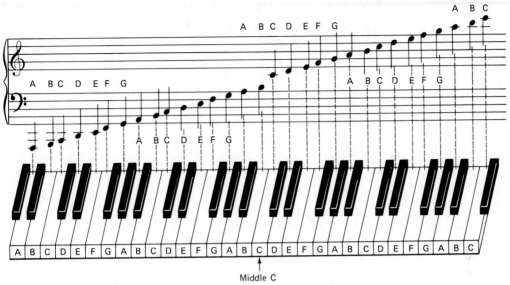

Notes on the grand staff and their positions on the piano keyboard.

Following is a chart that shows the relationships of the duration symbols:

One whole note lasts as long as 2 half notes or 4 quarter notes, and so on. As shown, the flags of several eighth notes or sixteenth notes in succession are usually joined by a horizontal **beam**.

To lengthen the duration of a tone (and add rhythmic variety), we can make it a **dotted note**; adding a dot (·) to the right of a note increases its duration by half. Thus, 1 quarter note ordinarily equals 2 eighth notes, but 1 dotted quarter note equals 3 eighth notes:

Frequently, a dotted note is followed by one that is much shorter; this long-short pattern, called *dotted rhythm*, strongly emphasizes the beat (and is therefore often used in marches).

A *tie* (⌢) is another way to lengthen the duration of a note. When two notes in a row are the same pitch and are connected by a tie, the first note is lengthened by the duration of the second. In the following example, the tone on *dell* lasts as long as 1 dotted quarter note plus 1 quarter note; the two tied notes become one continuous sound:

The farm - er   in   the dell,   The farm - er   in   the dell,

We can also add rhythmic variety by shortening the duration of a note. One method is the *triplet*, three notes of equal duration notated as a group within a curved line and the number 3. Such a group lasts only as long as if it were two notes of equal value:

NOTATING SILENCE (RESTS)

Duration of silence is notated by using a symbol called a *rest*. Rests are pauses; their durations correspond to those of notes:

whole rest   half rest   quarter rest   eighth rest   sixteenth rest

NOTATING METER

A *time signature* (or *meter signature*) shows the meter of a piece. It appears at the beginning of the staff at the start of a piece (and again later if the meter changes) and consists of two numbers, one on top of the other. The upper number tells how many beats fall in a measure; the lower number tells what kind of note gets the beat (2 = a half note, for instance, and 4 = a quarter note). Thus a $\frac{2}{4}$ time signature shows that there are 2 beats to the measure (duple meter) and a quarter note gets 1 beat. Duple meter may also be shown as $\frac{2}{2}$ (or by its symbol, ¢); quadruple meter is usually $\frac{4}{4}$ (or c). The most common triple meter is $\frac{3}{4}$.

A page from the orchestral score of Tchaikovsky's Romeo and Juliet.

THE SCORE

An orchestral *score* shows the music for each instrumental or vocal category in a performing group; often, a score will show more than twenty different staves of notation (see the illustration above).

ELEMENTS [5] MELODY

For many of us, music means melody. Though it is easier to recognize than define, we do know that a *melody* is a series of single notes which add up to a recognizable whole. A melody begins, moves, and ends; it has direction, shape, and continuity. The up-and-down movement of its pitches conveys tension and release, expectation and arrival. This is the melodic curve, or line.

As you get further into the music explored in this book, you'll find a wealth of melodies: vocal and instrumental, long and short, simple and complex. This section will help you sort them out by introducing some terms and basic melodic principles.

A melody moves by small intervals called *steps* or larger ones called *leaps*. A *step* is the interval between two adjacent tones in the *do-re-mi* scale (from *do* to *re*, from *re* to *mi*, etc.). Any interval larger than a step is a *leap* (*do* to *mi*, for example). Besides moving up or down by step or leap, a melody may simply repeat the same note. A melody's range—the distance between its lowest and highest tones—may be wide or narrow; melodies written for instruments tend to have a wider range than those for voices, and they frequently have wide leaps and rapid notes that would be difficult to sing. Often the highest tone of a melody will be the *climax*, or emotional focal point.

Note durations as well as pitches contribute to the distinctive character of a melody, and the specific order of long and short notes is important. A well-known melody can be almost unrecognizable if it is not sung or played in proper rhythm.

How the tones are performed can also vary the effect of a melody: they may be sung or played in a smooth, connected style called *legato* or in a short, detached style called *staccato*.

Many melodies are made up of shorter parts called *phrases*. Phrases may have similar pitch and rhythm patterns that help unify the melody, or they may contrast, furnishing variety. They often appear in balanced pairs (a phrase of rising pitches, say, followed by one of falling pitches). In analyzing music, letters are customarily used to represent sections of a piece: lowercase letters (a, b, etc.) for phrases and other relatively short sections, and capital letters (A, B, etc.) for longer sections. If two sections, such as phrases, differ significantly, we use different letters: a b. If one exactly repeats another, the letter is repeated: a a. If a section is a varied repetition of a previous one, the repeated letter has a prime mark: a a'. A repetition of a melodic pattern at a higher or lower pitch is called a *sequence*.

36

A resting place at the end of a phrase—a point of arrival—is called a *cadence*; it may be partial, setting up expectations (an **incomplete cadence**), or it may give a sense of finality (a **complete cadence**).

Now let's consider some examples of familiar melodies, starting with *Row, Row, Row Your Boat*:

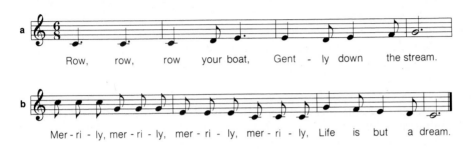

Sing it only up to the word *stream*. Notice that on *stream* the melody comes to a resting place which ends the first phrase; but it seems incomplete, as though it had posed a question. Now sing the rest—the second phrase, beginning on *merrily*—and notice how it ends conclusively and seems to answer the question. Thus the first phrase ends with an incomplete cadence and the second with a complete cadence. Each phrase is the same length, a formula typical of many melodies called *tunes*; the two phrases create a feeling of symmetry and balance, one beginning with repeated notes and then moving upward by step, the second moving downward by leap and then by step. The climax comes on the first *merrily*.

Next, sing the entire nursery tune *Mary Had a Little Lamb*:

It also has two balancing phrases, the first ending with an incomplete cadence and the second with a complete cadence. But here the second phrase begins exactly like the first before proceeding to a different, more conclusive ending (an a a' pattern). Melodic repetition, both exact and (as here) varied, plays an important unifying role in music.

Our final example, *America*, has phrases that are *not* of equal length:

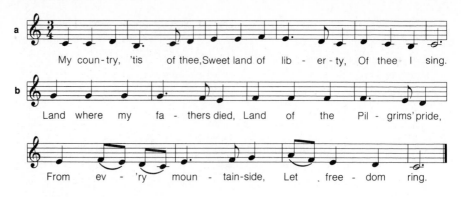

a

My coun-try, 'tis of thee, Sweet land of lib - er - ty, Of thee I sing.

b

Land where my fa - thers died, Land of the Pil - grims' pride,

From ev - 'ry moun - tain-side, Let free - dom ring.

The second phrase (starting from *Land*) is longer than the first and creates a feeling of continuation rather than balance or symmetry. An interesting aspect of *America* is the way a repeated rhythmic pattern (for *My country, 'tis of thee, Sweet land of liberty, Land where my fathers died*, and *Land of the Pilgrims' pride*) unifies the melody. *America* also contains a sequence: the melody for *Land of the Pilgrims' pride* is simply a repetition a little lower of the preceding *Land where my fathers died*.

These three melodies are complete in themselves. Frequently, however, a melody will serve as a starting point for a more extended piece of music and, in stretching out, will go through all kinds of changes. This kind of melody is called a **theme**.

ELEMENTS

[6] HARMONY

When folksingers accompany themselves on a guitar, they add support, depth, and richness to the melody; we call this *harmonizing*. Most music in western culture is a blend of melody and harmony (much nonwestern music, on the other hand, emphasizes melody and rhythm rather than harmony).

Harmony refers to the way chords are constructed and how they follow each other. A *chord* is a combination of three or more tones sounded at once. Essentially, a chord is a group of simultaneous tones, and a melody is a series of individual tones heard one after another. As a melody unfolds, it gives clues for harmonizing, but it does not always dictate a specific series—or *progression*—of chords; a melody may be harmonized in several musically convincing ways. Chord progressions enrich a melody by adding emphasis, surprise, suspense, or finality. New chords and progressions continually enter the language of music, but the basic chordal vocab-

(Wide World)

The folksinger Joan Baez blends melody and harmony by accompanying herself on the guitar.

ulary has remained fairly constant. We'll look now at a few principles of harmony.

CONSONANCE AND DISSONANCE

Some chords are considered stable and restful, others unstable and tense. A stable tone combination is called a *consonance*; consonances are points of arrival, rest, and resolution. An unstable tone combination is a *dissonance*; its tension demands an onward motion to a stable chord. Thus dissonant chords are "active"; traditionally, they have been considered harsh and have expressed pain, grief, and conflict. A dissonance has its *resolution* when it moves to a consonance. When a resolution is delayed or is accomplished in surprising ways—when the composer plays with our sense of expectation—a feeling of drama or suspense is created.

Consonance and dissonance exist in varying degrees; some consonant chords are more stable than others, and some dissonant chords are tenser than others. Also, dissonance has been used more freely over the centuries, so that a chord considered intolerably harsh at one time may later come to seem mild.

THE TRIAD

A great variety of chords are used in music. Some consist of three different tones; others have four, five, or even more. The simplest, most basic chord is the **triad** (pronounced *try'-ad*), which has three tones; to indicate that the three tones are played at one time, it is notated:

A triad is made up of alternate tones of the scale, such as the first (*do*), third (*mi*), and fifth (*sol*). The bottom tone is called the *root*; the others are a third and a fifth above the root. (From *do* to *mi* in the scale is an interval of a third; from *do* to *sol* is an interval of a fifth.)

A triad built on the first, or tonic, note of the scale (*do*) is called the **tonic chord** (*do-mi-sol*); it is the main chord of a piece, the most stable and conclusive, and traditionally would begin and end a composition. Next in importance is the triad built on the fifth note of the scale (*sol*), the **dominant chord** (*sol-ti-re*). The dominant chord is strongly pulled toward the tonic chord—it sets up tension that is resolved by the tonic, and the progression from dominant to tonic gives a strong sense of conclusion. This has great importance in music. The progression from the dominant to the tonic chord (often used at the end of a phrase, a melody, or an entire piece) is called a **cadence**. (As noted in Section 5, this term also means a resting point at the end of a phrase.)

BROKEN CHORDS (ARPEGGIOS)

When the individual tones of a chord are sounded one after another, it is called a **broken chord**, or **arpeggio**. *The Star-Spangled Banner* begins with a broken chord:

Here the notes of the tonic chord are heard in succession rather than together.

Throughout this book, the importance of harmony will be more and more apparent. It helps give music variety and movement; and its effects are endless, varying with the style of a particular era and the desires of individual composers.

ELEMENTS

(© Katrina Thomas/Photo Researchers)

Street musicians. Informal music making is a source of pleasure for both players and listeners.

The audience at an outdoor concert of the New York Philharmonic orchestra. Whether in a public park or a concert hall, live performances have a special electricity.

(© Jan Halaska 1980/Photo Researchers)

(© 1983 Waring Abbott)

Concert by Huey Lewis and The News. The exchange between singer and audience contains a bit of magic, something direct and spellbinding.

KEY [7]

Almost all familiar melodies are built around a central tone toward which the other tones gravitate and on which the melody usually ends. To feel this gravitational pull (which is rooted in cultural conditioning), sing *America* (page 38), pausing for a few seconds between *freedom* and *ring*; you'll probably feel uneasy until you supply the last tone. This central tone is the **keynote**, or **tonic**. A keynote can be any of the twelve tones of the octave; when, for example, a piece is in the key of C, the tonic or keynote is C.

Key involves not only the central tone but also a central chord and scale. *Chord* was defined in Section 6; the basic chord of a piece in C is a tonic triad with C as its root, or bottom tone. A *scale* is made up of the basic pitches of a piece of music arranged in order from low to high or high to low. A piece in the key of C has a basic scale, *do-re-mi-fa-sol-la-ti-do*, with C as its *do*, or tonic. *Key*, then, refers to the presence of a central note, scale, and chord within a piece, and all the other tones are heard in relationship to them. Another term for key is **tonality**. After 1900, some composers abandoned tonality; but even today much of the music we hear is tonal.

THE MAJOR SCALE

The basic scales of western music from the late 1600s to 1900 were the *major* and *minor*, and they continue to be widely used today.

The **major scale**—the familiar *do-re-mi*, etc.—has two kinds of intervals in a specific pattern: the **half step**, the smallest interval traditionally used in western music; and the **whole step**, twice as large as the half step. The illustrations show the pattern of whole and half steps in the major scale (below) and a major scale with C as the beginning tone (at the top of the following page).

The C major scale uses only the white keys of the piano (the half steps come between E and F and between B and C, which are not separated by

Pattern of whole and half steps making up the major scale.

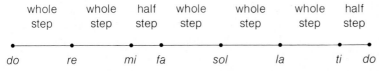

whole step	whole step	half step	whole step	whole step	whole step	half step
do	re	mi	fa	sol	la	ti do

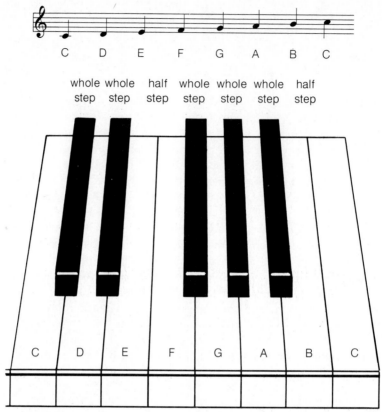

Major scale beginning on C.

black keys). We can construct similar major scales by starting the same pattern of intervals on any of the twelve tones of the octave (thus there are twelve possible major scales); the other major scales use one or more black keys of the piano, but the pattern sounds the same.

THE MINOR SCALE

Along with the major scale, the minor scale is fundamental to western music. The *minor scale*—like the major—consists of seven different tones and an eighth tone that duplicates the first an octave higher, but it differs from the major scale in its pattern of intervals, or whole and half steps. Since (again, like the major) it can begin on any of the twelve tones of the octave, there are twelve possible minor scales. Here is a comparison between a major and a minor scale both starting on C.

C major scale:

whole step	whole step	half step	whole step	whole step	whole step	half step
C	D	E	F	G	A	B	C

C minor scale:

whole step	half step	whole step	whole step	half step	whole step	whole step
C	D	E♭	F	G	A♭	B♭	C

The crucial difference is that in the minor scale there is only a half step between the second and third tones; this greatly changes the sound of the scale and the mood of music using it. Music based on minor scales tends to sound serious or melancholy; also, the tonic triad built from a minor scale is a minor chord, which sounds darker than a major chord.

Joshua Fought the Battle of Jericho is a tune based on a minor scale:

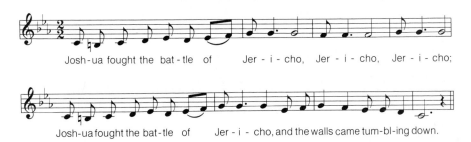

Josh-ua fought the bat-tle of Jer - i - cho, Jer - i - cho, Jer - i - cho;

Josh-ua fought the bat-tle of Jer - i - cho, and the walls came tum-bl-ing down.

THE KEY SIGNATURE

When a piece of music is based on (for example) a major scale with D as its keynote, we say that it is in the key of D major; when it is based on a minor scale with the keynote F, it is in the key of F minor. Each major and minor scale has a specific number of sharps or flats, from none to seven; and to indicate the key of a piece, a *key signature*—consisting of sharp and flat signs following the clef at the beginning of the staff—is used. To illustrate, here is the key signature for D major, which contains two sharps:

Key signatures make it unnecessary to put a sharp or flat sign before every sharped or flatted note in the piece.

THE CHROMATIC SCALE

The twelve tones of the octave—*all* the black and white keys in one octave on the piano—form the *chromatic scale*. The tones of the chromatic scale (unlike those of the major or minor scale) are all the same distance apart, one half step:

The word *chromatic* comes from the Greek *chroma, color*; and the traditional function of the chromatic scale is to color or embellish the tones of the major and minor scales. It does not define a key, but it gives a sense of motion and tension. It has long been used to evoke grief, loss, or sorrow. In the twentieth century it has also become independent of major and minor scales and is used as the basis for entire compositions.

MODULATION: CHANGE OF KEY

Most short melodies we know remain in one key from start to end; but in longer pieces, variety and contrast are created by using more than one key. A shift from one key to another within the same piece is called a *modulation*. A modulation is like a temporary shift in the center of gravity— it brings a new central tone, chord, and scale. Though modulations are sometimes subtle and difficult to spot, they produce subconscious effects that increase our enjoyment.

TONIC KEY

No matter how often a piece changes key, there usually is one main key, called the *tonic* or *home key*. The tonic key is the central key around which the whole piece is organized. Traditionally, a piece would usually begin in the home key and practically always end in it. A composition in the key of C major, for example, would begin in the home key, modulate to several other keys—say, G major and A minor—and finally conclude in the home key of C major. The other keys are subordinate to the tonic.

Modulating away from the tonic key is like visiting: we may enjoy ourselves during the visit, but after a while we're glad to go home. In music, modulations set up tensions that are resolved by returning to the home key. For centuries, the idea of a central key was a basic principle of music.

But after 1900, some composers wrote music that ignored the traditional system. The results of this revolutionary step are explored in Part VI, The Twentieth Century.

MUSICAL TEXTURE [ELEMENTS **8**]

At any moment within a piece, we may hear one unaccompanied melody, several melodies, or one melody with harmony. The term *musical texture* describes these possibilities; it refers to how many different layers of sound are heard at once, whether they are melody or harmony, and how they are related to each other. Texture is described as transparent, dense, thin, thick, heavy, or light; and variations in texture create contrast and drama. We'll now look at three basic textures: *monophonic*, *polyphonic*, and *homophonic*.

MONOPHONIC TEXTURE

The texture of a single unaccompanied melodic line is *monophonic*, meaning literally *one sound*. If you sing alone, you make monophonic music. Performance of a single melodic line by more than one instrument or voice is playing or singing in *unison* and results in a fuller, richer-sounding monophonic texture.

POLYPHONIC TEXTURE

Simultaneous performance of two or more melodic lines of relatively equal interest produces *polyphonic* (*many-sounding*) texture. In polyphony several melodic lines compete for attention, adding a dimension that has been compared to perspective in painting: each line enriches the others. The technique of combining several melodic lines into a meaningful whole is called *counterpoint* (and the term *contrapuntal texture* is sometimes used in place of *polyphonic texture*). To fully enjoy polyphony, you may have to hear a piece several times; it's often helpful to listen first for the top line, then for the bottom line, and then for the middle lines.

Polyphonic music often contains *imitation*, which occurs when a melodic idea is presented by one voice or instrument and then restated immediately by another. A *round*—a song in which several people sing the same melody but each starts at a different time—uses imitation; *Row, Row, Row Your Boat*, on the following page, is a familiar example:

Here, the imitation is "strict": each voice sings exactly the same melody. But in polyphonic texture imitation is often freer, with the imitating line starting like the first one but then going off on its own.

HOMOPHONIC TEXTURE

When we hear one main melody accompanied by chords, the texture is **homophonic**. Attention is focused on the melody, which is supported and colored by sounds of subordinate interest. When harmonized by chords, *Row, Row, Row Your Boat* is an example of homophonic texture:

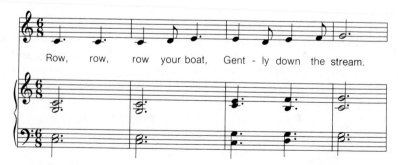

Accompaniments in homophonic music vary widely in character and importance, from subdued background chords to surging sounds that almost hide the main melody. When a subordinate line asserts its individuality and competes for the listener's attention, the texture is probably best described as being between homophonic and polyphonic.

CHANGES OF TEXTURE

Changing textures within a composition creates variety and contrast, as was noted above. A composer may, for instance, begin with a melody and a simple accompaniment and later weave the melody into a polyphonic web—or contrast a single voice with massive chords sung by a chorus. Georges Bizet's *Farandole* from *L'Arlésienne* Suite No. 2, is a good example of textural variety.

FARANDOLE FROM L'ARLÉSIENNE SUITE NO. 2, BY GEORGES BIZET

The *Farandole* comes from Bizet's music for the play *L'Arlésienne (The Woman from Arles),* which is set in southern France. Two contrasting themes are heard in this exciting orchestral piece. The first, in minor, is a march theme adapted from a southern French folk song. The lively second theme, in major, has the character of the *farandole,* a southern French dance.

Side C, band 3

[*8-record/cassette set:* Side 8, band 7]

Many changes of texture contribute to the *Farandole*'s exciting mood. The piece contains two kinds of homophonic texture: in one, the accompaniment and melody have the same rhythm; in the other, the rhythm of the accompaniment differs from that of the melody. The *Farandole* opens with the march theme and its accompaniment in the same rhythm. But when the lively dance theme is first presented, its accompanying chords do not duplicate the rhythm of the melody; instead, they simply mark the beat.

The *Farandole* also includes two kinds of polyphony: with and without imitation. Soon after the opening, the march theme is presented by the violins and then is imitated by the violas. At the end of the piece, polyphony results when the march and dance themes—previously heard in alternation—are presented simultaneously. In this concluding section, both themes are in major.

The *Farandole* also contains monophonic texture, which sets off the homophony and polyphony. Monophony is heard when the march theme is played by the strings in unison.

Listening Outline
To be read while music is heard

*FARANDOLE FROM L'ARLÉSIENNE SUITE NO. 2 (1879),
BY GEORGES BIZET (1839–1875)**

Allegro deciso (forceful allegro), march tempo, quadruple meter ($\frac{4}{4}$), D minor

Piccolo, 2 flutes, 2 oboes, 2 clarinets, 2 bassoons, 4 French horns, 2 trumpets, 2 cornets, 3 trombones, timpani, tambourine, bass drum, cymbals, 1st violins, 2d violins, violas, cellos, double basses

(About 3 minutes)

1. a. Full orchestra, *ff*, march theme; homophonic (accompaniment in same rhythm as melody), minor.

    b. Violins imitated by violas, march theme; polyphonic, minor.
2. a. High woodwinds, *ppp*, dance theme; faster tempo, homophonic (accompanying chords on beat), major; decorative rushes in violins, long crescendo to *ff* as dance theme is repeated.

ppp   *poco a poco crescendo* _____

    b. Full orchestra, *fff*, dance theme.
3. a. Strings only, *ff*, march theme in faster tempo; monophonic, minor.
    b. High woodwinds, *ppp*, dance theme; homophonic.
    c. Strings only, *ff*, continue march theme; monophonic, then homophonic as lower strings accompany melody.
    d. High woodwinds, *ppp*, dance theme; homophonic. Crescendo to
4. Full orchestra, *fff*, dance and march themes combined; polyphonic, major. Homophonic ending.

**L'Arlésienne* Suites No. 1 and No. 2 are sets of pieces from the theater music composed by Bizet. Suite No. 2 was arranged by Bizet's friend Ernest Guiraud after the composer's death.

MUSICAL FORM

The word *form* is associated with shape, structure, organization, and coherence. Form calls to mind the human body or the balanced arrangement of figures in a painting. *Form* in music is the organization of musical ideas in time. In the flow of time, a composer creates something cohesive out of the musical elements—pitch, tone color, dynamics, melody, harmony, and texture. In a logically organized piece, one thought grows from another and all the parts are interrelated; we perceive the form by recalling the various parts and how they relate, and with repeated listening the form becomes clearer and takes on an emotional meaning.

TECHNIQUES THAT CREATE MUSICAL FORM

Both in short tunes (such as those we explored in Section 5) and in much longer compositions, repetition, contrast, and variation are essential techniques. *Repetition* creates a sense of unity; *contrast* provides variety; and *variation*, in keeping some elements of a musical thought while changing others, provides both unity and variety.

Repetition

Musical repetition appeals to the pleasure we get in recognizing and remembering something, and the repetition of melodies or extended sections is a technique widely used for binding a composition together. The passage of time influences our reaction to repetition: when a musical idea returns, the effect is not duplication but balance and symmetry.

Contrast

Forward motion, conflict, and change of mood all come from contrast. Opposition—of loud and soft, strings and woodwinds, fast and slow, major and minor—propels and develops musical ideas. Sometimes such contrast is complete, but at other times the opposites have common elements that give a sense of continuity.

Variation

In the variation of a musical idea, some of its features will be retained while others are changed. For example, a melody might be restated with a different accompaniment, or its pitches might stay the same while its rhythm is changed. A whole composition can be created from variations on one idea.

TYPES OF MUSICAL FORM

Composers have traditionally organized musical ideas by using certain forms or patterns, and listeners can respond more fully when they recognize these. It's important to note, though, that two compositions having the same form may be different in every other respect. We'll look now at two basic types of musical form. (Remember, from Section 5, that lower-case letters represent phrases or short sections and capital letters represent longer sections.)

Three-Part (Ternary) Form: A B A

During the last few centuries *three-part form (A B A)* has probably been used most frequently. It can be represented as *statement* (A), *contrast* or *departure* (B), *return* (A). When the return of A is varied, the form is outlined A B A' (Wagner's Prelude to Act III of *Lohengrin*, analyzed in Section 1, is in A B A' form). The contrast between A and B can be of any kind, A and B can be of equal or unequal length, and the way A returns after B differs from piece to piece—A may come unexpectedly, or it may be clearly signaled (if B comes to a definite end with a cadence and a pause), or there may be a transition smoothly linking the two.

   The sections of an A B A composition can be subdivided; for example, as follows:

A   B   A
a b a   c d c   a b a

In some pieces, a listener might mistake subsection b within the first A for the arrival of B; but as the music progresses, the greater contrast one hears with B will make it clear that b is a subsection.

DANCE OF THE REED PIPES FROM NUTCRACKER SUITE, BY PETER ILYICH TCHAIKOVSKY

Side B, band 10
[*8-record/cassette set:*]
[*Side 10, band 3*]

The *Nutcracker* Suite is a set of dances from Tchaikovsky's fairy-tale ballet *The Nutcracker. Dance of the Reed Pipes* is a particularly clear example of A B A' form. Section A features three flutes playing a staccato melody which conveys a light, airy feeling and is repeated several times. The B section contrasts in tone color, melody, and key—it features a trumpet melody accompanied by brasses and cymbals. This melody moves by step within a narrow range, in contrast to the opening flute melody, which has a wide range and lots of leaps as well as steps. The F sharp minor key of the middle section contrasts with the D major key of the opening section. The concluding A' section, in D major, is a shortened version of the opening A section.

Listening Outline   To be read while music is heard

DANCE OF THE REED PIPES FROM NUTCRACKER SUITE (1892),
BY PETER ILYICH TCHAIKOVSKY (1840–1893)

Three-part (ternary) form: A B A'

Moderato assai (very moderate), duple meter ($\frac{2}{4}$), D major

3 flutes, 2 oboes, English horn, 2 clarinets, bass clarinet, 2 bassoons, 4 French horns, 2 trumpets, 3 trombones, tuba, timpani, cymbals, 1st violins, 2d violins, violas, cellos, double basses

(About 2½ minutes)

A   1. *a.* Low pizzicato strings, *p,* introduce
    b. 3 flutes, staccato melody in major, pizzicato strings accompany. Melody repeated.

    c. English horn melody, legato, flutes accompany, staccato.
    d. 3 flutes, staccato melody, pizzicato strings accompany. Melody repeated. Cadence.

B   2. *a.* Trumpet melody in minor, brasses and cymbals accompany.

    b. Strings repeat trumpet melody. Flutes lead back to

A'   3. 3 flutes, staccato melody in major, strings accompany. Melody repeated. Cadence.

Two-Part (Binary) Form: A B

A composition divided into two large sections is in *two-part form (A B)*. Two-part form gives a sense of *statement* (A) and *counterstatement* (B). If either of its large sections is immediately repeated, or both are, the form might be represented by A A B, A B B, or A A B B. As in three-part form, differences between A and B may be of any kind, and the two sections may be equal or unequal in length and may have subsections. The B section almost always returns to the home key and gives a sense of finality.

BADINERIE FROM SUITE NO. 2 IN B MINOR, BY JOHANN SEBASTIAN BACH

The *Badinerie* (French for *jest* or *banter*) is the lighthearted finale of Bach's Suite No. 2 in B Minor for solo flute, string orchestra, and harpsichord. It is in two-part (binary) form and is outlined A A B B, because each part is repeated. Parts A and B differ in key and length but are similar in melody and rhythm. The first part begins in B minor and then modulates to F sharp minor, and the longer second part begins in F sharp minor and then modulates back to the tonic key of B minor. Section A opens with a descending phrase that reappears at the beginning of section B but at a lower pitch. Each section of this playful miniature is rounded off by a cadence.

Side A, band 5

[8-record/cassette set:]
[Side 2, band 7]

Listening Outline To be read while music is heard

BADINERIE FROM SUITE NO. 2 IN B MINOR (1735–1739),
BY JOHANN SEBASTIAN BACH (1685–1750)

Two-part (binary) form: A A B B

Duple meter ($\frac{2}{4}$), B minor

Solo flute, string orchestra, harpsichord

(About 1½ minutes)

A   1. Flute, descending phrase in minor,

phrase repeated, running notes lead to cadence in minor. Section A repeated.

B   2. Descending phrase, lower in pitch than section A,

running notes, flute melody descends and leads to cadence in minor. Section B repeated.

LISTENING FOR FORM

Music is continuous in its flow and does not always fall into clearly defined units. Short pieces, especially, may seem elusive, and some music seems to fit none of the usual patterns. But such music is not formless—it has unique forms that can be discovered through repeated hearings. It's important for listeners to lean on memory, to put related ideas together by recognizing and recalling them and finding their relationships. Through alert listening their overall shape will be made clear.

MUSICAL STYLE [ELEMENTS 10]

In music, *style* refers to a characteristic way of using melody, rhythm, tone color, dynamics, harmony, texture, and form. How these elements are put together can result in a distinctive or unique sound, and we can speak of the musical style of one composer, a group of composers, a country, or a period in history. Compositions created in the same part of the world or around the same time are often similar in style, but individuals using the same musical vocabulary can create a personal manner of expression.

Musical styles change from one historical era to the next, but these changes are continuous, so that any boundary between one stylistic period and another is only approximate. Although there are some sudden turning points, even the most revolutionary new styles are usually foreshadowed in earlier compositions; and few changes of style sweep away the past entirely.

Western art music can be divided into the following stylistic periods:

Middle Ages (450–1450)   Romantic (1820–1900)
Renaissance (1450–1600)   Twentieth century to 1950
Baroque (1600–1750)   1950 to the present
Classical (1750–1820)

The following chapters describe the general features of each period and show how it differs from the preceding one. Awareness of the characteristics of a style will let you know what to listen for in a composition and help you recognize innovative or unique features.

Music is probably as old as the human race; and we know—from art and other evidence—that it existed in ancient Egypt, Israel, Greece, and Rome, but hardly any notated music has survived from these civilizations. The first stylistic period to be considered in this book is the European Middle Ages, from which notated music *has* come down to us—allowing compositions created over 1,000 years ago to come alive today.

THE MIDDLE AGES AND RENAISSANCE

II

1 Music in the Middle Ages (450–1450)
2 Music in the Renaissance (1450–1600)

Sacred music predominated during the Middle Ages. This miniature from a twelfth-century psalter shows King David playing the harp, and ten other musicians.

[1] MUSIC IN THE MIDDLE AGES (450–1450)

A thousand years of European history are spanned by the phrase *Middle Ages*. The "dark ages"—a time of migration, upheavals, and wars—began about 450 with the disintegration of the Roman Empire. But the later Middle Ages (until about 1450) were a period of cultural growth: romanesque churches and monasteries (1000–1150) and gothic cathedrals (1150–1450) were constructed, towns grew, and universities were founded.

During the Middle Ages a very sharp division existed among three main social classes: nobility, peasantry, and clergy. The nobles were sheltered within fortified castles; but the peasants lived miserably, and many were bound to the soil and subject to feudal overlords. This was an age of faith: all segments of society felt the powerful influence of the Roman Catholic church. Monks in monasteries held a virtual monopoly on learning; most people, including the nobility, were illiterate. Just as the cathedral dominated the medieval landscape and the medieval mind, so was it the center of musical life. Most important musicians were priests and worked for the church. Boys received music education in church schools, and an important occupation in monasteries was liturgical singing. Women were not allowed to sing in church but did make music in convents, and some—like Hildegard of Bingen (1098–1179), abbess of Rupertsberg—wrote music for their choirs.

Although most medieval music was vocal—the church frowned upon instruments because of their earlier role in pagan rites—instruments did serve as accompaniment and after about 1100 were used increasingly in church. (The organ was most prominent.) In the later Middle Ages, instruments were a source of controversy between composers, who wanted to create elaborate compositions, and the church, which wanted music only as a discreet accompaniment to the religious service.

THE CHURCH MODES

The *church modes* were the basic scales of western music in the Middle Ages and (despite their name) were used in secular as well as sacred music. Like major and minor scales, they consist of seven different tones and an eighth tone that duplicates the first an octave higher; but their patterns of whole and half steps are different. (Much western folk music follows the patterns of the church modes: for example, *What Shall We Do with the Drunken Sailor?* is in a mode called *Dorian*; *When Johnny Comes Marching Home* is in the *Aeolian* mode.)

56

(Lauros-Giraudon/Art Resource)

Architecture changed during the Middle Ages from the romanesque style, seen in the eleventh-century nave at the left, to the gothic of the thirteenth-century Cathedral of Reims above.

GREGORIAN CHANT

For over 1,000 years (though it is not common today), the official music of the Roman Catholic church has been *Gregorian chant*, which consists of melody set to sacred Latin texts and sung without accompaniment. (It is monophonic in texture.) Gregorian chant was meant to create the atmosphere for specific prayers and rituals in the church service and has a calm, otherworldy quality (resulting partly from the use of church modes) that represents the voice of the church rather than any individual. Its rhythm is

57

(Bildarchiv Foto Marburg)

During the Middle Ages, artists were concerned more with religious symbolism than with lifelike representation. Sculptures from the late-twelfth-century church of St. Trophine in Arles (in southern France) show Christ surrounded by symbols of the four evangelists.

flexible, without meter, and has little sense of beat; this gives it a floating, almost improvisational character. Melodies may be simple or elaborate but tend to move by step within a narrow range of pitches.

Gregorian chant is named after Pope Gregory I (the Great, reigned 590–604), who was credited by medieval legend with having created it; actually, however, it evolved over many centuries. At first, the chants were passed along by oral tradition, but later they were notated (the illustration shows an example of medieval chant notation). Most of the several thousand chants known today date from A.D. 600 to 1300, and the earliest surviving manuscripts date from about the ninth century. The composers—like the artists who decorated the early medieval churches—remain almost completely unknown.

ALLELUIA: VIDIMUS STELLAM (WE HAVE SEEN HIS STAR)

Side A, band 1

$\begin{bmatrix} \textit{8-record/cassette set:} \\ \textit{Side 1, band 1} \end{bmatrix}$

An elaborate and jubilant Gregorian chant is the Alleluia from the Mass for Epiphany (it is shown on the following page in medieval notation). The word *alleluia* is a Latinized form of the Hebrew *hallelujah* (*praise ye the*

Medieval chant notation for Alleluia: Vidimus stellam.

Lord). In this chant, many notes are sung to single syllables of text. The long series of tones on *ia* is an expression of wordless joy and religious ecstasy. The monophonic texture of the chant is varied by an alternation between a soloist and a choir singing in unison. The chant is in A B A form; the opening Alleluia melody is repeated after a middle section that is set to a biblical verse.

Solo voice, *Alleluia* phrase. Chorus, *Alleluia* phrase repeated with long series of tones on *ia*.	A

Solo voices:	*Vidimus stellam*	We have seen His star
	ejus in Oriente,	in the East,
	et venimus cum muneribus	and are come with gifts
	adorare	to worship
Chorus:	*Dominum.*	the Lord.

B

Chorus, *Alleluia* phrase with long series of tones on *ia*.	A

A
Alleluia
[First time by soloist, repetition by choir]   [Choir]

Al - le - lu - ia.

no meter

texture: monophonic

SECULAR MUSIC IN THE MIDDLE AGES

Despite the domination of Gregorian chant (and the fact that for centuries only sacred music was notated), there was much music outside the church. The first large body of secular songs that survives in decipherable notation was composed during the twelfth and thirteenth centuries by French nobles called *troubadours* and *trouvères*. Most of these songs are about love, but there are also songs about the Crusades, dance songs, and spinning songs. In southern France, there were women troubadours—such as Beatriz de Dia—who addressed their songs to men. The notation of troubadour and trouvère melodies does not indicate rhythm, but it's likely that

(*Heidelberg University Library*)

Many secular songs in the Middle Ages dealt with love. The illustration shows the German poet-composer Frauenlob (c. 1255–1318) with a group of musicians.

many had a regular meter with a clearly defined beat (thus they differ from the nonmetrical rhythm of Gregorian chant).

There was also music performed by wandering minstrels—*jongleurs*—who were acrobats as well and were on the lowest social level. They usually sang songs written by others and played instrumental dances on harps, fiddles (bowed string instruments), and lutes (plucked string instruments).

DANSE ROYALE (ROYAL DANCE; THIRTEENTH CENTURY)

Danse royale (Royal Dance), one of the earliest surviving pieces of instrumental music, is a medieval dance (an *estampie*). It is monophonic in texture, and the music manuscript does not indicate which instrument plays the melodic line. In our recording, the melody is performed on a *shawm*, a double-reed ancestor of the modern oboe. During the Middle Ages, the shawm's piercingly brilliant tone was favored for outdoor music like marches and dances. A rhythmical background is provided by two medieval drums called *tabors*. *Danse royale* is in triple meter and has a strong, fast beat.

[*8-record/cassette set:* Side 1, band 2]

THE DEVELOPMENT OF POLYPHONY: ORGANUM

For centuries, western music was basically monophonic. But sometime between 700 and 900, the first steps were taken in a revolution that eventually transformed music: monastery choirs began to add a second melodic line to Gregorian chant. Medieval music that consists of Gregorian chant and one or more additional melodic lines is called *organum*.

At first, the second line was improvised and simply duplicated the chant melody at a different pitch—the two lines were parallel, note against note, at an interval of a fourth (such as *do* to *fa*) or a fifth (such as *do* to *sol*):

Sit glo - ri - a Do - mi - ni in se - cu - la

Between 900 and 1200, however, organum became truly polyphonic, as the additional melody became more independent. The second melody might develop its own curve instead of remaining strictly parallel to the main melody (sometimes its motion was contrary to that of the chant). Around 1100, the two lines were no longer restricted to note-against-note style but could differ rhythmically. The chant, on the bottom, was often sung in very long notes while the added melody, on top, moved in shorter notes.

After 1150, Paris became the center of polyphonic music. Two successive choirmasters of the Cathedral of Notre Dame—Leonin and Perotin, the first notable composers known by name—and their followers are referred to as the *school of Notre Dame*, and from about 1170 to 1200 these Notre Dame composers developed rhythmic innovations. Earlier polyphonic music probably had the free, unmeasured rhythms of Gregorian chant; but Leonin and Perotin, for the first time in music history, used *measured rhythm*, with definite time values and a clearly defined meter.

Medieval polyphony had relatively few triads, which in later periods became the basic consonant chords. A triad contains two intervals of a third (such as *do* to *mi* and *mi* to *sol*); medieval music theorists considered this a dissonance—though in the later Middle Ages triads and thirds were used more often, making polyphonic music fuller and richer (by our standards).

FOURTEENTH-CENTURY MUSIC: THE "NEW ART" IN FRANCE

The fourteenth century was a time of disintegration in Europe: it saw the Hundred Years' War (1337–1453), the black death (bubonic plague), and a weakening of both the feudal system and the authority of the church.

Given this atmosphere, it's not surprising that secular music became more important than sacred music in the fourteenth century.

Composers wrote polyphonic music that was *not* based on Gregorian chant, including drinking songs and pieces that imitated bird calls, barks of dogs, and hunters' shouts. By the early fourteenth century they had evolved a new system of music notation that allowed them to specify almost any rhythmic pattern. Syncopation—rarely used earlier—now became important. Changes in musical style in the fourteenth century were so profound that French and Italian music was called the *new art* (*ars nova*, in Latin). We'll study a mass by Guillaume de Machaut, the foremost French composer of the time.

NOTRE DAME MASS (MID-FOURTEENTH CENTURY), BY GUILLAUME DE MACHAUT

Guillaume de Machaut (about 1300–1377), who was famous as both musician and poet, was born in the French province of Champagne. Though a priest, he spent most of his life as a court official for various royal families. Machaut traveled to many courts and presented beautifully decorated copies of his music to noble patrons; these make him one of the first important composers whose works have survived. The decline of the church is reflected in his output, which consists mainly of love songs for one or two voices and instrumental accompaniment. But he also wrote sacred music, and his *Notre Dame* Mass, the best-known composition of the fourteenth century, is of great historical importance: it is the first polyphonic treatment of the mass ordinary by a known composer.

The **mass ordinary** consists of texts that remain the same from day to day throughout most of the church year. The five sung prayers of the ordinary are the Kyrie, Gloria, Credo, Sanctus, and Agnus Dei. Since the fourteenth century, these five texts have often been set to polyphonic music and have inspired some of the greatest choral works. In each age, composers have responded to the mass in their own particular style. This centuries-old tradition of the mass gives invaluable insight into the long span of music and its changing styles.

The *Notre Dame* Mass is written for four voices, some of which were probably performed or doubled by instruments. How Machaut wanted his mass performed and which instruments were used to support the voices are unknown. We also do not know when or why the mass was composed. We'll examine the Agnus Dei of the mass as an example of fourteenth-century polyphony.

Agnus Dei

Machaut's music for the Agnus Dei—a prayer for mercy and peace—is solemn and elaborate. It is in triple meter. Complex rhythmic patterns

[*8-record/cassette set:*
Side 1, band 5]

contribute to the Agnus Dei's intensity. The two upper parts are rhythmically active and contain syncopation, a characteristic of fourteenth-century music. The two lower parts move in longer notes and play a supporting role. In our recording, one low part is played on an instrument, and the three other parts are sung by vocal soloists who are reinforced by instruments.

The Agnus Dei is based on a Gregorian chant, which Machaut furnished with new rhythmic patterns and placed in the tenor, one of the two lower parts. Since the chant, or cantus firmus, is rhythmically altered within a polyphonic web, it is more a musical framework than a tune to be recognized. The harmonies of the Agnus Dei include stark dissonances, hollow-sounding chords, and full triads. Thus the Agnus Dei sounds fuller than some earlier medieval works.

Like the chant melody on which it is based, the Agnus Dei is in three sections. It may be outlined as follows:

Agnus Dei (I)	Agnus Dei (II)	Agnus Dei (III)
A	B	A

The same text appears in each section, except for a change from *miserere nobis (have mercy on us)* to *dona nobis pacem (grant us peace)* in the concluding Agnus Dei (III). A and B are similar in mood, rhythm, and texture and end with the same hollow-sounding chord. The division into three sections is thought to symbolize the Trinity. In Machaut's time, music was meant to appeal to the mind as much as to the ear.

Agnus dei, qui tollis peccata mundi: miserere nobis.	Lamb of God, who taketh away the sins of the world, have mercy on us.	A
Agnus dei, qui tollis peccata mundi: miserere nobis.	Lamb of God, who taketh away the sins of the world, have mercy on us.	B
Agnus dei, qui tollis peccata mundi: dona nobis pacem.	Lamb of God, who taketh away the sins of the world, grant us peace.	A

MIDDLE AGES
RENAISSANCE

2

MUSIC IN THE RENAISSANCE (1450–1600)

The fifteenth and sixteenth centuries in Europe have come to be known as the *Renaissance*. People then spoke of a "rebirth," or "renaissance," of creativity; it was a period of exploration and adventure which saw the voyages of Columbus and Magellan and produced Leonardo da Vinci—

(Marburg/Art Resource)

Above: The Birth of Venus (1480), by Botticelli. Renaissance sculptors and painters once again depicted the nude human body, a subject of shame and concealment during the Middle Ages.

(Scala/Art Resource)

Left: David (1504) by Michelangelo.

who was a painter, sculptor, architect, engineer, scientist, and fine musician.

The dominant intellectual movement, called *humanism*, focused on human life and accomplishments, and the humanists—though devout Christians—were captivated by the pagan cultures of ancient Greece and Rome. Humanism strongly influenced Renaissance art: for example, sculptors and painters once again depicted the nude human body, and they treated the madonna not as childlike or unearthly but as a beautiful young woman.

The Catholic church was far less powerful in the Renaissance than in the Middle Ages, for the unity of Christendom was exploded by the Protestant Reformation led by Martin Luther (1483–1546). No longer did the church monopolize learning. Aristocrats and the upper middle class now considered education a status symbol, and they hired scholars to teach their children. The invention of printing with movable type (around 1450) accelerated the spread of learning. Before 1450, books were rare and extremely expensive because they were copied by hand. By 1500, 15 to 20 million copies of 40,000 editions had been printed in Europe.

The Renaissance in music occurred between 1450 and 1600 (though some historians place its beginning as early as 1400). As with the other arts, musical horizons were expanded: printing widened the circulation of music, and the number of composers and performers increased. Indeed, every educated person was expected to be trained in music, in keeping with the Renaissance ideal of the "universal man." As in the past, musicians worked in churches, courts, and towns; but though the church remained an important patron (and church choirs increased in size), musical activity gradually shifted to the courts.

CHARACTERISTICS OF RENAISSANCE MUSIC

Words and Music

In the Renaissance, as in the Middle Ages, vocal music was more important than instrumental music. The humanistic interest in language influenced vocal music, creating a close relationship between words and music: Renaissance composers (much more than medieval composers) wrote music to enhance the meaning and emotion of the text.

Renaissance composers often used *word painting,* a musical representation of specific poetic images. For example, the words *descending from heaven* might be set to a descending melodic line, and *running* might be heard with a series of rapid notes. Yet, despite this emphasis on capturing the emotion and imagery of a text, Renaissance music may seem calm and restrained to us. While there *is* a wide range of emotion in Renaissance music, it usually is expressed in a moderate, balanced way, with *no* extreme contrasts of dynamics, tone color, and rhythm.

(National Gallery, London)

During the Renaissance, music was an important leisure activity; every educated person was expected to play an instrument and read notation. This painting shows a lutenist accompanying himself and two other singers.

Texture

The texture of Renaissance music is chiefly polyphonic. A typical choral piece has four, five, or six voice parts of nearly equal melodic interest. Imitation among the voices is common: each presents the same melodic idea in turn, as in a round. Homophonic texture, with successions of chords, is also used, especially in light music, like dances. The texture may vary within a piece to provide contrast and bring out aspects of the text.

Renaissance music sounds fuller than medieval music. The bass register is used for the first time, expanding the pitch range to more than 4 octaves. With this new emphasis on the bass line came richer harmony. Composers began to think in terms of chords as well as individual melodies. Now all the melodic lines were conceived at the same time. (During the Middle Ages, a melodic line was conceived and then another was added on top of it, with relatively little attention to total harmonic effect.) Renaissance music sounds mild and relaxed, because stable, consonant chords are favored; triads occur often, while dissonances are played down.

Renaissance choral music did not need instrumental accompaniment. For this reason, the period is sometimes called the "golden age" of *a cappella (unaccompanied)* choral music. Even so, instruments were often combined with voices. They might duplicate the vocal lines to reinforce the sound, or they might take the part of a missing singer. But parts written exclusively for instruments are rarely found in Renaissance choral music.

Rhythm and Melody

In Renaissance music, rhythm is more a gentle flow than a sharply defined beat. This is because each melodic line has great rhythmic independence: when one singer is at the beginning of his or her melodic phrase, the others may already be in the middle of theirs. This technique makes singing Renaissance music both a pleasure and a challenge, for each singer must maintain an individual rhythm. But pitch patterns in Renaissance melodies are easy to sing. The melody usually moves along a scale with few large leaps.

SACRED MUSIC IN THE RENAISSANCE

The two main forms of sacred Renaissance music, both polyphonic choral works, are the **motet**, set to a sacred Latin text other than the ordinary of the mass; and the **mass**, made up of five sections—Kyrie, Gloria, Credo, Sanctus, and Agnus Dei. The motet and the mass are alike in style, but the mass is longer.

The Renaissance Motet

AVE MARIA . . . VIRGO SERENA
(HAIL, MARY . . . SERENE VIRGIN; 1502),
BY JOSQUIN DESPREZ

Side A, band 2
[8-record/cassette set:]
[Side 1, band 6]

Josquin Desprez (about 1440–1521) was a master of Renaissance music. Like many leading composers of the time, he was Flemish and had an international career; he spent much of his life in Italy, serving in dukes' private chapels and in the Papal Choir, and in his later years he worked for Louis XII of France and held several church posts in Flanders. His compositions, which included masses, motets, and secular vocal pieces, strongly influenced other composers and were praised enthusiastically by music lovers (including Martin Luther).

Josquin's four-voice motet *Ave Maria . . . virgo serena* is an outstanding Renaissance choral work. This Latin prayer to the Virgin is set to delicate and serene music. The opening uses polyphonic imitation, a technique typical of the period. The short melodic phrase on *Ave Maria* is presented by the soprano voice and then imitated in turn by the alto, tenor, and bass. The next two words, *gratia plena (full of grace)*, have a different melody, which also is passed from voice to voice. Notice that each voice enters while the preceding one is in the middle of its melody. This overlapping creates a feeling of continuous flow. Josquin adapted the melody for the opening phrases from a Gregorian chant, but the rest of the motet was not based on a chant melody.

Josquin skillfully varies the texture of this motet; two, three, or four voices are heard at one time. In addition to the imitation among individual voices, there is imitation between pairs of voices: duets between the high voices are imitated by the two lower parts. Sometimes the texture almost becomes homophonic, as at the words *Ave, vera virginitas*. Here, also, is a change from duple to triple meter, and the tempo momentarily becomes more animated. But soon the music returns to duple meter and a more peaceful mood. *Ave Maria* ends with slow chords that express Josquin's personal plea to the Virgin: *O Mother of God, remember me. Amen.*

Ave Maria	Hail Mary,	Each soprano phrase
gratia plena	full of grace,	imitated in turn by
dominus tecum,	the Lord is with thee,	alto, tenor, and bass.
virgo serena.	serene Virgin.	Duple meter.
Ave, cuius conceptio,	Hail, whose conception,	High duet imitated by three lower voices.
solemni plena gaudio,	full of great jubilation,	All four voices.
coelestia terrestria	fills Heaven and Earth	Increased rhythmic
nova replet laetitia.	with new joy.	animation reflects "new joy."

Ave, cuius nativitas	Hail, whose birth	High duet imitated by
nostra fuit solemnitas,	brought us joy,	low duet.
ut lucifer lux oriens	as Lucifer, the morning star,	Soprano phrase
verum solem praeveniens.	went before the true sun.	imitated by alto,
		tenor, and bass.
Ave, pia humilitas,	Hail, pious humility,	High duet imitated by
sine viro fecunditas,	fruitful without a man,	low duet.
cuius annuntiatio	whose Annunciation	High duet.
nostra fuit salvatio.	brought us salvation.	Low duet.
Ave, vera virginitas,	Hail, true virginity,	Triple meter.
immaculata castitas,	immaculate chastity,	
cuius purificatio	whose purification	
nostra fuit purgatio.	brought our cleansing.	
Ave, praeclara omnibus	Hail, glorious one	Duple meter, high
angelicis virtutibus,	in all angelic virtues,	duets imitated by
cuius assumptio	whose Assumption	lower voices.
nostra glorificatio.	was our glorification.	Brief pause.
O mater Dei,	O Mother of God,	Sustained chords.
memento mei. Amen.	remember me. Amen.	

The Renaissance Mass

POPE MARCELLUS MASS (1562–1563), BY GIOVANNI PIERLUIGI PALESTRINA

During the sixteenth century, Italian composers attained the excellence of earlier Flemish masters such as Josquin. Among the most important Italian Renaissance composers was Giovanni Pierluigi Palestrina (about 1525–1594), who devoted himself to church music and accordingly had a career centered in Rome (one of his positions was music director of St. Peter's). Palestrina's music includes 104 masses and some 450 other sacred works; its restraint and serenity reflect an emphasis on spirituality (for centuries, church authorities have regarded his masses as models of church music), and its technical perfection is a model for students of counterpoint.

Palestrina's *Pope Marcellus* Mass (dedicated to Pope Marcellus II, who reigned briefly in 1555) is his most famous work. It is written for an a capella choir of six voice parts: soprano, alto, two tenors, and two basses. We'll focus on the first section, the Kyrie.

Kyrie

Instructor's records: Side 1, band 1

The Kyrie has a rich polyphonic texture. Its six voice parts constantly imitate each other, yet blend beautifully. This music sounds fuller than Josquin's *Ave Maria*, in part because six voices are used rather than four. The elegantly curved melodies summon the spirit of Gregorian chant. They flow smoothly and can be sung easily. Upward leaps are balanced at once by downward steps, as in the opening melody:

Soprano

Ky - rie e - lei - - - - - son,

The Kyrie of the *Pope Marcellus* Mass is written in three sections:

1. *Kyrie eleison.*   Lord, have mercy upon us.
2. *Christe eleison.*   Christ, have mercy upon us.
3. *Kyrie eleison.*   Lord, have mercy upon us.

This text is short, and words are repeated with different melodic lines to express calm supplication. The rhythm flows continuously to the end of each section, when all voices come together on sustained chords. Each of the three sections begins in a thin texture with only some of the voices sounding, but as the other voices enter, the music becomes increasingly full and rich.

SECULAR MUSIC IN THE RENAISSANCE

Vocal Music: The Renaissance Madrigal

During the Renaissance, secular vocal music became increasingly popular; throughout Europe, poems in various languages were set to music, numerous song collections became available, and music was an important leisure activity. Renaissance secular music was written for groups of solo voices and for solo voice with instrumental accompaniment. As mentioned above, word painting was common; and secular music had more rapid changes of mood than sacred music.

An important form of vocal music was the *madrigal*, a piece for several solo voices set to a short poem, usually about love. Like a motet, it has homophonic and polyphonic textures, but it more often uses word painting and unusual harmonies. Madrigals began in Italy around 1520 and were published there by the thousands in the sixteenth century. In 1588 a volume of translated Italian madrigals was published in London, setting off a spurt of madrigal writing by English composers. The English madrigal became lighter and more humorous than its Italian model, with simpler melody and harmony.

AS VESTA WAS DESCENDING (1601), BY THOMAS WEELKES

Among the finest English madrigalists was Thomas Weelkes (about 1575–1623), an organist and church composer. Weelkes's *As Vesta Was Descending* comes from *The Triumphes of Oriana* (1601), an anthology of English

[*8-record/cassette set:*
  Side 1, band 8]

madrigals written to honor Queen Elizabeth, who was often called Oriana. The text of this six-voice madrigal pictures Vesta (the Roman goddess of the hearth) coming down a hill with her attendants, "Diana's darlings." (Diana was the Roman goddess of chastity, hunting, and the moon.) At the same time, the "maiden queen," Oriana (Elizabeth), is climbing the hill with her shepherd gallants. Vesta's attendants desert her and race down the hill to join Oriana.

As Vesta Was Descending has the light mood typical of English madrigals. Word painting is plentiful. For example, the word *descending* is sung to downward scales, and *ascending* to upward ones.

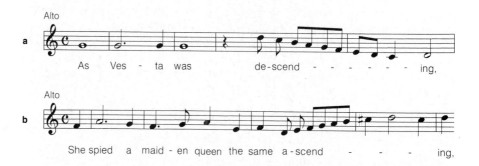

When Vesta's attendants run down the hill, "first *two* by *two*, then *three* by *three together*, leaving their goddess all *alone*," we hear first *two* voices, then *three* voices, then *six* voices, and finally a *solo* voice. In the extended concluding section, "*Long* live fair Oriana," a joyous phrase is imitated among the voices. And in the bass this phrase is sung in long notes, with the longest note on the word *long*.

As Vesta was from Latmos hill descending,   Descending scales
she spied a maiden queen the same ascending,   Ascending scales.
attended on by all the shepherds swain,
to whom Diana's darlings
came running down amain.   Rapid descending figures.

First two by two,   Two voices.
then three by three together,   Three voices; all voices. Solo voice.

leaving their goddess all alone, hasted thither,
and mingling with the shepherds of her train
with mirthful tunes her presence entertain.
Then sang the shepherds and nymphs of Diana,
Long live fair Oriana!   Brief joyful phrase imitated among voices; long notes in bass.

THE MIDDLE AGES

(Scala/ Art Resource)

Interior of the Sainte-Chapelle in Paris (1243–1248). During the Middle Ages, religious beliefs and knowledge were strengthened by the biblical scenes depicted in stained glass windows.

(National Gallery of Art, Washington, D.C., Andrew W. Mellon Collection)

Madonna and Child Enthroned, by an anonymous Byzantine artist (late thirteenth century).
Like Gregorian chant, medieval painting often expressed an otherworldly feeling.
It represented the voice of the church, rather than of any individuals.

THE RENAISSANCE

(Scala/Art Resource)

Saint Anne, the Virgin and Child, by Leonardo da Vinci (1506–1510). The Renaissance was an age of curiosity and individualism, exemplified in the remarkable life of Leonardo da Vinci (1452–1519)—who was an important painter, sculptor, architect, engineer, and scientist, and a fine musician as well. Renaissance painters emphasized balance and human beauty and used perspective to create an illusion of depth.

(Metropolitan Museum of Art, John Stewart Kennedy Fund, 1910)

Mars and Venus United by Love, by Paolo Veronese (1576). Classical mythology was an important source of inspiration for Renaissance art. Veronese, and the other Venetian painters of his time, reveled in rich colors and textures.

Instrumental Music

Though still subordinate to vocal music, instrumental music did become more important during the Renaissance. Traditionally, instruments accompanied voices or played music intended for singing, and even in the early 1500s instrumental music was largely adapted from vocal music. But during the sixteenth century instrumental music became increasingly emancipated from vocal models: more music was written specifically for instruments, composers began to exploit instruments' particular capacities when writing instrumental solos, and purely instrumental forms (such as theme and variations) were developed. Much of this instrumental music was intended for dancing—a popular Renaissance entertainment—and a wealth of dance music has come down to us.

Renaissance instruments produced softer, less brilliant sounds than the instruments we hear today. Most came in families of three to eight, ranging from soprano to bass (recorders and viols—bowed string instruments— were among the most important), and often several members of a family were played together. But composers did not specify instruments: a piece might be performed by different instruments, depending on what was available, and today's standardized orchestras and other ensembles did not exist.

RICERCAR IN THE TWELFTH MODE
(SIXTEENTH CENTURY), BY ANDREA GABRIELI

Andrea Gabrieli (about 1520–1586) was organist at St. Mark's Cathedral in Venice from 1564 until his death. He was an important composer of both sacred and secular vocal music, as well as instrumental music. Gabrieli's Ricercar in the Twelfth Mode was written for four unspecified instruments (soprano, alto, tenor, and bass). In our recording, the ricercar is performed by a group of recorders ranging from soprano to bass. (A *ricercar* is a polyphonic instrumental composition employing imitation. That this one is "in the twelfth mode" means that it is based on a scale corresponding to C major.)

[*8-record/cassette set:*
Side 1, band 7]

This short, lively piece is composed of several contrasting sections; its form is A B CC A. Gabrieli unifies the ricercar by bringing back the opening material (A) after the two middle sections. Most of section C is in triple meter and contrasts with the duple meter of sections A and B. The work features imitation among the individual instruments and rapid echoes between the two lower and two upper parts. Though relatively simple, the piece is an early step toward the more elaborate instrumental music that developed in the baroque period.

THE BAROQUE PERIOD

Organ pipes of the Groote Kerke at Haarlem in the Netherlands.

[1] BAROQUE MUSIC (1600–1750)

Though the word *baroque* has at various times meant bizarre, flamboyant, and elaborately ornamented, modern historians use it simply to indicate a particular style in the arts. An oversimplified but useful characterization of baroque style is that it fills space—canvas, stone, or sound—with action and movement. Painters, sculptors, and architects became interested in forming a total illusion, like a stage setting. Artists such as Bernini, Rubens, and Rembrandt exploited their materials to expand the potentials of color, detail, ornament, and depth; they wanted to create totally structured worlds.

Such a style was very well suited to the wishes of the aristocracy, who also thought in terms of completely integrated structures. In France, for example, Louis XIV held court in the Palace of Versailles, a magnificent setting that fused baroque painting, sculpture, and architecture into a symbol of royal wealth and power. The baroque style was also shaped by the

(Alinari/Art Resource)

Bernini's Ecstacy of St. Theresa (1645–1652) fills space with action and movement.

76

(Scala/Art Resource)

The Palace of Versailles, in France, fused baroque architecture, sculpture, and painting into a symbol of royal wealth and power.

needs of churches, which used the emotional and theatrical qualities of art to make worship more attractive. The middle class, too, influenced the development of the baroque style. In Holland, for instance, prosperous merchants and doctors commissioned realistic depictions of landscapes and scenes from everyday life.

It's also helpful to think of baroque style against the backdrop of seventeenth-century scientific discovery. The work of Galileo (1564–1642) and Newton (1642–1727) represented a new approach to science based on the union of mathematics and experiment; they discovered mathematical laws governing bodies in motion. Such scientific advances led to new inventions and the gradual improvement of medicine, mining, navigation, and industry during the baroque era. Baroque art is a complex mixture of rationalism, sensuality, materialism, and spirituality.

In music, the baroque style flourished from about 1600 to 1750. Its two giants were George Frideric Handel and Johann Sebastian Bach (Bach's death in 1750 marks the end of the period), but many other masters—Monteverdi, Purcell, Corelli, Vivaldi—were largely forgotten until the "baroque revival" of the 1940s and 1950s.

During the baroque period (and until about 1800), most music was written to order; it was commissioned by aristocratic courts, churches, opera houses, and municipalities, all of which also employed musicians—and invariably demanded *new* music. Thus composers were an integral part of baroque society; and even though they wrote their music for specific needs of their patrons, its quality is so high that much of it has become standard in today's concert repertory.

77

The baroque period can be divided into three phases: early (1600–1640), middle (1640–1680), and late (1680–1750). The early phase was one of the most revolutionary periods in music history. Italian composers of the early baroque invented opera—a drama sung to orchestral accompaniment—and the operas of Claudio Monteverdi (1567–1643) convey unprecedented passion and dramatic contrast. Early baroque composers favored homophonic textures, which they felt could project words more clearly than the polyphony typical of Renaissance music; and, to depict extreme emotions, they used dissonances with a new freedom. They also stressed contrasts of sound—solo singers against a chorus, voices against instruments.

During the middle phase (1640–1680), the new musical style spread from Italy throughout Europe. The church modes of the middle ages gradually gave way to major and minor scales, which were the tonal basis for most compositions by about 1680; and instrumental music took on a new importance.

We will focus mainly on the late baroque period (1680–1750), which produced most of the baroque music heard today. Many aspects of harmony (including the emphasis on the dominant-tonic attraction) arose during this period, and for the first time instrumental music became as important as vocal music. Polyphony returned to favor; in fact, late baroque composers gloried in it.

Let's look more closely at some features of late baroque style. (From now on, the word *baroque* will pertain to the late baroque phase.)

CHARACTERISTICS OF BAROQUE MUSIC

Unity of Mood

A baroque piece usually expresses one basic mood—what begins joyfully will remain joyful throughout. Emotional states like joy, grief, and agitation were represented. (At the time, these moods were called *affections*.) Composers molded a musical language to depict the affections; specific rhythms or melodic patterns were associated with specific moods. This common language gives a family resemblance to much late baroque music.

The prime exception to this baroque principle of unity of mood occurs in vocal music. Drastic changes of emotion in a text may inspire corresponding changes in the music. But even in such cases, one mood is maintained at some length before it yields to another.

Rhythm

Unity of mood in baroque music is conveyed, first of all, by continuity of rhythm. Rhythmic patterns heard at the beginning of a piece are repeated throughout it. This rhythmic continuity provides a compelling drive and energy—the forward motion is rarely interrupted. The beat is emphasized far more in baroque music than in most Renaissance music, for example.

Melody

Baroque melody also creates a feeling of continuity. An opening melody will be heard again and again in the course of a baroque piece. And even when a melody is presented in varied form, its character tends to remain constant. There is a continuous expanding, unfolding, and unwinding of melody. This sense of directed motion is frequently the result of a melodic sequence, that is, successive repetition of a musical idea at higher or lower pitch levels. Many baroque melodies sound elaborate and ornamental, and they are not easy to sing or remember. The baroque melody gives the impression of dynamic expansion rather than of balance and symmetry. A short opening phrase is often followed by a longer phrase with an unbroken flow of rapid notes.

Terraced Dynamics

Paralleling continuity of rhythm and melody in baroque music is a continuity of dynamic level: the volume tends to stay constant for a stretch of time. When the dynamics do shift, it's sudden, as though one had physically stepped from one level to another. This alternation between loud and soft is called **terraced dynamics.** *Gradual* changes through crescendo and decrescendo are *not* prominent features of baroque music. However, singers and instrumentalists no doubt made some subtle dynamic inflections for expressive purposes.

The main keyboard instruments of the baroque period were the organ and harpsichord, both well suited for continuity of dynamic level. An organist or harpsichordist could not obtain a crescendo or decrescendo by varying finger pressure, as pianists today can. A third keyboard instrument, the clavichord, could make gradual dynamic changes, but only within a narrow range—from about *ppp* to *mp*. Sound was produced on it by means of brass blades striking the strings. The clavichord was usually not used in large halls, since its tone was too weak. But for home use by amateurs it was ideal; its cost was low and its expressive sound satisfying. It had especially wide popularity in Germany.

Texture

We've noted that late baroque music is predominantly polyphonic in texture: two or more melodic lines compete for the listener's attention. Usually, the soprano and bass lines are the most important. Imitation between the various lines, or "voices," of the texture is very common. A melodic idea heard in one voice is likely to make an appearance in the other voices as well.

However, not all late baroque music was polyphonic. A piece might shift in texture, especially in vocal music, where changes of mood in the words demand musical contrast. Also, baroque composers differed in their treatment of musical texture. Bach inclined toward a consistently polyphonic texture, whereas Handel used much more contrast between polyphonic and homophonic sections.

Chords and the Basso Continuo (Figured Bass)

Chords became increasingly important during the baroque period. In earlier times, there was more concern with the beauty of individual melodic lines than with chords formed when the lines were heard together. In a sense, chords were mere by-products of the motion of melodic lines. But in the baroque period chords became significant in themselves. As composers wrote a melodic line, they thought of chords to mesh with it. Indeed, sometimes they composed a melody to fit a specific chord progression. This interest in chords gave new prominence to the bass part, which served as the foundation of the harmony. The whole musical structure rested on the bass part.

The new emphasis on chords and the bass part resulted in the most characteristic feature of all baroque music, an accompaniment called the *basso continuo*, or *figured bass.* This is made up of a bass part together with numbers (figures) which specify the chords to be played above it. The continuo—to use the common abbreviation for *basso continuo*—is usually played by at least two instruments: an organ or a harpsichord and a low melodic instrument like the cello or bassoon. With the left hand, the organist or harpsichordist plays the bass part, which is also performed by the cello or bassoon. With the right hand, the keyboard player improvises chords or even a melodic line, following the indications of the numbers. These numbers specify only a basic chord, not the exact way in which the chord should be played. Thus, the performer is given a great deal of freedom. (This shorthand system is similar in principle to the chord indications found on the modern song sheets from which jazz pianists improvise.)

The basso continuo offered the advantage of emphasizing the all-important bass part, besides providing a steady flow of chords. Practically, the use of numbers, rather than chords with all their notes written out, saved time for busy baroque composers. It also saved paper at a time when paper was expensive.

Words and Music

Like their Renaissance predecessors, baroque composers used music to depict the meaning of specific words. *Heaven* might be set to a high tone, and *hell* to a low one. Rising scales represented upward motion; descending scales depicted the reverse. Descending chromatic scales were associated with pain and grief. This descriptive musical language was quite standardized: a lament for a lost love might call forth the same descending chromatic scale used to depict suffering in the *Crucifixus* of the mass.

Baroque composers emphasized words by writing many rapid notes for a single syllable of text; this technique also displayed a singer's virtuosity. The individual words and phrases of a text are repeated over and over as the music continuously unfolds.

THE BAROQUE ORCHESTRA

During the baroque period, the orchestra evolved into a performing group based on instruments of the violin family. By modern standards, the baroque orchestra was small, consisting of from ten to thirty or forty players. Its instrumental makeup was flexible and could vary from piece to piece. At its nucleus were the basso continuo (harpsichord plus cello, double bass, or bassoon) and upper strings (first and second violins and violas). Use of woodwind, brass, and percussion instruments was variable. To the strings and continuo could be added recorders, flutes, oboes, trumpets, horns, trombones, or timpani. One piece might use only a single flute, while another would call for two oboes, three trumpets, and timpani. Trumpets and timpani joined the orchestra mainly when the music was festive. This flexibility contrasts with the standardized orchestra of later periods, composed of four sections: string, woodwind, brass, and percussion.

The baroque trumpet had no valves but was given rapid, complex melodic lines to play in a high register. Because the instrument was difficult to play and had a traditional association with royalty, the trumpeter was the aristocrat of the baroque orchestra. When prisoners of war were exchanged, trumpeters, if they had been captured, were treated like military officers.

Bach, Handel, Vivaldi, and others chose their orchestral instruments with care and obtained beautiful effects from specific tone colors. They loved to experiment with different combinations of instruments. However, in the baroque period tone color was distinctly subordinate to other musical elements—melody, rhythm, and harmony. Composers frequently rearranged their own or other composers' works for different instruments. A piece for string orchestra might become an organ solo, losing little in the process. Often, one instrument was treated like another. An oboe would play the same melody as the violins, or the flute and trumpet would imitate each other for extended sections of a piece.

BAROQUE FORMS

It has been noted that a piece of baroque music—particularly instrumental music—usually has unity of mood. Yet many baroque compositions include a set of pieces, or movements, that contrast. A *movement* is a piece that sounds fairly complete and independent but is part of a larger composition. Usually, each movement has its own themes, comes to a definite end, and is separated from the next movement by a brief pause. Thus, a baroque composition in three movements may contain contrasts between a fast and energetic opening, a slow and solemn middle, and a conclusion that is quick, light, and humorous.

All the form types described in "Musical Form" in Part I appear in baroque music. Three-part form (A B A), two-part form (A B), and continuous or undivided form are all common. A variation form found in many baroque works is the **ground bass,** or **basso ostinato** (*obstinate*, or *persistent, bass*), a musical idea repeated over and over in the bass while the melodies above it constantly change. (One famous example of the ground bass is the aria *Dido's Lament* from *Dido and Aeneas*, an opera by the English composer Henry Purcell, who lived from about 1659 to 1695.)

[8-record/cassette set: Side 2, band 3]

Regardless of form, baroque music features contrasts between bodies of sound. Often there is a quite regular alternation between a small and a large group of instruments, or between instruments and voices with instrumental accompaniment. This exploration of contrasting sounds was pursued with great imagination and provides a key to the understanding and enjoyment of baroque music.

[BAROQUE 2] THE CONCERTO GROSSO AND RITORNELLO FORM

We've seen that the contrast between loud and soft sounds—between large and small groups of performers—is a basic principle of baroque music. This principle governs the concerto grosso, an important form of orchestral music in the late baroque period. In the **concerto grosso,** a small group of soloists is pitted against a larger group of players called the **tutti** (*all*). Usually, between two and four soloists play with anywhere from eight to twenty or more musicians for the tutti. The tutti consists mainly of string instruments, with a harpsichord as part of the basso continuo. A concerto grosso presents a contrast of texture between the tutti and the soloists, who assert their individuality and appeal for attention through brilliant and fanciful melodic lines. The soloists were the best and highest-paid members of the baroque orchestra, because their parts were more difficult than those of the other players. Concerti grossi were frequently performed by private orchestras in aristocratic palaces.

The concerto grosso consists of *several movements that contrast in tempo and character.* Most often there are three movements: (1) fast, (2) slow, (3) fast. The opening movement is usually vigorous and determined,

clearly showing the contrast between tutti and soloists. The slow movement is quieter than the first, often lyrical and intimate. The last movement
is lively and carefree, sometimes dancelike.

The first and last movements of concerti grossi are often in *ritornello
form,* which is based on alternation between tutti and solo sections. In
ritornello form the tutti opens with a theme called the *ritornello (refrain).*
This theme, always played by the tutti, returns in different keys throughout the movement. But it usually returns in fragments, not complete. Only
at the end of the movement does the entire ritornello return in the home
key. Although the number of times a ritornello (tutti) returns varies from
piece to piece, a typical concerto grosso movement might be outlined as
follows:

1.   *a.*   Tutti (*f*), ritornello in home key
    b.   Solo
2.   *a.*   Tutti (*f*), ritornello fragment
    b.   Solo
3.   *a.*   Tutti (*f*), ritornello fragment
    b.   Solo
4.   Tutti (*f*), ritornello in home key

In contrast to the tutti's ritornello, the solo sections offer fresh melodic
ideas, softer dynamics, rapid scales, and broken chords. Soloists may also
expand short melodic ideas from the tutti. The opening movement of
Bach's *Brandenburg* Concerto No. 5 is a fine example of ritornello form in
the concerto grosso.

BRANDENBURG CONCERTO NO. 5 IN D MAJOR (1721), BY JOHANN SEBASTIAN BACH

Bach's six *Brandenburg* Concertos are so called because he dedicated them
to the margrave of Brandenburg—although he had actually composed
them for the orchestra of his own employer, the prince of Cöthen. Each of
the six is written for a different and unusual combination of instruments.

The *Brandenburg* Concerto No. 5 uses a string orchestra and a group of
soloists consisting of a flute, a violin, and a harpsichord. This was the first
time that a harpsichord had been given the solo role in a concerto grosso.
In 1719, the prince of Cöthen bought a new harpsichord; Bach probably
wanted to show off this instrument (as well as his skill as a keyboard
player), and so he gave it a solo spot. The tutti is written for violins, violas,
cellos, and double bass. During the tutti sections the solo violinist plays
along, as does the harpsichordist, who supplies the figured bass.

The *Brandenburg* Concerto No. 5 has three movements: (1) fast, (2) slow,
(3) fast. We'll focus on the first movement.

First Movement:

Allegro

The allegro movement opens with the ritornello, which is an almost continuous flow of rapid notes. After the ritornello ends very definitely, the soloists present short melodic ideas, the flute and violin imitating each other
playfully. The appearance of the soloists brings a lower dynamic level and
the new tone color of the flute. After a while, the tutti returns loudly with a
brief fragment of the ritornello, only to give way again to the soloists. This
alternation between brief, loud ritornello fragments in the tutti and longer,
softer solo sections continues throughout the movement.

The soloists' music tends to be brilliant, fanciful, and personal when
compared with the more vigorous and straightforward tutti sections. Solo
sections are also more polyphonic in texture than the tutti and stress imitation between the flute and violin. The soloists play new material of their
own or varied fragments from the ritornello. These solo sections build tension and make the listener anticipate the tutti's return. Listen especially for
the suspenseful solo section that begins with a new theme in minor and
ends with the fluttery sound of trills in the flute and violin. (A *trill* is an
ornament consisting of the rapid alternation of two tones that are a whole
or half step apart.)

Only the harpsichord plays during the long final solo section. And it is
spectacular! Bach builds a tense high point for the movement through irresistible rhythm and dazzling scale passages that require a virtuoso's skill.
His audience must have marveled at this brilliant harpsichord solo within a
concerto grosso. Audiences still do.

Side A, band 3

[*8-record/cassette set:*
Side 2, band 5]

Listening Outline   To be read while music is heard

BRANDENBURG CONCERTO NO. 5 IN D MAJOR (1721),
BY JOHANN SEBASTIAN BACH

First Movement: Allegro

Ritornello form, duple meter ($\frac{2}{2}$), D major

Flute, violin, harpsichord (solo group); string orchestra, continuo (tutti)

(About 11 minutes)

Tutti   1. *a.* Strings, *f*, ritornello.

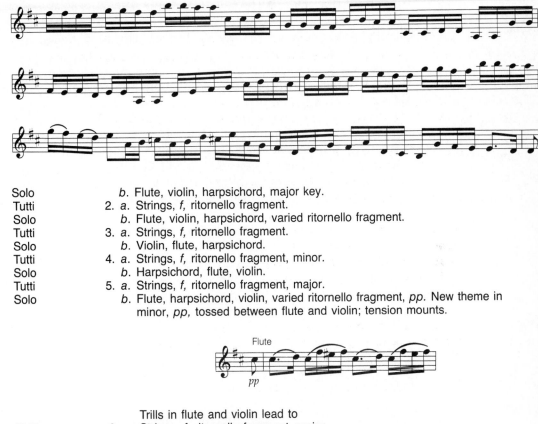

Solo		*b.* Flute, violin, harpsichord, major key.
Tutti	2. *a.*	Strings, *f,* ritornello fragment.
Solo		*b.* Flute, violin, harpsichord, varied ritornello fragment.
Tutti	3. *a.*	Strings, *f,* ritornello fragment.
Solo		*b.* Violin, flute, harpsichord.
Tutti	4. *a.*	Strings, *f,* ritornello fragment, minor.
Solo		*b.* Harpsichord, flute, violin.
Tutti	5. *a.*	Strings, *f,* ritornello fragment, major.
Solo		*b.* Flute, harpsichord, violin, varied ritornello fragment, *pp.* New theme in minor, *pp,* tossed between flute and violin; tension mounts.

Trills in flute and violin lead to

Tutti	6. *a.*	Strings, *f,* ritornello fragment, major.
Solo		*b.* Violin, flute, harpsichord.
Tutti	7. *a.*	Strings, *f,* longer ritornello fragment.
Solo		*b.* Violin, harpsichord, flute, varied ritornello fragment.
Tutti	8. *a.*	Strings, *f,* ritornello fragment.
Solo		*b.* Violin and flute play carefree idea with rapid harpsichord scales in background.
		c. Long harpsichord solo featuring virtuoso display. Mounting tension resolved in
Tutti	9.	Strings, *f,* ritornello.

THE FUGUE [BAROQUE **3**]

One cornerstone of baroque music is the fugue. A fugue can be written for a group of instruments or voices, or for a single instrument like an organ or harpsichord. The *fugue* is a polyphonic composition based on one main theme, called a *subject.* Throughout a fugue, different melodic lines, or "voices," imitate the subject. The top melodic line—whether sung or played—is the soprano voice, and the bottom is the bass. A fugue's texture usually includes three, four, or five voices. Though the fugue's subject remains fairly constant throughout, it takes on new meanings when shifted to different keys or combined with different melodic and rhythmic ideas.

The form of a fugue is extremely flexible; in fact, the only constant feature of fugues is how they begin—the subject is almost always presented in a single, unaccompanied voice. By thus highlighting the subject, the composer tells us what to remember and listen for. In getting to know a fugue, try to follow its subject through the different levels of texture. After its first presentation, the subject is imitated in turn by all the remaining voices.

The opening of a fugue in four voices may be represented as follows:

Soprano   Subject .... etc.

Alto   Subject .... etc.

Tenor   Subject .... etc.

Bass   Subject .... etc.

In this case, the top voice announces the subject and then the lower voices imitate it. However, the subject may be announced by *any* voice—top, bottom, or middle—and the order in which the remaining voices imitate it is also completely flexible.

This may seem reminiscent of a round like *Row, Row, Row Your Boat,* but in a fugue the game of follow the leader (exact imitation of the subject) does not continue indefinitely. The dotted lines in the fugue diagram just given show that *after a voice has presented the subject, it's free to go its own way with different melodic material.* A fugue's opening differs from a round's in another way: in a round, each voice presents the melody on the same tones. If the melody begins with the tones C–D–E, each voice will begin with these tones, whether at a higher or lower register. But in the opening of a fugue, *the subject is presented in two different scales.* The first time, it is based on the notes of the *tonic scale.* But when the second voice presents the subject, it is in the *dominant scale*—five scale steps higher than the tonic— and it is then called the *answer.* A subject beginning with the notes C–D–E, for example, would be imitated by an answer five steps higher, on G–A–B. This alternation of subject and answer between the two scales creates variety.

In many fugues, the subject in one voice is constantly accompanied in another voice by a different melodic idea called a *countersubject.* A constant companion, the countersubject always appears with the subject, sometimes below it, sometimes above it.

After the opening of a fugue, when each voice has taken its turn at presenting the subject, a composer is free to decide how often the subject will be presented, in which voices, and in which keys. Between presentations of the subject, there are often transitional sections called *episodes,* which offer either new material or fragments of the subject or countersubject. Episodes do *not* present the subject in its entirety. They lend variety to the fugue and make reappearances of the subject sound fresh. Bach called one composer of fugues "pedantic" because he "had not shown enough fire to reanimate the theme by episodes."

Several musical procedures commonly appear in fugues. One is *stretto,* in which a subject is imitated before it is completed; one voice tries to catch the other. Another common procedure is *pedal point* (or *organ point*), in which a single tone, usually in the bass, is held while the other voices produce a series of changing harmonies against it. (The term is taken from organ music, where a sustained low tone is produced by the organist's foot on a key of the pedal keyboard.)

A fugue subject can be varied in four principal ways:

1. It can be turned upside down, a procedure known as *inversion.* If the subject moves *upward* by leap, the inversion will move *downward* the same distance; if the subject moves *downward* by step, the inversion will move *upward* by step. In inversion, each interval in the subject is reversed in direction.
2. The subject may be presented *retrograde,* that is, by beginning with the last note of the subject and proceeding backward to the first.
3. The subject may be presented in *augmentation,* in which the original time values are lengthened.
4. The subject may appear in *diminution,* with shortened time values.

Fugues usually convey a single mood and a sense of continuous flow. They may be written as independent works or as single movements within larger compositions. Very often an independent fugue is introduced by a short piece called a *prelude.*

Bach and Handel each wrote hundreds of fugues; their fugues represent the peak among works in the form. In the baroque period, as a friend of Bach observed, "Skill in fugue was so indispensable in a composer that no one could have attained a musical post who had not worked out a given subject in all kinds of counterpoint and in a regular fugue." Fugal writing has continued into the nineteenth and twentieth centuries, but is not used as frequently as in the baroque period. Yet to this day, musicians study how to write fugues as part of their training.

ORGAN FUGUE IN G MINOR (LITTLE FUGUE; ABOUT 1709), BY JOHANN SEBASTIAN BACH

One of Bach's best-known organ pieces is the *Little* Fugue in G Minor, so called to differentiate it from another, longer fugue in G minor. The opening section of this fugue corresponds to the diagram on page 86. Each of the fugue's four voices takes its turn at presenting the tuneful subject, which is announced in the top voice and then appears in progressively lower voices, until it reaches the bass, where it is played by the organist's feet on the pedal keyboard. Like many baroque melodies, the subject gathers momentum as it goes along, beginning with relatively long time values (quarter notes) and then proceeding to shorter ones (eighth and sixteenth notes).

Side A, band 4

[*8-record/cassette set:*
Side 2, band 6]

Starting with its second appearance, the subject is accompanied by a countersubject that moves in short time values.

After the opening section, the subject appears five more times, each time preceded by an episode. The first episode uses both new material and a melodic idea from the countersubject.

This episode contains downward sequences, which are melodic patterns repeated in the same voice but at lower pitches.

For harmonic contrast, Bach twice presents the subject in major keys rather than minor. The final statement of the subject—in minor—exploits the powerful bass tones of the pedal keyboard. Though the fugue is in minor, it ends with a major chord. This was a frequent practice in the baroque period; major chords were thought more conclusive than minor.

THE ELEMENTS OF OPERA $\begin{bmatrix} \text{BAROQUE} \\ \mathbf{4} \end{bmatrix}$

The baroque era witnessed the development of a major innovation in music—*opera*, or drama that is sung to orchestral accompaniment. In Section 5, we'll look at baroque opera; but first, a general discussion of opera is in order.

In opera, characters and plot are revealed through song rather than speech. Once we accept this convention, opera offers us great pleasure, since the music not only delights the ear but also depicts mood, character, and action and heightens the emotional effect of the story. Opera demands performers who can sing and act simultaneously, and in addition to solo singers—the stars—it uses secondary soloists, choruses, nonsinging "extras," and sometimes dancers, all in costume. In the orchestra pit are the instrumentalists and the conductor. Scenery, lighting, and stage machinery are intricate, since operas often include fires, floods, storms, and supernatural effects. A large opera's personnel—from conductor to stage director and assorted vocal coaches, rehearsal accompanists, technicians, and stagehands—may reach a startling total of several hundred people.

The creation of an opera results from the joint efforts of a composer and a dramatist. The text, called a *libretto*, is usually written by the dramatist, or *librettist*, and then set to music by the composer, but the two usually collaborate to ensure that the text meets the composer's musical needs. W. H. Auden once observed—correctly—that "no good opera plot can be sensible." Opera characters are people overwhelmed by love, lust, hatred, and revenge; they wear fantastic disguises and commit extraordinary acts of violence. Yet the music makes them human and real. A great opera composer is a master of musical timing and characterization and has a keen sense of the theater; through the music, the composer paces and controls the drama.

Some operas are serious, some comic, some both. Most are entirely sung, though some contain spoken dialogue. The range of characters is broad—gods, empresses, dukes, servants, priests, prostitutes, peasants, clowns, cowboys. For the opera soloists who create all these roles, the basic voice categories (soprano, alto, tenor, and bass) are divided more finely: the *voice categories of opera* include coloratura soprano (with a very high range), lyric soprano and lyric tenor, dramatic soprano and dramatic tenor, basso buffo (who takes comic roles), and basso profundo (with a very low range).

Like plays, operas have from one to five acts subdivided into scenes. An act presents a variety of vocal and orchestral contrasts. For many opera fans, the main attraction is the *aria*, a song for solo voice with orchestral accompaniment, usually lasting several minutes. An aria is an outpouring of melody that expresses an emotional state; it is a complete piece with a definite beginning, high point, and end (at which the audience often responds with an ovation). Composers often lead into an aria with a *recitative*, a vocal line that imitates speech and is used to move the action forward. In a recitative, words are sung quickly, often on repeated tones, and with one note to each syllable—as opposed to an aria, where one syllable may be stretched over many notes. Besides arias, there are compositions for two or more singers: duets (two singers), trios (three), quartets (four), quintets (five), and sextets (six). Pieces for three or more singers are called *ensembles*. The opera chorus—courtiers, sailors, peasants, prisoners, or whatever—creates atmosphere and comments on the action.

The nerve center of an opera performance is the orchestra pit—a sunken area directly in front of the stage. An opera orchestra has the same instruments as a symphony orchestra but usually a smaller string section. It supports the singers, depicts mood and atmosphere, and highlights the drama. The conductor's awesome responsibility is to hold everything together. (A *conductor* beats time, indicates expression, cues in musicians, and controls the balance among instruments or voices.)

Most operas open with a purely orchestral composition called an *overture* or *prelude* (orchestral introductions to acts other than the first are always called *preludes*). Since the eighteenth century, the music for the overture has been drawn from material in the opera itself. Many overtures are complete compositions that frequently appear on symphony orchestra programs.

OPERA IN THE BAROQUE ERA

Opera was born in Italy. Its "parents" were a small group of nobles, poets, and composers called the *Camerata* (Italian for *fellowship* or *society*) who began meeting in Florence around 1575 to create a new vocal style based on the music of ancient Greek tragedy. (Since no ancient Greek music had survived, they relied on literary accounts of it.) This new style followed the rhythms and pitch fluctuations of speech. It was sung by a soloist with only a simple chordal accompaniment and was thus homophonic; the Camerata rejected polyphony because it would obscure the all-important text.

Euridice, by Jacopo Peri, which was performed in Florence in 1600, is the earliest opera that has been preserved; seven years later, Monteverdi composed *Orfeo*, the first *great* opera. Both are based on the Greek myth of Orpheus and Eurydice.

Much baroque opera was composed for ceremonial occasions at court; its subject matter, classical mythology and ancient history, fascinated aristocratic patrons and also flattered them, since they identified with the Greek and Roman heroes and gods. But in 1637, the first public opera house opened in Venice, and between then and 1700 there were seventeen opera houses in Venice alone and many in other Italian cities—ample evidence that opera was born in the right place at the right time. Court opera was designed to display magnificence and splendor; similarly, the public opera houses had stage machinery and sets that bordered on the colossal: gods would ride across the sky in chariots, ships would toss, boulders would split.

Baroque opera marked the rise of virtuoso singers, particularly the *castrato*, a male singer castrated before puberty. (A *virtuoso* is a performing artist of extraordinary technical mastery.) Castration of boy singers was common in Italy from 1600 to 1800, usually with the consent of impoverished parents who hoped their sons would go on to wealth and stardom. A castrato (plural, *castrati*) combined the lung power of a man with the vocal range of a woman and had a unique sound—not like a woman's—that intrigued listeners. Some baroque operas cannot be done today, because contemporary singers are unable to manage the fiendishly difficult castrato parts.

Late baroque operas consisted largely of arias linked by recitatives. Usually, the recitative is speechlike and accompanied only by a basso continuo;

91

this is a *secco recitative*. When the recitative is supported by strings as well as continuo, it is called an *accompanied recitative*. The form of a typical aria is A B A, and an aria in A B A form is called a *da capo aria*: after the B section, the term *da capo* is written, meaning *from the beginning* and indicating a repetition of the A section. However, the repetition was not literal, because the singer was expected to *embellish* the returning melody with ornamental tones.

By combining virtuosity, nobility, and extravagance, baroque opera expressed the spirit of a grand age.

ORFEO (ORPHEUS, 1607), BY CLAUDIO MONTEVERDI

The earliest operatic masterpiece, *Orfeo*, was created by Claudio Monteverdi (1567–1643), a monumental figure in the history of music whose works not only were highly influential in their time but also form a bridge between the sixteenth and seventeenth centuries. He composed *Orfeo* for the court of Mantua, where he was music director—a position which evidently earned him little money and even less respect. Later, life improved for him; in 1613, he was appointed music director of St. Mark's in Venice, the most important church position in Italy, and he remained there until his death. Only three of his twelve operas are preserved, but they truly blend music and drama. To achieve emotional intensity, he used dissonance with unprecedented freedom and daring and introduced new orchestral effects, and his vocal lines respond marvelously to the inflections of Italian while maintaining melodic flow.

Fittingly enough, Monteverdi's first opera is about Orpheus, the supremely gifted musician of Greek myth. Orpheus, son of the god Apollo, is ecstatically happy after his marriage to Eurydice. But this joy is shattered when his bride is killed by a poisonous snake. Orpheus goes down to hades hoping to bring her back to life. Because of his beautiful music, he is granted this privilege—on the condition that he not look back at Eurydice while leading her out of hades. But in a moment of anxiety, Orpheus does look back, and Eurydice vanishes. Nonetheless, there is a happy ending, of sorts. Apollo pities Orpheus and brings him to heaven, where he can gaze eternally at Eurydice's radiance in the sun and stars.

When *Orfeo* was composed, in 1607, no expense was spared to make it a lavish production. There were star soloists, a chorus, dancers, and a large orchestra of about forty players. The aristocratic audience was wildly enthusiastic and recognized the historic significance of the performance.

Monteverdi creates variety in *Orfeo* by using many kinds of music—recitatives, arias, duets, choruses, and instrumental interludes. He uses the opera orchestra to establish atmosphere, character, and dramatic situation. With the simplest of musical means, Monteverdi makes his characters come alive. Through vocal line alone he quickly characterizes the hero's joy and despair. Monteverdi sets his text in a very flexible way, freely alternating recitatives with more melodious passages, depending on the meaning of the words.

Act II
Recitative: *Tu se' morta (You are dead)*

Monteverdi's mastery of the then-novel technique of recitative is shown in *Tu se' morta*, sung by Orpheus after he is told of Eurydice's death. Orpheus resolves to bring her back from hades, and he bids an anguished farewell to the earth, sky, and sun. His vocal line is accompanied only by a basso continuo played by a small portable organ and a bass lute. (In modern performances, other instruments are sometimes substituted.)

[8-record/cassette set: Side 2, band 2]

The texture is homophonic as the accompaniment simply gives harmonic support to the voice. The vocal line is rhythmically free, with little sense of beat or meter, and its phrases are irregular in length. This flexible setting of text is meant to suggest the passionate speech of an actor declaiming his lines. Monteverdi frequently uses word painting, the musical representation of poetic images that was favored by baroque composers. For example, words like *stelle (stars)* and *sole (sun)* are sung to climactic high tones, while *abissi (abysses)* and *morte (death)* are sung to somber, low tones. Three times during the recitative the melodic line rises to a climax and then descends. Through such simple means, Monteverdi makes Orpheus's passion come alive.

Tu se' morta, se' morta, mia vita,	You are dead, you are dead, my dearest,
ed io respiro; tu se' da me partita,	And I breathe; you have left me,
se' da me partita per mai più,	You have left me forevermore,
mai più non tornare, ed io rimango—	Never to return, and I remain—
no, no, che se i versi alcuna cosa ponno,	No, no, if my verses have any power,
n'andrò sicuro a' più profondi abissi,	I will go confidently to the deepest abysses,
e, intenerito il cor del re de l'ombre,	And, having melted the heart of the king of shadows,
meco trarrotti a riveder le stelle,	Will bring you back to me to see the stars again,
o se ciò negherammi empio destino,	Or, if pitiless fate denies me this,
rimarrò teco in compagnia di morte.	I will remain with you in the company of death.
Addio terra, addio cielo, e sole, addio.	Farewell earth, farewell sky, and sun, farewell.

[BAROQUE **6**] THE BAROQUE SONATA

One of the main developments in instrumental music was the baroque *sonata*, a composition in several movements for one to eight instruments. (In later periods, the term *sonata* took on a more restricted meaning.) Composers often wrote **trio sonatas**, so called because they had three melodic lines: two high ones and a basso continuo. A trio sonata is actually played by four instruments, however—two high instruments, such as violins, flutes, or oboes; and a keyboard instrument plus a cello or bassoon for the continuo.

TRIO SONATA IN E MINOR, OP. 3, NO. 7 (1689), BY ARCANGELO CORELLI*

Corelli's Trio Sonata in E Minor is a fine example of the baroque trio sonata. Corelli (1653–1713), the most prominent Italian violinist and composer of string music around 1700, was also an eminent teacher who laid the foundations of modern violin technique; he wrote only instrumental music— sixty sonatas and twelve concertos, all for strings.

In the E Minor Trio Sonata, the basso continuo is for organ and cello; the upper lines are taken by two violins that play in the same high register. The violins are the center of attention; they seem to be rivals, taking turns at the melodic ideas, intertwining, and sometimes rising above each other in pitch. Though the bass line is subordinate to the two upper voices, it is no mere accompaniment. It imitates melodic ideas presented by the violins.

The sonata has four short movements. The first movement is solemn, dignified, and slow, in quadruple meter; the second is a vigorous, fugue-like allegro in duple meter; the third is a soulful adagio in triple meter; and the fourth is a dancelike allegro in A A B B form, also in triple meter.

[*Instructor's records: Side 1, bands 2–3*]

[BAROQUE **7**] ANTONIO VIVALDI

Antonio Vivaldi (1678–1741), a towering figure of the late Italian baroque, was the son of a violinist at St. Mark's Cathedral in Venice. He became a priest, but left the ministry after about a year because of poor health; for

---

*The abbreviation *op.* stands for *opus*, Latin for *work*. An opus number is a way of identifying a piece or set of pieces. Usually, within a composer's output, the higher a composition's opus number, the later it was written.

most of his life, he was a violin teacher, composer, and conductor at a Venetian music school for orphaned and illegitimate girls. It was for the school's all-female orchestra—considered one of the best in Italy—that he composed many of his finest works. Though he was famous and influential as a virtuoso violinist and a composer, his popularity waned shortly before his death in 1741; he died in poverty and was almost forgotten until the baroque revival of the 1940s and 1950s.

Vivaldi is best known for his 450 or so concerti grossi and solo concertos (a *solo concerto* is a piece for a *single* soloist and an orchestra). He exploited the resources of the violin and many other instruments and is noted for fast movements with vigorous, tuneful themes and impassioned, lyrical slow movements.

LA PRIMAVERA (SPRING), CONCERTO FOR VIOLIN AND STRING ORCHESTRA, OP. 8, NO. 1, FROM THE FOUR SEASONS (1725)

Vivaldi's most popular work is the concerto *La Primavera (Spring)* from *The Four Seasons*, a set of four solo concertos for violin, string orchestra, and basso continuo. Each of these concertos depicts sounds and events associated with one of the seasons, such as the bird songs heard in spring and the gentle breezes characteristic of summer. The descriptive effects in the music correspond to images and ideas found in the sonnets that preface each of the four concertos. To make his intentions absolutely clear, Vivaldi placed lines from the poems at the appropriate passages in the musical score and even added such descriptive labels as *the sleeping goatherd* and *the barking dog*. The *Spring, Summer, Autumn,* and *Winter* concertos are examples of baroque *program music,* or instrumental music associated with a story, poem, idea, or scene. They are forerunners of the more elaborate program music that developed during the romantic period.

Like most of Vivaldi's concertos, *Spring* has three movements: (1) fast, (2) slow, (3) fast. Both the first movement (which we'll study) and the last are in ritornello form.

First Movement:

Allegro

The allegro, in E major, opens with an energetic orchestral ritornello depicting the arrival of spring. Each of the ritornello's two phrases is played loudly and then repeated softly, in the terraced dynamics typical of baroque music. After the ritornello, the movement alternates between extended solo sections containing musical tone painting and brief tutti sections presenting part of the ritornello theme. In the first solo section, bird songs are imitated by high trills and repeated notes played by the violin soloist and two violins from the orchestra. In the second descriptive epi-

[*8-record/cassette set:*
Side 2, band 4]

sode, murmuring streams are suggested by soft running notes in the violins. The next solo section contains string tremolos and rapid scales representing thunder and lightning. Following the storm, the ritornello appears in minor instead of in major. All the pictorial passages in this movement provide contrasts of texture and dynamics between returns of the ritornello theme. The allegro's tunefulness, rhythmic vitality, and light, homophonic texture evoke the feeling of springtime.

Listening Outline   To be read while music is heard

LA PRIMAVERA (SPRING),
CONCERTO FOR VIOLIN AND STRING ORCHESTRA, OP. 8, NO. 1,
FROM THE FOUR SEASONS (1725), BY ANTONIO VIVALDI

First Movement: Allegro

Ritornello form, quadruple meter ($\frac{4}{4}$), E major

Solo violin, string orchestra, harpsichord (basso continuo)

(About 3½ minutes)

Spring has   1. *a.* Tutti, ritornello opening phrase, *f*, repeated *p*
come

         closing phrase, *f*, repeated *p*, major key.

Song of the   *b.* Solo violin joined by two violins from orchestra, high trills and repeated
birds   notes.
         2. *a.* Tutti, ritornello closing phrase, *f*.
Murmuring   *b.* Violins, *p*, running notes, cellos, *p*, running notes below sustained tones in
streams   violins.

3. *a.* Tutti, ritornello closing phrase, *f.*

Thunder and
lightning

b. String tremolos, *f,* upward rushing scales introduce high solo violin, brilliant virtuoso passages answered by low string tremolos.

4. *a.* Tutti, ritornello closing phrase in minor key, *f.*

Song of the
birds

b. Solo violin joined by two violins from orchestra, high repeated notes and trills, minor key.

5. *a.* Tutti, ritornello opening phrase varied, *f,* ends in major key.

b. Solo violin, running notes accompanied by basso continuo.

6. Tutti, ritornello closing phrase, *f,* repeated *p,* major key.

JOHANN SEBASTIAN BACH

BAROQUE

8

The masterpieces of Johann Sebastian Bach (1685–1750) mark the high point of baroque music. Bach came from a long line of musicians and passed on this musical heritage; four of his sons were also composers. He was born in Eisenach, Germany, and began his musical career as a church organist and then as court organist and later concertmaster of the court orchestra in Weimar.

His most lucrative and prestigious post was as court conductor for the prince of Cöthen—more important, this was the first position in which he was not involved with church or organ music. For six years (1717–1723) he directed and composed for the prince's small orchestra; the *Brandenburg* Concertos grew out of this productive period.

Bach's next position was as cantor (director of music) of St. Thomas Church in Leipzig, with responsibility for the four main municipal churches. Bach remained here for the last twenty-seven years of his life. He rehearsed, conducted, and usually composed an extended work for chorus, soloists, and orchestra for each Sunday and church holiday and was responsible for the musical education of some fifty-five students in the St. Thomas school. He also became director of the Leipzig Collegium Musicum, a student organization that gave weekly concerts at a coffeehouse. An eminent teacher of organ and composition, he gave organ recitals and was often asked to judge the construction of organs. In his last years, his eyesight deteriorated, yet he continued to compose, conduct, and teach; when he died in 1750, he had become completely blind.

Bach was a deeply religious man—a Lutheran—who wrote the letters *J. J.* for *Jesu Juva* (*Jesus help*) at the beginning of each sacred composition and *S. D. G.* for *Soli Deo Gloria* (*to God alone the glory*) at the end. His love of music was so great that as a young man he would walk up to 30 miles to hear a famous organist. He was married twice and had twenty children, of whom nine survived him and four became well-known musicians.

Bach was by no means considered the greatest composer of his day,

(Granger Collection)

Johann Sebastian Bach.

though he was recognized as the most eminent organist, harpsichordist, and improviser (*improvisation* is the term used for music created at the same time as it is performed). He was little known outside Germany; and by the time of his maturity, the baroque style had started to go out of fashion and many people thought his works too heavy, complex, and polyphonic. His music was largely forgotten for years after his death, though a few later composers were aware of his genius; but in 1829 Felix Mendelssohn presented the *St. Matthew Passion*, and Bach's music has been the daily bread of every serious musician since then.

BACH'S MUSIC

Bach created masterpieces in every baroque form except opera. Throughout, he fused technical mastery with emotional depth. The excellence and number of his compositions for orchestra, small groups, and various solo instruments show how prominent instrumental music had become in the baroque period. His vocal music—the bulk of his output—was written mostly for the Lutheran church and was often based on familiar hymns. But his personal style was drawn from Italian concertos and French dance pieces as well as German church music.

Bach's works are unique in their combination of polyphonic texture and rich harmony and are used as models by music students today. Baroque music leans toward unity of mood, and this is particularly true of Bach, who liked to elaborate a single musical idea in a piece, creating unity by an insistent rhythmic drive. By his time, there was little difference in style between sacred and secular music; he often created sacred music simply by rearranging secular works, and his church music uses operatic forms like aria and recitative. Sometimes he composed music to demonstrate what could be done with a specific form (his *Art of the Fugue*, for example) or instrument (for instance, his six suites for solo cello). His *Well-Tempered Clavier*, a collection of forty-eight preludes and fugues, two in each major and minor key, was composed to explore and demonstrate a system of tuning (the title means, roughly, *The Well-Tuned Keyboard Instrument*).

THE BAROQUE SUITE [BAROQUE **9**]

In the baroque period (and later), music was written that—while meant for listening—was related to specific dance types in tempo, meter, and rhythm. The baroque *suite* is a set of dance-inspired movements, all in the same key but different in tempo, meter, and character; it is performed by a solo instrument, a small group, or an orchestra. The movements have various national origins: the moderately paced *allemande* from Germany, the fast *courante* and the moderate *gavotte* from France, the slow and solemn *sarabande* from Spain, and the fast *gigue* (jig) from England and Ireland.

The movements of a suite are usually in two-part form with each section repeated: A A B B. The A section, which opens in the tonic key and modulates to the dominant, is balanced by the B section, which begins in the dominant and returns to the tonic. Otherwise, the sections contrast very little, since they use the same thematic materials.

Suites often begin with a movement that is *not* dance-inspired. One common opening is the **French overture**, usually written in two parts—the first slow and dignified, with dotted rhythms; the second quick and lighter in mood, often beginning like a fugue.

Bach wrote four suites for orchestra, which were probably performed in a Leipzig coffeehouse by the Collegium Musicum.

SUITE NO. 3 IN D MAJOR (1729–1731), BY JOHANN SEBASTIAN BACH

2 oboes, 3 trumpets, timpani, strings, basso continuo
First Movement: Overture

The suite opens with a majestic French overture, which exploits the bright sounds of trumpets. After a slow opening section with dotted rhythms, we hear the energetic fast section. This begins like a fugue, with an upward-moving theme introduced by the first violins and then imitated by the other instruments.

The fast section is like a concerto grosso in its alternation of solid tutti passages with lightly scored ones highlighting the first violins. After the fast section, the slow tempo, dotted rhythms, and majestic mood of the opening return.

Second Movement: Air

[8-record/cassette set:
Side 3, band 1]

The second movement, the air, contains one of Bach's best-loved melodies. It is scored for only strings and continuo and is serene and lyrical, in contrast to the majestic and bustling French overture. The title suggests that the movement is written in the style of an Italian aria. Like the opening movement, the air is not related to dance. In its A A B B form, the B section is twice as long as the A section. The air combines a steadily moving bass (which proceeds in upward and downward octave leaps) with a rhapsodic and rhythmically irregular melody in the violins.

Third Movement: Gavotte

All the movements that follow the overture and the air are inspired by dance, beginning with the gavotte, which is written in duple meter and in a moderate tempo and uses the full orchestra again. It may be outlined as follows: gavotte I (A A B B); gavotte II (C C D D); gavotte I (A B). Notice the contrast between the sections for full orchestra and those without trumpets and timpani.

Fourth Movement: Bourrée

The bourrée is an even livelier dance, also in duple meter. Its form is A A B B, and it is the shortest movement of the suite.

Fifth Movement: Gigue

[8-record/cassette set:
Side 3, band 2]

The suite concludes with a rollicking gigue in $\frac{6}{8}$ time, also in the form A A B B. Here, Bach's manner is simple and direct. Listen for the splendid effect when timpani and trumpets periodically join the rest of the orchestra.

THE CHORALE AND CHURCH CANTATA

In Bach's time, the Lutheran church service (which lasted about 4 hours) was filled with music, and his church had not only a choir of twelve or so boys and men but also an orchestra of fourteen to twenty-one players. Each service included several *chorales*, hymn tunes sung to a German religious text. These were often preceded by a *chorale prelude*, a short composition played by the organist and based on a hymn tune. Chorales were also employed in the principal means of musical expression in the service—the church *cantata*.

The cantata designed for Lutheran services of Bach's day was usually written for chorus, vocal soloists, organ, and small orchestra. Its text, in German, was either original or drawn from the Bible or familiar hymns and was meant to reinforce the minister's sermon. It might last about half an hour and include choruses, recitatives, arias, and duets—in fact, it closely resembled baroque opera.

The cantor, or music director, had to provide cantatas for every Sunday and holiday; Bach wrote about 295, of which about 195 are still in existence.

CANTATA NO. 140: WACHET AUF, RUFT UNS DIE STIMME (AWAKE, A VOICE IS CALLING US; 1731), BY JOHANN SEBASTIAN BACH

Wachet auf, ruft uns die Stimme (Cantata No. 140), Bach's best-known cantata, is based on a chorale tune which was then about 130 years old and widely familiar. It has the form A B A, and the last movement of the cantata presents it unadorned:

101

There are nine melodic phrases; 1 to 3, the A section, are repeated immediately; phrase 3 reappears at the end of the B section (phrase 9) and beautifully rounds off the melody.

The cantata has seven movements: (1) chorus and orchestra, (2) recitative for tenor, (3) duet for bass (Jesus) and soprano (the soul), (4) tenor chorale, (5) recitative for bass (Jesus), (6) duet for bass (Jesus) and soprano (soul), (7) chorale (chorus doubled by orchestra). We'll consider movements 1, 4, and 7.

First Movement: Chorus and Orchestra

2 oboes, English horn, French horn,
1st violins, 2d violins, violas,
basso continuo (organ, bassoon, cello)

[8-record/cassette set:
  Side 3, band 3]

In the chorale text of the first movement, watchmen on the towers of Jerusalem call on the wise virgins (Christians) to awake because the bridegroom (Christ) is coming. The movement opens with an orchestral ritornello that may have been intended to suggest a procession or march. There are dotted rhythms (long-short, long-short), a rising figure with syncopation, and a series of rising scales.

At the ritornello's closing cadence the sopranos enter and sing the first phrase of the chorale in long notes. Soon the three lower voices engage in an imitative dialogue based on a new motive in shorter note values. Throughout, the orchestra continues to play still shorter notes.

Thus there are three layers of sound: the chorale phrases in long notes in the soprano; the imitative dialogue in shorter note values in the three lower voices; and the ever-busy orchestra playing motives from the ritornello in even shorter notes. The chorale tune (in the soprano) is presented not as a continuous whole but rather phrase by phrase, with breaks between. After each phrase, the voices pause while the orchestra continues to play interludes made up of either the whole ritornello or sections from it. Sometimes the motives in the three lower voices illustrate the text, as when they have rising scale figures at the word *hoch (high)* and exclamations at the repeated *wo (where)*.

Once during the movement, the three lower voices become emancipated from the soprano and jubilantly sing a melody in rapid notes on *Alleluja*. This, perhaps, is the most exciting moment in the movement.

		Orchestral ritornello.
Wachet auf, ruft uns die Stimme	"Awake," the voice of watchmen	
		Brief orchestral interlude.
der Wächter sehr hoch auf der Zinne,	calls us from high on the tower,	Rising scales in lower voices depict *hoch (high).*
		Brief orchestral interlude.
wach auf, du Stadt Jerusalem!	"Awake, you city of Jerusalem!"	
		Orchestral ritornello.
Mitternacht heisst diese Stunde;	Midnight is this very hour;	
		Brief orchestral interlude.
sie rufen uns mit hellem Munde:	they call to us with bright voices:	
		Brief orchestral interlude.
wo seid ihr klugen Jungfrauen?	"Where are you, wise virgins?"	
		Long orchestral interlude.
Wohl auf, der Bräut'gam kömmt,	Take cheer, the Bridegroom comes,	
		Brief orchestral interlude.
steht auf, die Lampen nehmt!	arise, take up your lamps!	
Alleluja!	Hallelujah!	Altos, jubilant melody in rapid notes. Imitation by tenors, then basses.
Alleluja!	Hallelujah!	Sopranos, chorale in long notes.
		Orchestral interlude.
Macht euch bereit	Prepare yourselves	
		Orchestral interlude.
zu der Hochzeit	for the wedding,	
		Brief orchestral interlude.
ihr müsset ihm entgegen gehn.	you must go forth to meet him.	
		Orchestral ritornello.

Fourth Movement: Tenor Chorale
Violins and violas in unison, basso continuo

The chorale tune returns in the fourth movement, the most popular of the cantata. Bach liked this section so much that toward the end of his life he rearranged it as a chorale prelude for organ. With miraculous ease, he sets two contrasting melodies against each other. First we hear the unison strings supported by the continuo playing a warm, flowing melody that Bach may have intended as a dancelike procession of the maidens as they "all follow to the joyful hall and share the Lord's supper." This melody is repeated and varied throughout while the tenors sing the chorale tune against it.

Side A, band 6

[*8-record/cassette set:*]
[*Side 3, band 4*]

The chorale tune moves in faster rhythmic values than it did in the opening movement, but here, too, it is broken into component phrases linked by the instrumental melody. It's helpful to listen several times to this movement, first focusing on the rapid rhythms of the graceful string melody, then on the sturdy, slower rhythms of the chorale tune, and finally on all lines at once.

Zion hört die Wächter singen,	Zion hears the watchmen singing,
das Herz tut ihr vor Freuden springen,	for joy her very heart is springing,
sie wachet und steht eilend auf.	she wakes and rises hastily.

(*Continued on page 105, following color section.*)

THE BAROQUE PERIOD

(Giraudon/Art Resource)

Henry IV Receiving the Portrait of Maria de' Medici, *by Peter Paul Rubens (1622–1625). Baroque artists became interested in forming a total illusion, like a stage setting. Both baroque painting and opera were often created for the nobility and designed to display magnificent extravagance.*

(Metropolitan Museum of Art, Harris Brisbane Dick Fund, 1946)

Rape of the Sabine Women, by Nicolas Poussin (1636–1637). The French painter Poussin combined dynamic motion with logic and balance.

Worship of the Holy Name of Jesus, by Giovanni Battista Gaulli (1670–1683). Baroque painters emphasized grandeur, movement, and drama. This painting of angels, saints, and sinners is a ceiling fresco in the Jesuit church Il Gesù, in Rome. It breaks through its frame and creates the illusion that the spectator is gazing into heaven. Its monumentality is comparable to that of Bach's Mass in B Minor.

(Scala/Art Resource)

(Metropolitan Museum of Art, Bequest of Benjamin Altman, 1913)

Self-Portrait, *by Rembrandt van Rijn (1660). The Dutch painter Rembrandt's masterful use of light and dark contributes to the sense of psychological truth in his portraits and self-portraits.*

(Continued from page 104)

Ihr Freund kommt von Himmel prächtig,	From heaven comes her friend resplendent,
von Gnaden stark, von Wahrheit mächtig,	sturdy in grace, mighty in truth,
Ihr Licht wird hell, ihr Stern geht auf.	her light shines bright, her star ascends.
Nun komm, du werte Kron,	Now come, you worthy crown,
Herr Jesu, Gottes Sohn.	Lord Jesus, God's own Son,
Hosianna!	Hosanna!
Wir folgen all'	We all follow
zum Freudensaal	to the joyful hall
und halten mit das Abendmahl.	and share the Lord's Supper.

Seventh Movement: Chorale
Chorus doubled by orchestra

Bach rounds off Cantata No. 140 by bringing back the chorale once more.
For the first time since the first movement, all voices and instruments take
part. Here the chorale is set in a relatively simple, homophonic texture for
four voices, with the instruments simply doubling them, not playing melodies of their own. Now the chorale is heard as a continuous melody, without interludes between its phrases. The rich sound, full harmonies, and
regular rhythms express praise of God, faith in him, and joy in being in his
kingdom. No doubt the congregation joined in the singing of the final
chorale, which so firmly expressed their unity and belief.

[*8-record/cassette set: Side 3, band 5*]

Gloria sei dir gesungen	Gloria be sung to you
mit Menschen- und englischen Zungen,	with men's and angel's tongues,
mit Harfen und mit Zimbeln schon.	with harps and beautiful cymbals.
Von zwölf Perlen sind die Pforten	Of twelve pearls are the gates
an deiner Stadt; wir sind Konsorten	at your city; we are consorts
der Engel hoch um deinen Thron.	of the angels high about your throne.
Kein Aug' hat je gespürt,	No eye has ever sensed,
kein Ohr hat je gehört	no ear has ever heard
solche Freude.	such a delight.
Des sind wir froh,	Of this we rejoice,
io, io!	io, io,
ewig in dulci jubilo.	forever in sweet joy.

[**11**] THE ORATORIO

Together with the opera and cantata, the oratorio stands as a major development in baroque vocal music. Like opera, the **oratorio** is a large-scale composition for chorus, vocal soloists, and orchestra; it usually is set to a narrative text. Oratorio differs from opera in that it has no acting, scenery, or costumes. Most oratorios are based on biblical stories, but usually they are not intended for religious services. Today they are performed in either concert halls or churches.

An oratorio contains a succession of choruses, arias, duets, recitatives, and orchestral interludes. The chorus is especially important and serves either to comment on or to participate in the drama. A narrator's recitatives usually relate the story and connect one piece with another. Oratorios are longer than cantatas (they sometimes last over 2 hours) and have more of a story line.

Oratorios first appeared in early seventeenth-century Italy as musical dramatizations of biblical stories and were performed in prayer halls called *oratorios*. During the baroque period, the oratorio spread to other countries and assumed many forms. *Messiah*, by George Frideric Handel, has for decades been the best-known and most-loved oratorio.

[**12**] GEORGE FRIDERIC HANDEL

George Frideric Handel (1685–1759), a master of Italian opera and English oratorio, was born one month before J. S. Bach, in Halle, Germany. He was not from a musical family—his father wanted him to study law—but by the time he was nine, his musical talent was so outstanding that he was allowed to study with a local organist and composer. By eleven, he himself was able to compose and give organ lessons. At eighteen, he set out for Hamburg, where he was drawn to the renowned opera house, and became a violinist and harpsichordist in the orchestra. When he was twenty, one of his operas was successfully produced.

At twenty-one, Handel went to Italy; there he wrote widely acclaimed operas and mingled with princes, cardinals, and famous musicians. Re-

(Metropolitan Museum of Art, bequest of Alexandrine Sinsheimer, 1959)

George Frideric Handel.

turning to Germany in 1710, he took a well-paid position as music director for Elector Georg Ludwig of Hanover; but after a month he asked for a leave to go to London, where his opera *Rinaldo* was being produced. It was a triumph, and a year later Handel asked for another English leave—which was granted for a "reasonable time" that turned out to be the next half-century (1712–1759).

Handel became England's most important composer and a favorite of Queen Anne. He was the director of the Royal Academy of Music (a commercial opera company) and composed a number of brilliant operas for outstanding sopranos and castrati. When the Royal Academy folded, he formed his own company to produce his works (for years, he had a triple career as impresario, composer, and performer). It eventually went bankrupt and Handel suffered a breakdown; but he recovered and managed to continue producing operas on his own. To these he added his oratorios, opening a glowing new chapter in music history.

Late in life, Handel was still conducting and giving organ concerts, though he was almost blind. When he died in 1759, 3,000 mourners attended his funeral in Westminster Abbey. He was stubborn, wealthy, generous, and cultivated. But above all, he was a master composer whose dramatic sense has rarely been equaled.

HANDEL'S MUSIC

Handel shares Bach's stature among composers of the late baroque. Although he wrote a great deal of instrumental music—suites, organ concertos, concerti grossi—the core of his huge output consists of English oratorios and Italian operas.

His oratorios are usually based on stories from the Old Testament and have titles like *Israel in Egypt* and *Joshua*; but they are not church music—they were for paying audiences in public theaters. Most have plots and characters, though they were performed without acting, scenery, or costumes. (*Messiah*, which deals with a New Testament subject and has no plot, is an exception.) The chorus is the focus of a Handelian oratorio and is combined flexibly and imaginatively with the orchestra. Handel's music has more changes in texture than Bach's. He liked to combine two different melodic ideas polyphonically, and he achieved sharp changes of mood by shifting between minor and major keys.

Handel's thirty-nine Italian operas are less well known today than his oratorios; but after two centuries of neglect, they are being revived successfully by modern opera companies. Their arias—often written to display the virtuosity of singers—show his outstanding ability to evoke a mood or emotion.

MESSIAH (1741)

Messiah lasts about 2½ hours and was composed in just twenty-four days. Handel wrote it before going to Ireland to attend performances of his own works that were being given to dedicate a concert hall. About five months after his arrival in Dublin (in 1742), Handel gave the first performance of *Messiah*; the occasion was a benefit for people in debtors' prisons. The rehearsals attracted wide attention: one newspaper commented that *Messiah* was thought "by the greatest Judges to be the finest Composition of Musick that ever was heard." Normally, the concert hall held 600 people; but to increase the capacity, women were asked not to wear hoopskirts, and men were asked to leave their swords at home.

Although the premiere was a success, the first London performance (1743) was poorly received, mainly because of the religious opposition to the use of a Christian text in a theater. It took *Messiah* almost a decade to find popularity in London. Not until it was performed yearly at a benefit for a London orphanage did it achieve its unique status. A contemporary wrote that *Messiah* "fed the hungry, clothed the naked, fostered the orphan."

Messiah is in three parts. Part I starts with the prophecy of the Messiah's coming and makes celestial announcements of Christ's birth and the redemption of humanity through his appearance. Part II has been aptly described by one Handel scholar as "the accomplishment of redemption by the sacrifice of Jesus, mankind's rejection of God's offer and mankind's utter defeat when trying to oppose the power of the Almighty." Part III expresses faith in the certainty of eternal life through Christ as redeemer.

Unlike most of Handel's oratorios, *Messiah* is meditative rather than dramatic; it lacks plot action and specific characters. *Messiah* is Handel's only English oratorio that uses the New Testament as well as the Old. Charles Jennings, a millionaire and amateur literary man, compiled the text by taking widely separated passages from the Bible—Isaiah, Psalms, and Job from the Old Testament; Luke, I Corinthians, and the Book of Revelations from the New.

Over the years, Handel rewrote some movements in *Messiah* for different performers and performances. In Handel's own time, it was performed with a smaller orchestra and chorus than we are used to. Handel's own chorus included twenty singers, all male, and his small orchestra had only strings and continuo, with trumpets and timpani used in some sections. Today we sometimes hear arranged versions; Mozart made one, and still later versions are often played by orchestras of one hundred and choruses of several hundred.

Messiah has over fifty movements, and Handel ensures variety by skillfully contrasting and grouping them. We will focus on two movements from Part I and the famous *Hallelujah* chorus which ends Part II.

Ev'ry Valley Shall Be Exalted
Aria for tenor
Andante

The aria *Ev'ry valley shall be exalted* is striking in its vivid word painting, so characteristic of baroque music. On a single syllable of *exalted (raised up),* forty-six rapid notes form a rising musical line.

Side A, band 7
[*8-record/cassette set: Side 3, band 7*]

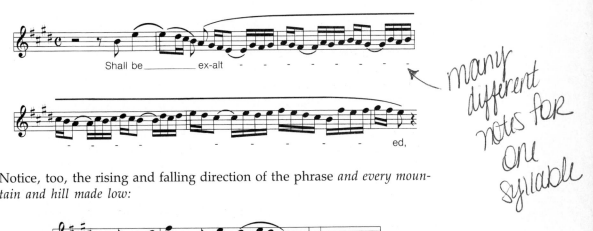

Shall be_____ ex-alt - - - - - - - - - - - - - - - - ed,

Notice, too, the rising and falling direction of the phrase *and every mountain and hill made low:*

and ev-'ry moun-tain and hill____ made low;

The crooked straight is represented as follows:

the crook - ed straight,

Plain (smooth or level), in the line and the rough places plain, is expressed by sustained tones and a long, legato melodic line.

Ev'ry valley shall be exalted, and ev'ry mountain and hill made low, the crooked straight, and the rough places plain. (Isaiah 40:4)

For unto Us a Child Is Born
Chorus

[*8-record/cassette set: Side 4, band 1*] The twelfth movement, *For unto us a Child is born,* is some of Handel's most joyful music. The texture is light, often with only one or two voices singing at a time. After the sopranos announce a motive, it is imitated by the tenors; then both voices—with different rhythms—are combined.

For un - to us a Child is born,

The words *and the government shall be upon His shoulder* bring a new melodic idea in dotted rhythm:

and the gov - ern - ment shall be up - on His shoul - - - - der;

Handel keeps the dynamics subdued until the chordal outburst on *Wonderful, Counsellor.* This change of texture and dynamics is a master's stroke.

With such a close fusion of words and music, it may be disconcerting to learn that most of the melodic ideas in this chorus came from Handel's Italian duet for the words *No, I will not trust you, blind love, cruel Beauty! You are too treacherous, too charming a deity!* (The musical idea for *Wonderful* is new.) But remember that in Handel's time there was little difference in style between sacred and secular music.

For unto us a Child is born, unto us a Son is given, and the government shall be upon His shoulder, and His Name shall be called: Wonderful, Counsellor, the Mighty God, the Everlasting Father, the Prince of Peace! (Isaiah 9:6)

Hallelujah Chorus

In the *Hallelujah* chorus, Handel offers sweeping variety by sudden changes among monophonic, polyphonic, and homophonic textures. The monophonic texture is very full-sounding as all the voices and instruments perform in unison at *for the Lord God Omnipotent reigneth*. The texture becomes polyphonic when this proclamation is set against joyful repeated exclamations of *Hallelujah* in quick rhythms. Polyphony gives way to homophony as the chorus sings *The kingdom of this world* to hymnlike music. Words and phrases are repeated over and over, as has been common practice in choral music for several centuries. (Below, braces connect lines sung at the same time.) Handel took his text from the Revelation of St. John, which celebrates God as the almighty and everlasting ruler.

Side A, band 8

[*8-record/cassette set:*
Side 4, band 2]

	Orchestral introduction
Hallelujah!	Chorus joins, homophonic, quick exclamations
for the Lord God Omnipotent reigneth;	Monophonic, longer notes
Hallelujah!	Homophonic, quick exclamations
for the Lord God Omnipotent reigneth;	Monophonic, longer notes
Hallelujah!	Homophonic, quick exclamations
{ for the Lord God Omnipotent reigneth; { Hallelujah!	Longer-note melody against quick exclamations, polyphonic
The kingdom of this world is become the Kingdom of our Lord and of His Christ:	Hymnlike in longer notes, homophonic
and He shall reign for ever and ever,	Bass melody, monophonic
	Other voices imitate, polyphonic
{ King of Kings, and Lord of Lords. { for ever and ever, Hallelujah, Hallelujah!	Long repeated tones against quick exclamations; phrases repeated at higher pitches
and He shall reign for ever and ever,	Polyphonic, imitation
{ King of Kings, and Lord of Lords, { for ever and ever, Hallelujah, Hallelujah!	Long repeated tones against quick exclamations
and He shall reign for ever and ever,	Polyphonic
King of Kings, and Lord of Lords.	Homophonic
and He shall reign for ever and ever,	Polyphonic
{ King of Kings, and Lord of Lords, { for ever and ever, for ever and ever,	Quick exclamations
Hallelujah, Hallelujah, Hallelujah, Hallelujah!	
	Pause
Hallelujah!	Sustained chords, homophonic

demonstrates 3 different textures

THE CLASSICAL PERIOD

Mozart as a child with his father and sister, depicted in 1763–1764 by Louis Carrogis de Carmontelle.

[**1**] THE CLASSICAL STYLE (1750–1820)

In looking at the baroque era, we found that the scientific methods and discoveries of geniuses like Galileo and Newton vastly changed people's view of the world. By the middle of the eighteenth century, faith in the power of reason was so great that it began to undermine the authority of the social and religious establishment. Philosophers and writers—especially Voltaire (1694–1778) and Denis Diderot (1713–1784)—saw their time as a great turning point in history and referred to it as the "age of enlightenment." They believed in progress, holding that reason, not custom or tradition, was the best guide to human conduct. Their attacks on the privileges of the aristocracy and clergy reflected the outlook of the middle class, which was struggling for its rights. This new climate of opinion prepared the way for the American and French revolutions at the end of the eighteenth century.

Revolutions in thought and action were paralleled by shifts of style in the visual arts. During the early eighteenth century, the heavy, monumental baroque style gave way to the more intimate rococo style, with its light colors, curved lines, and graceful ornaments. The painters Antoine Watteau (1684–1721) and Jean Honoré Fragonard (1732–1806) depicted an enchanted world peopled by elegant men and women in constant pursuit of pleasure. But by the later eighteenth century there was yet another change in taste, and rococo art was thought frivolous, excessively ornamented, and lacking in ethical content. The rococo style was superseded by the neoclassical style, which attempted to recapture the "noble simplicity and calm grandeur" of ancient Greek and Roman art. Neoclassical artists emphasized firm lines, clear structures, and moralistic subject matter. The painter Jacques Louis David (1748–1825), who took part in the French Revolution, sought to inspire heroism and patriotism through his scenes of ancient Rome.

In music history, the transition from the baroque style to the full flowering of the classical (which parallels this trend in the visual arts) is called the *preclassical* period. It extends from roughly 1730 to 1770 and thus was developing even as Bach and Handel were creating baroque masterpieces. The preclassical composers—who included Bach's sons Carl Philipp Emanuel (1714–1788) and Johann Christian (1735–1782)—concentrated on simplicity and clarity, discarding much that had enriched late baroque music. They favored tuneful melody, simple harmony, and contrasts of

(Frick Collection, New York)

The rococo painter Jean Honoré Fragonard showed the game of love in The Meeting, 1774.

mood and theme. The term *style galant* (*gallant style*) was applied to their light, graceful music.

The term *classical* is confusing because it has so many different meanings; it may refer to Greek or Roman antiquity, to any enduring creation or accomplishment (such as a *movie classic*), and—for many people—to any music that is *not* rock, jazz, folk, or popular. Music historians borrowed the term *classical* from art history, where it is more appropriate, since the painting, sculpture, and architecture of the late eighteenth and early nineteenth centuries were often influenced by Greek and Roman models. But the music of this period has little direct relationship to antiquity. The significant parallel between "classical" music and "neoclassical" art is a common stress on balance and clarity of structure. These traits can be found in the fully developed classical style in music, which flourished from about 1770 to 1820.

The master composers of the classical style were Joseph Haydn (1732–1809), Wolfgang Amadeus Mozart (1756–1791), and Ludwig van Beethoven (1770–1827). These three worked during a time that witnessed the American and French revolutions, the Napoleonic Wars, and a dramatic shift in power from the aristocracy and the church to the middle class. Like

(German Theater Museum)

Most of Haydn's music was composed for a wealthy aristocratic family. Shown here is a performance of a Haydn comic opera in 1775 at the palace Esterháza.

everyone else, musicians were strongly affected by these changes, and in the careers of Haydn, Mozart, and Beethoven we can trace the slow emancipation of the composer. Haydn, as we will see, was content to spend most of his life as a skilled servant to a wealthy aristocratic family. Mozart broke away from this pattern to try his luck as a free-lancer but died tragically in poverty. Beethoven succeeded where Mozart failed—he was able to work independently. This was partly because his commanding personality (which prompted the nobility to give him gifts and treat him as an equal) allowed him to take advantage of the new social mobility, and partly because of the wider middle-class market for music.

During the classical period, in fact, though music was still an important part of court life (and many aristocrats were excellent musicians), the middle class had a great influence on music. Prosperous merchants, doctors, lawyers, and government officials not only organized public concerts (palace concerts usually being closed to townspeople) but also wanted to be surrounded by music at home. As a result, the demand for printed music, instruments, and music lessons vastly increased. Moreover, composers in the classical period took middle-class tastes into account; for example, their comic operas sometimes ridiculed the aristocracy. Composers were also influenced by folk and popular music. Haydn, Mozart, and Beethoven all wrote dance music for public balls in Vienna—one of the music centers of Europe and a city in which they were all active.

Let's now consider some characteristics of the classical style.

CHARACTERISTICS OF THE CLASSICAL STYLE

Contrast of Mood

Great variety and contrast of mood received new emphasis in classical music. While a late baroque piece may convey a single emotion, a classical composition will fluctuate in mood. Dramatic, turbulent music might lead into a carefree dance tune. Not only are there contrasting themes within a movement, but there also may be striking contrasts within a single theme.

Mood in classical music may change gradually or suddenly, expressing conflicting surges of elation and depression. But such conflict and contrast are under the firm control of the classical composer. Masters like Haydn, Mozart, and Beethoven were able to impart unity and logic to music of wide emotional range.

Rhythm

Flexibility of rhythm adds variety to classical music. A classical composition has a wealth of rhythmic patterns, while a baroque piece contains a few that are reiterated throughout. Baroque works convey a sense of continuity and perpetual motion, so that after the first few bars one can predict pretty well the rhythmic character of an entire movement. But the classical style also includes unexpected pauses, syncopations, and frequent changes from long notes to shorter ones. And the change from one pattern of note lengths to another may be either sudden or gradual.

Texture

In contrast to the polyphonic texture of late baroque music, classical music is basically homophonic. However, texture is treated as flexibly as rhythm. Pieces shift smoothly or suddenly from one texture to another. A work may begin homophonically with a melody and simple accompaniment but then change to a more complex polyphonic texture that features two simultaneous melodies or melodic fragments imitated among the various instruments.

Melody

Classical melodies are among the most tuneful and easy to remember. The themes of even highly sophisticated compositions may have a folk or popular flavor. Occasionally, composers simply borrowed popular tunes. (Mozart did, in his variations on *Twinkle, Twinkle, Little Star*, which he knew as the French song *Ah, vous dirai-je, maman*.) More often, they wrote original themes with a popular character.

Classical melodies often sound balanced and symmetrical because they are frequently made up of two phrases of the same length. The second phrase, in such melodies, may begin like the first, but it ends more conclusively. Such a melodic type, which may be diagramed a a', is easy to sing (it is frequently found in nursery tunes such as *Mary Had a Little Lamb*). Baroque melodies, on the contrary, tend to be less symmetrical, more elaborate, and harder to sing.

Dynamics and the Piano

The classical composers' interest in expressing shades of emotion led to the widespread use of gradual dynamic change—crescendo and decrescendo. They did not restrict themselves to the terraced dynamics (abrupt shifts from loud to soft) characteristic of baroque music. Crescendos and decrescendos were an electrifying novelty; audiences sometimes rose excitedly from their seats.

During the classical period, the desire for gradual dynamic change led to the replacement of the harpsichord by the piano. By varying the finger pressure on the keys, a pianist can play more loudly or softly. Although the piano was invented around 1700, it began to replace the harpsichord only around 1775. Almost all the mature keyboard compositions of Haydn, Mozart, and Beethoven were written for the piano, rather than for harpsichord, clavichord, and organ, which were featured in baroque music.

The End of the Basso Continuo

The basso continuo was gradually abandoned during the classical period. In Haydn's or Mozart's works, a harpsichordist did not need to improvise an accompaniment. One reason why the basso continuo became obsolete was that more and more music was written for amateurs, who could not master the difficult art of improvising from a figured bass. Also, classical composers wanted more control; they preferred to specify an accompaniment rather than trust the judgment of improvisers.

THE CLASSICAL ORCHESTRA

A new orchestra evolved during the classical period. Unlike the baroque orchestra, which could vary from piece to piece, it was a standard group of four sections: strings, woodwinds, brass, and percussion. In the late instrumental works of Mozart and Haydn, an orchestra might consist of the following:

Strings: 1st violins, 2d violins, violas, cellos, double basses
Woodwinds: 2 flutes, 2 oboes, 2 clarinets, 2 bassoons
Brass: 2 French horns, 2 trumpets
Percussion: 2 timpani

Notice that woodwind and brass instruments are paired and that clarinets have been added. Trombones were also used by Haydn and Mozart, but only in opera and church music, not in solely instrumental works.

The number of musicians in a classical orchestra was greater than in a baroque group, but practice varied considerably from place to place. Haydn directed a private orchestra of only twenty-five players from 1761 to 1790. But for public concerts in London in 1795, he led a large orchestra of sixty musicians.

Classical composers exploited the individual tone colors of orchestral instruments. Unlike baroque composers, they did not treat one instrument like another. Classical composers would not let an oboe duplicate the violin melody for the entire length of a movement. A classical piece has greater variety of tone color, and more rapid changes of color. A theme might begin in the full orchestra, shift to the strings, and then continue in the woodwinds.

Each section of the classical orchestra had a special role. The strings were the most important section, with the first violins taking the melody most of the time and the lower strings providing an accompaniment. The woodwinds added contrasting tone colors and were often given melodic solos. Horns and trumpets brought power to loud passages and filled out the harmony, but they did not usually play the main melody. Timpani were used for rhythmic bite and emphasis. As a whole, the classical orchestra had developed into a flexible and colorful instrument to which composers could entrust their most powerful and dramatic musical conceptions.

CLASSICAL FORMS

Instrumental works of the classical period usually consist of several movements that contrast in tempo and character. There are often four movements, arranged as follows:

1. Fast movement
2. Slow movement
3. Dance-related movement
4. Fast movement

Classical symphonies and string quartets usually follow this four-movement pattern, while classical sonatas may consist of two, three, or four movements. A *symphony* is written for orchestra; a *string quartet* for two violins, viola, and cello; and a *sonata* for one or two instruments. (The classical symphony, string quartet, and sonata are more fully described in Sections 2 to 6 and 8.) In writing an individual movement of a symphony, string quartet, or sonata, a classical composer could choose from several different forms. One movement of a composition might be in A B A form, while another might be a theme and variations.

Classical movements often contrast themes vividly. A movement may contain two, three, or even four or more themes of different character. This use of contrasting themes distinguishes classical music from baroque music, which often uses only one main theme. The classical composer sometimes signals the arrival of a new theme with a brief pause.

Though we speak of a classical style, we must remember that Haydn, Mozart, and Beethoven were three individuals with different personalities. They employed similar musical procedures and forms, but their emotional statements bear the particular stamp of each.

[CLASSICAL 2] SONATA-FORM *also*

ALLEGRO

An astonishing amount of important music from the classical period to the twentieth century is composed in sonata form (sometimes called *sonata-allegro form*). The term **sonata form** refers to the form of a *single* movement. It should not be confused with the term *sonata*, which is used for a whole composition made up of *several* movements. The opening fast movement of a classical symphony, sonata, or string quartet is usually in sonata form. This form is also used in slow movements and in fast concluding movements.

A sonata-form movement consists of three main sections: the exposition, where the themes are presented; the development, where themes are treated in new ways; and the recapitulation, where the themes return. These three main sections are often followed by a concluding section, the coda (Italian for *tail*). Remember that these sections are all within *one* *movement*.

A *single* sonata-form movement may be outlined as follows:

Exposition

First theme in tonic (home) key
Bridge containing modulation from home key to new key
Second theme in new key
Closing section in key of second theme

Development

New treatment of themes; modulations to different keys

Recapitulation

First theme in tonic key
Bridge
Second theme in tonic key
Closing section in tonic key

(Coda)   Last

In tonic key

A fast movement in sonata form is sometimes preceded by a slow introduction that creates a strong feeling of expectancy.

EXPOSITION

The *exposition* sets up a strong conflict between the tonic key and the new key, between the first theme (or group of themes) and the second theme (or group of themes). It begins with the first theme in the tonic, or home, key. There follows a *bridge, or transition,* leading to the second theme, which is in a new key. The modulation from the home key to a new key creates a feeling of harmonic tension and forward motion. The second theme often contrasts in mood with the first theme. A closing section ends the exposition in the key of the second theme. At the end of a classical exposition there is usually a repeat sign (:‖) to indicate that the whole exposition is to be repeated.

DEVELOPMENT

The *development* is often the most dramatic section of the movement. The listener may be kept off balance as the music moves restlessly through several different keys. Through these rapid modulations, the harmonic tension is heightened.

In this section, themes are *developed,* or treated in new ways. They are broken into fragments, or *motives*—short musical ideas developed within a composition. A motive may take on different and unexpected emotional meanings. A fragment of a comic theme, for example, may be made to sound aggressive and menacing through changes of melody, rhythm, or dynamics. Themes can be combined with new ideas or changed in texture. A complex polyphonic texture can be woven by shifting a motive rapidly among different instruments. The harmonic and thematic searching of the development builds a tension that demands resolution.

RECAPITULATION

The beginning of the *recapitulation* brings resolution, as we again hear the first theme in the tonic key. In the recapitulation, the first theme, bridge, second theme, and concluding section are presented more or less as they were in the exposition, with one crucial difference: all the principal material is now in the tonic key. Earlier, in the exposition, there was strong contrast between the first theme in the home key and the second theme and closing section in a new key; that basis for tension is resolved in the recapitulation by presenting the first theme, second theme, and closing section all in the tonic key.

CODA

An even more powerful feeling of conclusion is attained by following the recapitulation with yet another section. The *coda* rounds off a movement by repeating themes or developing them further. It always ends in the tonic key.

The amazing durability and vitality of sonata form result from its capacity for drama. The form moves from a stable situation toward conflict (in the exposition), to heightened tension (in the development), and then back to stability and resolution of conflict. The illustration below shows an outline.

Sonata form is exceptionally flexible and subject to endless variation. It is not a rigid mold into which musical ideas are poured. Rather, it may be viewed as a set of principles that serve to shape and unify contrasts of theme and key. Haydn, Mozart, and Beethoven repeatedly used sonata form, yet each maintained individuality. Movements in sonata form may differ radically in character, in length, and in the number and treatment of themes. Sonata form is so versatile that it is no surprise to find its use spanning more than two centuries.

A movement in sonata form moves from a stable situation toward conflict, to heightened tension, and then back to stability.

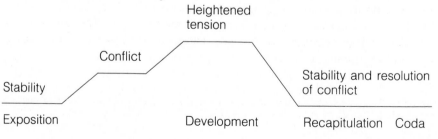

SYMPHONY NO. 40 IN G MINOR, K. 550,
BY WOLFGANG AMADEUS MOZART*

Fourth Movement:

Allegro assai (very fast)

The rapid sonata-form last movement from Mozart's Symphony No. 40 in G Minor, K. 550, conveys a feeling of controlled tension. The opening theme, in the tonic key of G minor, offers brusque contrasts of dynamics and rhythm. A soft upward arpeggio (broken chord) alternates repeatedly with a loud rushing phrase.

Side B, band 1

[8-record/cassette set:
  Side 5, band 2]

Excitement is maintained throughout the long bridge, which is based on the loud rushing phrase of the first theme. The bridge ends clearly with a brief pause, as do other sections in this movement.

The tender second theme, in the new key of B flat major, is a lyrical contrast to the brusque opening theme. It is softer, flows more smoothly, and uses longer notes.

Mozart weaves almost the entire development section from the upward arpeggio of the first theme. During the opening few seconds, there is an eruption of violence as the orchestra in unison plays a variation of the arpeggio and a series of jagged downward leaps. As the development continues, the texture becomes polyphonic and contrasts with the homophony of the exposition. Arpeggios press upon each other in quick imitation. Rapid shifts of key create restless intensity.

In the recapitulation, both the first and second themes are in the tonic key, G minor. This minor key now adds a touch of melancholy to the tender second theme, which was heard in major before. The passion and violence of this movement foreshadow the romantic expression to come during the nineteenth century.

*Note: In the nineteenth century, Mozart's more than 600 compositions were catalogued chronologically by Ludwig von Köchel. Hence, it is customary to refer to them by their "K." numbers.

Listening Outline

To be read while music is heard

SYMPHONY NO. 40 IN G MINOR, K. 550 (1788),
BY WOLFGANG AMADEUS MOZART

Fourth Movement: Allegro assai (very fast)

Sonata form, duple meter ($\frac{2}{2}$), G minor

Flute, 2 oboes, 2 clarinets, 2 bassoons, 2 French horns, 1st violins, 2d violins, violas, cellos, double basses

(About 4½ minutes)

EXPOSITION

First theme   1. Upward arpeggio, *p*, explosive rushing phrase, *f*, minor key.

→ also BROKEN CHORD

       High repeated tones, *f*, upward arpeggio, *p*, rushing phrase, *f*, leads into

Bridge   2. Long passage of continuously rushing notes, strings, *f*.

Second theme   3. *a.* Tender melody in violins, *p*, major key.

       b. Clarinet, *p*, tender melody somewhat varied.

Closing section   4. Suddenly loud, continuously rushing notes in strings, *f*. (Exposition may be repeated.)

DEVELOPMENT

       1. Orchestra in unison, *f*, upward arpeggio, jagged downward leaps.

124

2. Suddenly soft, upward arpeggio lightly tossed between violins and woodwinds.
3. Suddenly loud, string arpeggios interwoven with rushing notes. Arpeggios press upon each other in quicker imitation. Woodwinds rejoin imitative dialogue.

RECAPITULATION

First theme   1. Upward arpeggio, *p*, explosive rushing phrase, *f*, minor key. High repeated tones, *f*, upward arpeggio, *p*, rushing phrase, *f*, leads into

Bridge   2. Passage of continuously rushing notes, strings, *f*.

Second theme   3. a. Tender melody in violins, *p*, minor key.
   b. Woodwinds, *p*, tender melody somewhat varied.

Closing section   4. Suddenly loud, continuously rushing notes, full orchestra. Cadence.

THEME AND VARIATIONS [CLASSICAL **3**]

The form called *theme and variations* is widely used in the classical period, either as an independent piece or as one movement of a symphony, sonata, or string quartet. In a ***theme and variations,*** a basic musical idea—the theme—is repeated over and over and is changed each time. This form may be outlined as theme (A)–variation 1 (A′)–variation 2 (A″)–variation 3 (A‴), and so on; each prime mark indicates a variation of the basic idea.

Each variation is usually about the same length as the theme. Changes of melody, rhythm, harmony, accompaniment, dynamics, or tone color may be used to give a variation its own identity. The core melody may appear in the bass, or it may be repeated in a minor key instead of a major one. It may be heard together with a new melody. Each variation is unique and may differ in mood from the theme. The variations may be connected to each other or separated by pauses. For the theme itself, a composer may invent an original melody or borrow someone else's. Beethoven once borrowed a little waltz tune and put it through thirty-three brilliant variations. More modest examples of theme and variations have as few as three variations.

SYMPHONY NO. 94 IN G MAJOR (SURPRISE), BY JOSEPH HAYDN

Second Movement:

Andante

Side B, band 4

[*8-record/cassette set: Side 4, band 3*]

The second movement (andante) of Haydn's *Surprise* Symphony (Symphony No. 94 in G Major) is a theme and variations. The folklike, staccato theme begins softly but is punctuated by a sudden loud chord. This is the "surprise" of the symphony. There are four variations, in which the theme is changed in tone color, dynamics, rhythm, and melody. Sometimes the original melody is accompanied by a new one called a *countermelody*. Such combinations of two distinctive melodies result in a polyphonic texture. In one variation the theme is presented in minor instead of major. The last variation is followed by a closing section in which a gently dissonant accompaniment momentarily darkens the mood of the carefree theme.

The theme is composed of two parts, sections a and b, which are each repeated. This pattern is usually retained in the variations.

Listening Outline   To be read while music is heard

SYMPHONY NO. 94 IN G MAJOR (SURPRISE; 1791), BY JOSEPH HAYDN (1732–1809)

Second Movement: Andante

Theme and variations, duple meter ($\frac{2}{4}$), C major

2 flutes, 2 oboes, 2 bassoons, 2 French horns, 2 trumpets, timpani, 1st violins, 2d violins, violas, cellos, double basses

(About 5½ minutes)

THEME
Section a   Violins, *p*, staccato theme.

                   Section a repeated, *pp*, with pizzicato string accompaniment. Surprise chord, *ff*.
Section b   Violins, *p*, continuation of theme.

Section b repeated with flute and oboe.

VARIATION 1   *a.* Theme begins, *f*, higher countermelody in violins, *p*. Section a repeated.

b. Violins, *p*, continuation of theme and higher countermelody. Section b
repeated.

VARIATION 2   *a.* Theme in minor, *ff*, violin phrase in major, *p*. Section a repeated.

b. Violins, *f*, rapid downward scales, orchestra *f*. Violins alone, *p*, lead into

VARIATION 3   *a.* Oboe, *p*, theme in faster repeated notes, major key.

Flute and oboe, *p*, legato countermelody above staccato theme in violins, *p*.

b. Continuation of theme and countermelody. Section b repeated.

VARIATION 4   *a.* Theme in brasses and woodwinds, *ff*, fast notes in violins, *ff*. Violins, *p*, legato
version of theme, dotted rhythm (long-short).

127

b. Violins, *p*, continuation of theme, dotted rhythm. Full orchestra, *ff*, triumphant continuation of theme leads to suspenseful chord, *ff*, sudden *p*.
Theme in oboe, *p*, gently dissonant chords in strings, flute joins, *pp* conclusion.

[CLASSICAL 4] MINUET AND TRIO

The form known as ***minuet and trio***, or ***minuet***, is employed as the third movement of classical symphonies, string quartets, and other works. Like the movements of the baroque suite, the minuet originated as a dance. It first appeared at the court of Louis XIV of France around 1650 and was danced by aristocrats throughout the eighteenth century. The minuet was a stately, dignified dance in which the dancing couple exchanged curtsies and bows.

The minuet movement of a symphony or string quartet is written for listening, not dancing. It is in triple meter ($\frac{3}{4}$ time) and usually in a moderate tempo. The movement is in A B A form: minuet (A), trio (B), minuet (A). The trio (B) is usually quieter than the minuet (A) section and requires fewer instruments. It often contains woodwind solos. The trio section got its name during the baroque period, when a set of two dances would be followed by a repetition of the first dance. The second dance was known as a "trio" because it was usually played by three instruments. Classical composers did not restrict themselves to three instruments in the B sections of their minuets, but the name *trio* remained.

The A (minuet) section includes smaller parts a, b, and a' (variation of a). In the opening A (minuet) section, all the smaller parts are repeated, as follows: a (repeated) ba' (repeated). [In the musical score, the repeat sign (:‖) indicates each repetition.] The B (trio) section is similar in form: c (repeated) dc' (repeated). At the close of the B (trio) section, the repetition of the entire A (minuet) section is indicated by the words *da capo (from the beginning)*. This time, however, the minuet is played straight through without the repetitions: a ba'. The whole movement can be outlined:

Minuet	*Trio*	*Minuet*
A	B	A
a (repeated) ba' (repeated)	c (repeated) dc' (repeated)	a ba'

With its A B A form and its many repeated parts, the minuet is structurally the simplest movement of a symphony or string quartet.

In many of Beethoven's compositions, the third movement is not a minuet but a related form called a *scherzo*. Like a minuet, a *scherzo* is usually in A B A form and triple meter, but it moves more quickly, generating energy, rhythmic drive, and rough humor. (*Scherzo* is Italian for *joke*.)

EINE KLEINE NACHTMUSIK (A LITTLE NIGHT MUSIC), K. 525, BY WOLFGANG AMADEUS MOZART

Third Movement:

Minuet (Allegretto)

Mozart's *Eine kleine Nachtmusik* is a **serenade,** a work that's usually light in mood, meant for evening entertainment. It is written for a small string orchestra or for a string quartet plus a double bass. (The double bass plays the cello part an octave lower.) The third movement is a courtly minuet in A B A form. The A (minuet) section is stately, mostly loud and staccato, with a clearly marked beat. In contrast, the B (trio) section is intimate, soft, and legato. Its murmuring accompaniment contributes to the smooth flow of the music.

Side B, band 2

[*8-record/cassette set:*
Side 4, band 5]

Listening Outline   To be read while music is heard

*EINE KLEINE NACHTMUSIK, K. 525 (1787),
BY WOLFGANG AMADEUS MOZART*

Third Movement: Minuet (Allegretto)

A B A form, triple meter ($\frac{3}{4}$), G major

1st violins, 2d violins, violas, cellos, double bass

(About 2 minutes)

MINUET (A)   1. Stately melody, *f*, predominantly staccato. Repeated.

Legato phrase, *p*, leads to stately staccato phrase, *f*. Repeated.

TRIO (B)   2. Gracious legato melody, *p*, murmuring accompaniment. Repeated.

Climbing legato phrase, *f*, leads to legato melody, *p*. Repeated.

MINUET (A)   3. Stately melody, *f*, predominantly staccato.
Legato phrase, *p*, leads to stately staccato phrase, *f*.

CLASSICAL

5 RONDO

Many classical movements are in rondo form. A *rondo* features a tuneful main theme (A) which returns several times in alternation with other themes. Common rondo patterns are A B A C A and A B A C A B A. The main theme is usually lively, pleasing, and simple to remember, and the listener can easily recognize its return. Because the main theme is usually stated in the tonic key, its return is all the more welcome. The rondo can be used either as an independent piece or as one movement of a symphony, string quartet, or sonata. It often serves as a finale, because its liveliness, regularity, and buoyancy bring a happy sense of conclusion.

Rondo form is often combined with elements of sonata form to produce the sonata-rondo. The *sonata-rondo* contains a development section similar to that in sonata form and is outlined A B A–development section–A B A.

The popularity of the rondo did not end with the classical period. It has been used by twentieth-century composers such as Igor Stravinsky and Arnold Schoenberg.

STRING QUARTET IN C MINOR, OP. 18, NO. 4, BY LUDWIG VAN BEETHOVEN

Fourth Movement:

Side B, band 5

Rondo (Allegro)

[8-record/cassette set: Side 5, band 6]

The exciting rondo movement from Beethoven's String Quartet in C Minor, Op. 18, No. 4, may be outlined A B A C A B A. Its main theme, A, is a lively gypsy dance made up of two repeated parts: a a b b. An unexpected held tone in part b suggests the improvisatory playing of a gypsy fiddler. The main theme, in minor, contrasts with the other themes, which are in major. Theme B is a lyrical legato melody, while theme C is playful, with quick upward rushes. At its final return, the main theme (A) has a faster tempo, prestissimo, and leads into a frenzied concluding section.

Listening Outline   To be read while music is heard

"gypsy music"

STRING QUARTET IN C MINOR, OP. 18, NO. 4 (1798–1800), BY LUDWIG VAN BEETHOVEN

Fourth Movement: Rondo (Allegro)

Duple meter ($\frac{2}{2}$), C minor

1st violin, 2d violin, viola, cello

(About 4½ minutes)

A   1. Lively main theme in 1st violin, minor key.

B   2. Lyrical melody, legato, major key.

A   3. Lively main theme, minor key. Theme becomes more agitated.
C   4. Upward rushes in each instrument, playful downward phrase in 1st violin, major key.
A   5. Lively main theme, minor key. Crescendo to held chord, *ff*.
B   6. Lyrical melody, legato, major key. Melody repeated an octave higher. Playful phrases in violins, crescendo to *f*, sustained tones in 1st violin.
A   7. Lively main theme, *ff*, faster tempo (prestissimo), minor key. Concluding section builds, downward staccato scale, high repeated tones, *p*. Upward rushes, *ff*, at end.

[6] THE CLASSICAL SYMPHONY

The great contribution of the classical period to orchestral music is the symphony. Haydn wrote at least 104 symphonies, Mozart over forty, and Beethoven nine. Most of Haydn's symphonies were composed for his employers, who required a steady flow of works for their palace concerts. Beethoven, on the other hand, wrote a symphony only when inspired. His symphonies are longer than Haydn's or Mozart's and were conceived for performance in large concert halls.

A *symphony* is an extended, ambitious composition typically lasting between 20 and 45 minutes, exploiting the expanded range of tone color and dynamics of the classical orchestra. A classical symphony usually consists of four movements which evoke a wide range of emotions through contrasts of tempo and mood. A typical sequence is (1) a vigorous, dramatic fast movement; (2) a lyrical slow movement; (3) a dancelike movement (minuet or scherzo); and (4) a brilliant or heroic fast movement.

The opening movement is almost always fast and in sonata form. It is usually the most dramatic movement and stresses an exciting development of short motives. Sometimes a slow introduction leads to the opening fast movement and creates a feeling of anticipation.

It is in the slow second movement that we are most likely to find broad, songlike melodies. This movement, by and large, is either in sonata form, A B A form, or theme-and-variations form. Unlike the other movements in the symphony, the slow movement is generally *not* in the tonic key. For example, if the first, third, and fourth movements are in the tonic key of C major, the second movement may be in F major. The new key points up the expressive contrast of the slow movement.

In the symphonies of Haydn and Mozart, the third movement is generally a minuet and trio, which may be in a moderate or fairly quick tempo. This movement varies in character from a courtly dance to a peasant romp or a vigorous piece that is hardly dancelike. Beethoven liked fast, energetic scherzos for his third movements.

The fourth, concluding movement of a Haydn or Mozart symphony is fast, lively, and brilliant, but somewhat lighter in mood than the opening movement. (The agitated final movement of Mozart's Symphony No. 40 in G Minor is not typical.) Beethoven's concluding movement tends to be more triumphant and heroic in character and sometimes is meant as the climax of the whole symphony. The final movement of a classical symphony is most often in sonata or sonata-rondo form.

In most classical symphonies, each movement is a self-contained compo-

132

sition with its own set of themes. A theme in one movement will only rarely reappear in a later movement. (Beethoven's Fifth and Ninth Symphonies are exceptions.) But a symphony is unified partly by the use of the same key in three of its movements. More important, the movements balance and complement each other both musically and emotionally.

The importance of the symphony has lasted into the middle of the twentieth century. Its great significance is reflected in such familiar terms as *symphonic music, symphony hall,* and *symphony orchestra.*

THE CLASSICAL CONCERTO [CLASSICAL **7**]

A classical *concerto* is a three-movement work for an instrumental soloist and orchestra. It combines the soloist's virtuosity and interpretive abilities with the orchestra's wide range of tone color and dynamics. Emerging from this encounter is a contrast of ideas and sound that is dramatic and satisfying. The soloist is very much the star, and all of his or her musical talents are needed in this challenging dialogue.

The classical love of balance can be seen in the concerto, for soloist and orchestra are equally important. Between them, there's an interplay of melodic lines and a spirit of give-and-take. One moment the soloist plays the melody while the orchestra accompanies. Then the woodwinds may unfold the main theme against rippling arpeggios (broken chords) played by the soloist. Mozart and Beethoven—the greatest masters of the classical concerto—often wrote concertos for themselves to play as piano soloists; the piano is their favored solo instrument. But other solo instruments used in classical concertos include violin, horn, trumpet, clarinet, bassoon, and cello.

Like symphonies, concertos can last anywhere from 20 to 45 minutes. But instead of the symphony's four movements, a concerto has three: (1) fast, (2) slow, and (3) fast. A concerto has no minuet or scherzo.

In the first movement and sometimes in the last movement, there is a special unaccompanied showpiece for the soloist, the *cadenza* (Italian for *cadence*). Near the end of the movement, the orchestra suspends forward motion by briefly sustaining a dissonant chord. This is indicated in the score by a *fermata* (⌒), a sign meaning *pause,* which is placed over the chord. The suspense announces the entry of the soloist's cadenza. For several minutes, the soloist, *without orchestra,* displays virtuosity by playing dazzling scale passages and broken chords. Themes of the movement are varied and presented in new keys. At the end of a cadenza, the soloist plays a long trill followed by a chord that meshes with the reentrance of the orchestra.

In the classical era, the soloist, who was often the composer, generally improvised the cadenzas. In this case, the score contained only the fermata, indicating where the cadenza should be inserted. But after the eighteenth century, the art of improvisation declined, and composers began to write cadenzas directly into the score. This gave them more control over their compositions.

A classical concerto begins with a movement in sonata form of a special kind, containing *two* expositions. The first is played by the orchestra, which presents several themes in the home key. This opening section sets the mood for the movement and leads us to expect the soloist's entrance. The second exposition begins with the soloist's first notes. Music for the solo entry may be powerful or quiet, but its effect is dramatic because suspense has been built. Together with the orchestra, the soloist explores themes from the first exposition and introduces new ones. After a modulation from the home key to a new key, the second exposition then moves to a development section, followed by the recapitulation, cadenza, and coda. The slow middle movement may take any one of several forms, but the finale is usually a quick rondo or sonata-rondo.

[CLASSICAL 8] CLASSICAL CHAMBER MUSIC

Classical *chamber music* is designed for the intimate setting of a room (chamber) in a home or palace, rather than for a public concert hall. It is performed by a small group of two to nine musicians, with one player to a part. Chamber music is lighter in sound than classical orchestral music. During the classical period, it was fashionable for an aristocrat or a member of the well-to-do middle class to play chamber music with friends and to hire professional musicians to entertain guests after dinner.

Chamber music is subtle and intimate, intended to please the performer as much as the listener. A chamber music group is a team. Each member is essential, and each may have an important share of the thematic material. Therefore much give-and-take is called for among the instruments. Classical chamber music does not need a conductor; instead, each musician must be sensitive to what goes on and coordinate dynamics and phrasing with the other musicians.

The most important form in classical chamber music is the *string quartet*, written for two violins, a viola, and a cello. Haydn, Mozart, and Beethoven wrote some of their most important music in this form. The string quartet can be compared to a conversation among four lively, sensitive, and intelligent people. And it's not surprising that the string quartet evolved when conversation was cultivated as a fine art.

Like the symphony, the string quartet usually consists of four movements: (1) fast, (2) slow, (3) minuet or scherzo, (4) fast. (Sometimes the second movement is a minuet or a scherzo and the slow movement is third.)

Other popular forms of classical chamber music are the sonata for violin and piano, the piano trio (violin, cello, and piano), and the string quintet (two violins, two violas, and cello).

JOSEPH HAYDN

CLASSICAL

9

Joseph Haydn (1732–1809) was born in Rohrau, a tiny Austrian village. Until he was six, his musical background consisted of folk songs and peasant dances (which later had an influence on his style); but then his eager response to music was recognized and he was given training. At eight, he went to Vienna to serve as a choirboy in the Cathedral of St. Stephen.

When his voice changed, Haydn was dismissed, penniless, from St. Stephen's; he gave music lessons to children, struggled to teach himself com-

(Royal College of Music)

Joseph Haydn.

position, and took odd jobs (including playing violin in street bands). But gradually, aristocratic patrons of music began to notice his talent; and in 1761, when he was twenty-nine, his life changed for the better, permanently: he entered the service of the Esterházys, the richest and most powerful of the Hungarian noble families. For nearly thirty years, most of his music was composed for performances in the palaces of the family, especially Esterháza—which contained an opera house, a theater, two concert halls, and 126 guest rooms.

As a highly skilled servant, Haydn was to compose all the music requested by his patron, conduct the orchestra, coach singers, and oversee the instruments and the music library. This entailed a staggering amount of work; there were usually two concerts and two opera performances weekly, as well as daily chamber music. Though today this sort of patronage seems degrading, it was taken for granted at the time and had definite advantages for composers: they received a steady income and their works were performed. Haydn was conscientious about his professional duties, concerned about his musicians' interests, and—despite an unhappy marriage—good-humored and unselfish.

Word spread about the Esterházys' composer, and Haydn's music became immensely popular all over Europe. In 1791–1792 and again in 1794–1795, Haydn went to London, and reports of the time say that his appearances there were triumphs. (The twelve symphonies he composed for these visits are now known as the *London symphonies*.) A servant had become a celebrity; Haydn was wined and dined by the aristocracy, given an honorary doctorate at Oxford, and received by the royal family.

In 1795, he returned to Vienna rich and honored. At this time—in his late sixties—he composed six masses and two oratorios, *The Creation* (1798) and *The Seasons* (1801), which were so popular that choruses and orchestras were formed for the sole purpose of performing them. He died in 1809, at seventy-seven.

HAYDN'S MUSIC

Haydn was a pathfinder for the classical style, a pioneer in the development of the symphony and the string quartet. Both Mozart and Beethoven were influenced by his style. His music, like his personality, is robust and direct; it radiates a healthy optimism. Many of his works have a folk flavor, and *The Creation* and *The Seasons* reflect his love of nature.

Haydn was a master at developing themes; he could build a whole movement out of a single main theme, creating contrasts of mood through changes in texture, rhythm, dynamics, and orchestration. The contagious joy that springs from his lively rhythms and vivid contrasts makes it clear why London went wild.

THE CLASSICAL PERIOD

(Metropolitan Museum of Art, Bequest of William K. Vanderbilt, 1920)

Toilet of Venus, *by François Boucher (1751). During the early eighteenth century, the heavy, monumental baroque style gave way to a more intimate style, the rococo, with light colors, curved lines, and graceful ornaments. The French rococo painter Boucher chose subjects that were decorative and sweetly sensuous.*

(Metropolitan Museum of Art, Wolfe Fund, 1931)

Death of Socrates, by Jacques-Louis David (1787). By the late eighteenth century, the rococo style had been superseded by the neoclassical style, which attempted to recapture the "noble simplicity and calm grandeur" of ancient Greek and Roman art. Neoclassical artists such as the French painter David emphasized firm lines, clear structures, and moralistic subjects.

Napoleon at St. Bernard, by Jacques-Louis David (1800). By the beginning of the nineteenth century, social mobility had increased to a point where a low-born genius like Napoleon could become emperor of France. It is said that Beethoven originally planned to name his Third Symphony (Eroica; 1803–1804) "Bonaparte," because he saw Napoleon as the embodiment of heroism; but when he learned that Napoleon had proclaimed himself emperor, he tore out the title page and later renamed the symphony "Heroic Symphony composed to celebrate the memory of a great man."

(Cliché des Musées Nationaux, Paris)

(© Museo del Prado, Madrid)

The Third of May, 1808, *by Francisco Goya (1814). The classical period was a time of violent political and social upheaval, witnessing the American Revolution, the French Revolution, and the Napoleonic wars. The Spanish painter Goya vividly showed the execution of Spanish hostages by soldiers of Napoleon's army.*

Haydn's 104 symphonies—along with his 68 string quartets—are considered the most important part of his enormous output. Many of them have nicknames, such as *Surprise* (No. 94), *Military* (No. 100), *Clock* (No. 101), and *Drum Roll* (No. 103).

Some scholars believe that Haydn invented the string quartet form. He began writing the first of his lifelong series of string quartets for good reason—only three other musicians (two violinists and a cellist, in addition to Haydn as violist) were on hand during the summer of 1757, when he was invited to take part in chamber music performances at a castle.

Haydn's output also includes piano sonatas, piano trios, divertimentos, concertos, operas, and masses. The variety in his works is astounding. He was a great innovator and experimenter who hated arbitrary "rules" of composition. "Art is free," he said. "The educated ear is the sole authority, . . . and I think I have as much right to lay down the law as anyone."

TRUMPET CONCERTO IN E FLAT MAJOR (1796)

Haydn's Trumpet Concerto in E Flat Major has a remarkable history. After its premiere in 1800, it was forgotten for almost 130 years. It was first published only in 1929, but in the 1930s a phonograph recording brought it to a wide audience. Now, it may well be Haydn's most popular work.

Haydn wrote the concerto in 1796 for a friend, a trumpeter at the Viennese court who had recently invented a keyed trumpet that could produce a complete chromatic scale. The keyed trumpet was intended to replace the natural trumpet, which could produce only a restricted number of tones. But the keyed trumpet had a dull sound and was supplanted by the valve trumpet around 1840. Today, the concerto is performed on a valve trumpet. Like most concertos, it has three movements: (1) fast, (2) slow, (3) fast. We'll examine the third movement.

Third Movement:

Allegro

The third movement is a dazzling sonata-rondo in which Haydn gives the trumpeter's virtuosity free rein. The movement combines the recurring main theme characteristic of rondo form with the development section found in sonata form. It may be outlined as A B A B' A–development section–A B"–coda. Themes A and B are introduced by the orchestra and are then presented mainly by the trumpet, with orchestral support. The main theme, A, is a high-spirited melody that is well suited to the trumpet. Theme B is playful; it contains a short, downward-moving phrase that is repeated several times. Haydn's fondness for musical surprises is reflected in the coda, which contains sudden changes of dynamics, unexpected harmonic twists, and a suspenseful long pause.

[8-record/cassette set:
Side 4, band 4]

Listening Outline To be read while music is heard

TRUMPET CONCERTO IN E FLAT MAJOR (1796),
BY JOSEPH HAYDN

Third Movement: Allegro

Sonata-rondo form, duple meter ($\frac{2}{4}$), E flat major

Solo trumpet, 2 flutes, 2 oboes, 2 bassoons, 2 French horns, 2 trumpets, timpani, 1st violins, 2d violins, violas, cellos, double basses

(About 4½ minutes)

A   1. *a.* Main theme in violins, *p.*

      b. Main theme in full orchestra, *f,* violins, running notes and rising scale lead
       to
B   *c.* Violins, *f,* downward short phrase, repeated *p,*

      orchestra, *f,* brass fanfares, cadence, pause.
A   2. Main theme in trumpet, strings accompany, trumpet repeats main theme,
      orchestra, *f,* violins, *p,* lead to
B′   3. Trumpet, held tone, ushers in downward short phrases, upward phrases with
      trills, downward legato phrases, trumpet trill to cadence, trumpet fanfares,
      orchestra, *f.*
A   4. *a.* Trumpet, held tone, ushers in main theme.
      b. Main-theme phrase in full orchestra, *f.*
DEVELOPMENT
      5. Trumpet, main-theme phrases, *p,* violins, *p,* main-theme phrases in minor with
      trumpet fanfares, running notes in violins, *f,* trumpet and brasses join, suddenly
      soft, violins introduce
A   6. *a.* Trumpet, held tone, ushers in main theme.
      b. Orchestra, *f,* running notes and rising scale lead to
B″   7. *a.* Trumpet, downward short phrases, downward broken chords, octave leaps,
      trill to cadence.
      b. Violins, *p,* high woodwinds, *p,* trumpet fanfares, violins, *p,* lead to

138

8. *a.* Trumpet, main-theme phrase, strings, *p*, trumpet, downward chain of trills.
   b. Suddenly loud, full orchestra, sudden *pp*, string tremolos, suddenly loud, full orchestra, repeated notes in trumpet, long pause.
   c. Trumpet, main-theme phrases, orchestra, *p*, crescendo to *ff*, repeated notes in trumpet, closing chords in orchestra.

WOLFGANG AMADEUS MOZART

CLASSICAL

10

Wolfgang Amadeus Mozart (1756–1791), one of the most amazing child prodigies in history, was born in Salzburg, Austria. By the age of six, he could play the harpsichord and violin, improvise fugues, write minuets, and read music perfectly at first sight. At age eight, he wrote a symphony; at eleven, an oratorio; at twelve, an opera.

Mozart's father, Leopold, a court musician, was eager to show him off. Between the ages of six and fifteen Mozart was continually on tour; he played for Empress Maria Theresa in Vienna, Louis XV at Versailles, George III in London, and innumerable aristocrats. On his trips to Italy he was able to master the current operatic style, which he later put to superb use.

When he was fifteen, Mozart returned to Salzburg—then ruled by a prince-archbishop. The archbishop was a tyrant who did not appreciate Mozart's music and refused to grant him more than a subordinate seat in the court orchestra. With his father's help, Mozart tried repeatedly but unsuccessfully over the next decade to find a position elsewhere.

Ironically, and tragically, Mozart won more acclaim as a boy wonder than as an adult musician. Having begun his professional life as an international celebrity, he could not tolerate being treated like a servant; he became insubordinate when the archbishop forbade him to give concerts or to perform at the houses of the aristocracy, and his relations with his patron went from bad to worse. Moreover, his complete dependence on his father had given him little opportunity to develop initiative; and a contemporary observed that he was "too good-natured, not active enough, too easily taken in, too little concerned with the means that may lead him to good fortune."

When he was twenty-five, Mozart could stand it no more: he broke free of provincial Salzburg and became a free-lance musician in Vienna. His first few years there were very successful. His German opera *Die Entführung aus dem Serail (The Abduction from the Seraglio,* 1782) was acclaimed; concerts of his own music were attended by the emperor and nobility; his

(Austrian Information Service, New York)

Wolfgang Amadeus Mozart.

compositions were published; pupils paid him high fees; and he formed a friendship with Haydn, who told Mozart's father, "Your son is the greatest composer that I know; he has taste and, what is more, the most profound knowledge of composition." In 1786 came his opera *Le Nozze di Figaro (The Marriage of Figaro).* Vienna loved it, and Prague was even more enthusiastic; "they talk of nothing but *Figaro,*" Mozart joyfully wrote. This success led an opera company in Prague to commission *Don Giovanni* the following year.

Although *Don Giovanni* was a triumph in Prague, its dark qualities and dissonance did not appeal to the Viennese, and Mozart's popularity in Vienna began to decline. Vienna was a fickle city in any case, and it found Mozart's music complicated and hard to follow. His pupils dwindled; the elite snubbed his concerts. His last year of life—1791—when he was in desperate financial straits and his health was failing, would make a grim opera plot. He received a commission for a comic opera, *Die Zauberflöte (The Magic Flute),* and while working on it was visited by a mysterious stranger dressed all in gray who carried an anonymous letter commissioning a requiem, a mass for the dead. As Mozart's health grew worse, he came to believe that the requiem was for himself and rushed to finish it while on his deathbed. (In fact, the stranger was the servant of a nobleman who intended to claim the requiem as his own composition.)

The Magic Flute was premiered to resounding praise in Vienna, but its success came too late. Mozart died shortly before his thirty-sixth birthday.

(The requiem was completed by his favorite pupil.) His funeral was the poorest possible, and he was buried in a common grave for paupers.

MOZART'S MUSIC

Mozart was among the most versatile of all composers and wrote masterpieces in all the musical forms of his time—symphonies, concertos, chamber music, operas. All his music sings and conveys a feeling of ease, grace, and spontaneity as well as balance, restraint, and proportion. Yet mysterious harmonies contrast with its lyricism, and it fuses elegance with power. Not only do his compositions sound effortless; they were created with miraculous ease and rapidity—for example, he completed his last three symphonies in only six weeks.

Many of Mozart's concertos are among his greatest works. His piano concertos—composed mainly for his own performances—are particularly important; but he also wrote concertos for violin, horn, flute, bassoon, oboe, and clarinet.

Mozart was also a master of opera, with a supreme ability to coordinate music and stage action, a keen sense of theater, an inexhaustible gift of melody, and a genius for creating characters through tone. Most of his operas are comedies, composed to German or Italian librettos. His three masterpieces of Italian comic opera (all composed to librettos by Lorenzo da Ponte) are *The Marriage of Figaro* (1786), *Don Giovanni* (1787), and *Cosi fan tutte* (1790); his finest opera in German is *The Magic Flute* (1791). The comic operas have both humorous and serious characters—not mere stereotypes but individual human beings who think and feel. Emotions in his arias and ensembles continually evolve and change.

"I am never happier," Mozart once wrote, "than when I have something to compose, for that, after all, is my sole delight and passion." His delight and passion are communicated in his works, which represent late eighteenth-century musical style at its highest level of perfection.

DON GIOVANNI (1787)

Don Giovanni (Don Juan) is a unique blend of comic and serious opera, combining seduction and slapstick with violence and the supernatural. The old tale of Don Juan, the legendary Spanish lover, had attracted many playwrights and composers before Mozart. Mozart's Don Giovanni is an extremely charming but ruthless nobleman who will stop at nothing to satisfy his sexual appetite. Don Giovanni's comic servant, Leporello, is a grumbling accomplice who dreams of being in his master's place.

The Don attempts to rape a young noblewoman, Donna Anna; her father, the Commendatore (Commandant), challenges him to a duel. Don

Giovanni kills the old man, causing Donna Anna and her fiancé, Don Ottavio, to swear revenge. Pursued by his enemies, the Don deftly engages in new amorous adventures. During one of them, he hides in a cemetery, where he sees a marble statue of the dead Commandant. The unearthly statue utters threatening words, but Don Giovanni brazenly invites it to dinner. When the statue appears at the banquet hall, it orders the Don to repent his sins. Don Giovanni defiantly refuses and is dragged down to hell.

Act I:

Leporello's catalog aria (Madamina)

[8-record/cassette set: Side 5, band 4]

Leporello sings his famous "catalog" aria (Madamina) to Donna Elvira, a woman whom Don Giovanni had earlier seduced and deserted and who has now appeared on the scene. In mocking "consolation," Leporello tells her that she is but one of many and displays a fat catalog of his master's conquests. The music bubbles with Leporello's delight as he reels off the amazing totals: 640 in Italy, 231 in Germany, 100 in France, 91 in Turkey, and in Spain, 1,003! Mozart makes the most of comic description as Leporello proceeds to list the Don's seduction techniques for different types of women:

Allegro.	*Madamina, il catalogo è questo* *Delle belle, che amò il padron mio;*	My dear lady, this is a list Of the beauties my master has loved,
	Un catalogo egli è, che ho fatt'io, *Osservate, leggete con me.*	A list which I have compiled. Observe, read along with me.
Staccato woodwind chuckles.	*In Italia seicento e quaranta,*	In Italy, six hundred and forty;
	In Almagna duecento a trentuna,	In Germany, two hundred and thirty-one;
	Cento in Francia, in Turchia novantuna,	A hundred in France; in Turkey ninety-one.
Longer notes.	*Ma in Ispagna son già mille e tre!*	In Spain already one thousand and three!
Shorter notes.	*V'han fra queste contadine,* *Cameriere, cittadine,* *V'han contesse, baronesse,* *Marchesine, principesse,* *E v'han donne d'ogni grado,* *D'ogni forma, d'ogni età!* *In Italia seicento e quaranta, ecc.*	Among these are peasant girls Maidservants, city girls, Countesses, baronesses, Marchionesses, princesses, Women of every rank, Every shape, every age. In Italy six hundred and forty, etc.
Andante con moto, courtly minuet.	*Nella bionda egli ha l'usanza*	With blondes it is his habit
	Di lodar la gentilezza;	To praise their kindness;
Mock-heroic flourish.	*Nella bruna, la costanza;*	In brunettes, their faithfulness;

Nella bianca la dolcezza;	In the very blonde, their sweetness.	Suave melodic phrase.
Vuol d'inverno la grassotta, *Vuol d'estate la magrotta;* *È la grande maestosa,*	In winter he likes fat ones, In summer he likes thin ones. He calls the tall ones majestic.	Crescendo, melody slowly rises to high held tone.
La piccina è ognor vezzosa;	The little ones are always charming.	Sprightly quick notes.
Delle vecchie fa conquista *Pel piacer di porle in lista.*	He seduces the old ones For the pleasure of adding to the list.	
Sua passion predominante *È la giovin principiante.* *Non si picca se sia ricca,* *Se sia brutta, se sia bella,* *Se sia ricca, brutta, se sia bella;* *Purchè porti la gonnella,* *Voi sapete quel che fa!* *Purchè porti la gonnella, ecc.*	His greatest favorite Is the young beginner. It doesn't matter if she's rich, Ugly or beautiful; If she is rich, ugly or beautiful. If she wears a petticoat, *You* know what he does. If she wears a petticoat, etc.	

Act I:

Duet: *Là ci darem la mano (There you will give me your hand)*

The Don's seduction technique is put to use in the lovely duet *Là ci darem la mano*. Don Giovanni persuades the pretty peasant girl Zerlina to come to his palace, promising to marry her and change her life. The music magically conveys his persuasiveness and her gradual surrender, as the voices become more and more intertwined. Forgetting her fiancé, Masetto, Zerlina throws herself into the Don's arms and they sing together, "Let us go, my beloved."

Side B, band 3

[*8-record/cassette set: Side 5, band 5*]

Don Giovanni

Là ci darem la mano,	There you will give me your hand,	Andante, $\frac{2}{4}$, legato melody.
Là mi dirai di sì. *Vedi, non è lontano;* *Partiam, ben mio, da qui*	There you will tell me "yes." You see, it is not far; Let us leave, my beloved.	

Zerlina

Vorrei e non vorrei;	I'd like to, but yet I would not.	Legato melody repeated.
Mi trema un poco il cor. *Felice è ver, sarei,* *Ma può burlarmi ancor.*	My heart trembles a little. It's true I would be happy, But he may just be tricking me.	

143

(Beth Bergman)

Sherrill Milnes as Don Giovanni and Teresa Stratas as Zerlina in the duet Là ci darem la mano.

Don Giovanni

Quicker interchange between voices.	*Vieni, mio bel diletto!*

Come, my dearly beloved!

Zerlina

Mi fa pietà Masetto!

I'm sorry for Masetto.

Don Giovanni

Io cangierò tua sorte.

I will change your life!

Zerlina

Presto, non son più forte!

Soon I won't be able to resist.

Don Giovanni

Vieni! Vieni!
Là ci darem la mano!

Come! Come!
There you will give me your hand.

Legato melody now shared by both voices.

Zerlina

Vorrei, e non vorrei!

I'd like to, but yet I would not.

Don Giovanni

Là mi dirai di sì.   There you will tell me "yes."

Zerlina

Mi trema un poco il cor!   My heart trembles a little.

Don Giovanni

Partiam, mio ben, da qui!   Let us leave, my beloved.

Zerlina

Ma può burlarmi ancor!   But he may just be tricking me.

Don Giovanni

Vieni, mio bel diletto!   Come, my dearly beloved!

Zerlina

Mi fa pietà Masetto!   I'm sorry for Masetto.   Voices overlap.

Don Giovanni

Io cangierò tua sorte.   I will change your life.

Zerlina

Presto, non son più forte!   Soon I won't be able to resist.

Don Giovanni

Andiam! Andiam!   Let us go!

Zerlina

Andiam!   Let us go!

Don Giovanni and Zerlina

Andiam, andiam, mio bene,   Let us go, let us go, my beloved,   Allegro, $\frac{6}{8}$; together
                                                                               they sing a new,
                                                                               joyous tune.
A ristorar le pene   To soothe the pangs
D'un innocente amor! ecc.   Of an innocent love, etc.

SYMPHONY NO. 40 IN G MINOR, K. 550 (1788)

The Symphony No. 40 in G Minor is the most passionate and dramatic of
Mozart's symphonies. Although the work is classical in form and technique, it is almost romantic in emotional intensity. It staggers the imagination that Mozart could compose the G minor and two other great sympho-

nies—No. 39 in E Flat and No. 41 in C (*Jupiter*)—during the short period of six weeks. They are his last three symphonies.

Like most classical symphonies, the Symphony No. 40 in G Minor has four movements: (1) fast, (2) slow, (3) minuet, (4) fast.

First Movement:
Molto allegro

Side A, band 9

$$\left[\begin{array}{c} \textit{8-record/cassette set:} \\ \textit{Side 4, band 6} \end{array}\right]$$

A quiet but agitated opening theme in the violins sets the mood for the entire first movement, which is in sonata form. A throbbing accompaniment in the violas contributes to the feeling of unrest. Dominating the violin melody is the rhythmic pattern short-short-long, first heard in the opening three-note motive.

The persistence of this rhythmic pattern gives the music a sense of urgency. Yet the melody is balanced and symmetrical. Questioning upward leaps are answered by downward scales, and the second phrase of the melody is a sequential repetition of the first, one step lower. The exposition continues with a bridge section that presents a new staccato motive played loudly by the violins.

The lyrical second theme, in B flat major, contrasts completely with the agitated G minor opening. Mozart exploits the expressive resources of tone color by dividing the theme between strings and woodwinds. In the closing section of the exposition, Mozart uses a fragment from the opening theme to achieve a different emotional effect. The three-note motive now sounds gentle and plaintive as it is passed between clarinet and bassoon against a sighing string background.

In the development, the movement becomes feverish. The opening theme is led into different keys and is cut into smaller and smaller pieces. The development begins mysteriously as the opening phrase ends in an unexpected way and sinks lower and lower. Then a sudden explosion of polyphonic texture increases the excitement and complexity. Mozart brusquely shifts the opening phrase between low and high strings while combining it with a furious staccato countermelody. Soon after, he demolishes the opening phrase: we hear the beginning of the theme without its upward leap.

Then the final note is lopped off.

Finally, we are left with the irreducible minimum of the original theme, the three-note motive.

The tension resolves only with the entrance of the entire opening theme in the tonic key.

In the recapitulation, exposition material is given new expressive meaning. The bridge is expanded and made more dramatic. The lyrical second theme, now in G minor, is touching and sad.

Listening Outline To be read while music is heard

SYMPHONY NO. 40 IN G MINOR, K. 550 (1788), BY WOLFGANG AMADEUS MOZART

First Movement: Molto allegro

Sonata form, duple meter ($\frac{2}{2}$), G minor

Flute, 2 oboes, 2 clarinets, 2 bassoons, 2 French horns, 1st violins, 2d violins, violas, cellos, double basses

(About 7½ minutes)

EXPOSITION
First theme   1. *a.* Main theme in violins, *p*, throbbing accompaniment in violas, minor key.

Molto allegro
Violins

p

                b. Full orchestra, *f.*

Bridge   2. *a.* Violins, *p,* main theme takes new turn to

                b. Full orchestra, *f,* major key, staccato motive and insistent upward scales in violins. Pause.

Second theme   3. *a.* Lyrical melody, *p,* major key, strings and woodwinds.

p

                b. Woodwinds and strings, *p,* lyrical melody somewhat varied. Crescendo in full orchestra.

                c. Staccato phrase, *f,* downward scale to

Closing section 4. *a.* String sighs, *p,* three-note motive in woodwinds, violins, *f.* Varied repetition of string sighs and three-note motive.

                b. Downward scales, *f,* full orchestra, cadence in major key. (Exposition may be repeated.)

DEVELOPMENT

                1. *a.* High woodwinds, *p,* lead to

                b. Violins, *p,* main-theme phrase repeated on lower pitches.

                2. Sudden *f,* full orchestra, main-theme phrase combined with rapid countermelody.

                3. *a.* Sudden *p,* high violins and woodwinds, three-note motive.

                b. Sudden *f,* full orchestra, three-note motive.

                c. Sudden *p,* high flutes and clarinets, three-note motive carried down to

RECAPITULATION

First theme   1. *a.* Main theme in violins, *p,* throbbing accompaniment in violas, minor key.

                b. Full orchestra, *f.*

Bridge   2. *a.* Violins, *p,* main theme takes new turn to

                b. Full orchestra, *f,* staccato motive in violins and cellos. Insistent upward scales in violins, *f.* Pause.

Second theme   3. *a.* Lyrical melody, *p,* minor key, strings and woodwinds.

                b. Woodwinds and strings, *p,* lyrical melody somewhat varied. Crescendo in full orchestra.

                c. Staccato phrase, *f,* downward scale to

Closing section 4. *a.* String sighs, *p,* three-note motive in woodwinds, violins, *f.* Varied repetition of string sighs and three-note motive.

                b. Downward scales, *f,* full orchestra.

CODA   1. *a.* Sudden *p,* main-theme motive in strings.

                b. Full orchestra, *f,* cadence in minor key.

Second Movement:
Andante

The mood of the andante hovers between gentleness and longing. The andante is written in sonata form and is the only movement of this symphony in major (it is in E flat). This movement develops from a series of gently pulsating notes in the opening theme.

As the theme continues, the violins introduce an airy two-note rhythmic figure that will appear—with changes of dynamics and orchestration—in almost every section of the andante. The rhythmic figure will be, at different times, graceful, insistent, and forceful.

Later, Mozart uses the airy figures as a delicate countermelody to the repeated-note idea. Floating woodwinds interwoven with strings reveal Mozart's sensitivity to tone color as an expressive resource.

Third Movement:
Menuetto (Allegretto)

The minuet, in G minor, is serious and intense; it does not sound like an aristocratic dance. The form of the minuet is A B A:

[8-record/cassette set:
Side 5, band 1]

Minuet	Trio	Minuet
A	B	A
A (repeated) ba' (repeated)	c (repeated) dc' (repeated)	a ba'

Powerful syncopations give a fierce character to the A section (the minuet), which is predominantly loud and in minor.

Later, Mozart increases the tension through polyphonic texture and striking dissonances. At the end of the A section, there is a sudden drop in dynamics; the flute, supported by oboes and a bassoon, softly recalls the opening melody of the minuet.

The trio section (B) brings a shift from minor to major, from fierce energy to graceful relaxation.

This change of mood is underscored by a soft dynamic level and pastoral woodwind interludes. After the trio, a sudden forte announces the return of the fierce A section.

Fourth Movement:

Allegro assai

Mozart ends the symphony with the tense movement already described in Section 2.

[CLASSICAL 11] LUDWIG VAN BEETHOVEN

For many people, Ludwig van Beethoven (1770–1827) represents the highest level of musical genius. He opened new realms of musical expression and profoundly influenced composers throughout the nineteenth century.

Beethoven was born in Bonn, Germany, into a family of musicians. By the age of eleven, he was serving as assistant to the court organist, and at age twelve he had several compositions published. When he was sixteen, he played for Mozart, who reportedly said, "Keep your eyes on him; some day he will give the world something to talk about." Shortly before his twenty-second birthday, he left Bonn to study with Haydn in Vienna, where he spent the rest of his life.

Beethoven's first years in Vienna brought hard work, growing confidence, and public praise (although his studies with Haydn were not entirely successful and he went secretly to another teacher). This music-loving city was dazzled by his virtuosity and moved by his improvisations. And although he rebelled against social convention, asserting that an artist deserved as much respect as the nobility, the same aristocrats who had allowed Mozart to die in poverty showered Beethoven with gifts. In 1809,

(Granger Collection)

Ludwig van Beethoven.

three noblemen obligated themselves to give him an annual income, their only condition being that he remain in Vienna—an arrangement unprecedented in music history. Unlike earlier composers, Beethoven was never actually in the service of the Viennese aristocracy. He earned good fees from piano lessons and concerts, and publishers were quick to buy his compositions.

But during his twenty-ninth year, disaster struck: he felt the first symptoms of deafness, which his doctors could do nothing to halt. On October 6, 1802, Beethoven wrote an agonized letter addressed to his brothers from Heiligenstadt, a village outside Vienna. In the letter (now known as the *Heiligenstadt testament*), he said, "I would have ended my life—it was only my art that held me back." This victory over despair coincided with an important change in his musical style; works that he created after his emotional crisis—perhaps most significantly the gigantic Third Symphony, the *Eroica*, composed from 1803 to 1804—have a new power and heroism. (He planned to name the Third Symphony *Bonaparte*, after Napoleon; but when Napoleon proclaimed himself emperor, Beethoven struck out the dedication and later wrote on the new title page, "Heroic Symphony composed to celebrate the memory of a great man.")

As a man, Beethoven remains something of a mystery. He was self-educated and had read widely, but he was weak in elementary arithmetic.

He claimed the highest moral principles but was often unscrupulous in dealing with publishers. He was orderly and methodical when composing but dressed sloppily and lived in incredibly messy apartments. He fell in love with several women but never formed a lasting relationship. The contradictions in his personality are especially evident in his disastrous guardianship of his young nephew Karl, who eventually attempted suicide. Beethoven took consolation from nature for disappointments in his personal life, and ideas came to him as he walked in the countryside. His Sixth Symphony, the *Pastoral*, expresses his recollections of life in the country.

As Beethoven's hearing weakened, this once brilliant pianist was forced to stop performing in public—though he insisted on conducting his orchestral works long after he could do it efficiently. His sense of isolation grew with his deafness. Friends had to communicate with him through an ear trumpet and, during his last years, by writing in notebooks which he carried.

Despite this, and despite mounting personal problems, Beethoven had a creative outburst after 1818 that produced some of his greatest works: the late piano sonatas and string quartets, the *Missa solemnis*, and the Ninth Symphony—out of total deafness, new realms of sound.

BEETHOVEN'S MUSIC

For Beethoven, music was not mere entertainment but a moral force, "a higher revelation than all wisdom and philosophy." His music directly reflects his powerful, tortured personality.

Beethoven's demand for perfection meant long and hard work—sometimes he worked for years on a single symphony while also writing other compositions. He carried musical sketchbooks everywhere, jotting down and revising ideas; the final versions of his works were often hammered out laboriously.

Beethoven mostly used classical forms and techniques, but he gave them new power and intensity. The musical heir of Haydn and Mozart, he bridged the classical and romantic eras; many of his innovations were used by later composers. In his works, tension and excitement are built up through syncopations and dissonances. The range of pitch and dynamics is greater than ever before, so that contrasts of mood are more pronounced. Accents and climaxes seem titanic. Greater tension called for a larger musical framework, and so he expanded his forms; he was a musical architect who could create large-scale structures in which every note seems inevitable. But his music is not all stormy and powerful; much of it is gentle, humorous, noble, or lyrical.

More than his predecessors, he tried to unify contrasting movements by means of musical continuity. Sometimes one movement leads directly into the next, without the traditional pause; sometimes a musical bond is created by similar themes. He also greatly expanded the development section of sonata-form movements and made it more dramatic. His works often have climactic, triumphant finales toward which the previous movements seem to build—an important departure from the light, relaxed endings of Haydn and Mozart.

Beethoven's most popular works are the nine symphonies, written for larger orchestras than Haydn's or Mozart's. Each of them is unique in character and style, though the odd-numbered symphonies tend to be more forceful and the even-numbered ones calmer and more lyrical. In the finale of the Ninth Symphony (*Choral*), Beethoven took the unprecedented step of using a chorus and four vocal soloists, who sing the text of Schiller's *Ode to Joy*.

His thirty-two piano sonatas are far more difficult than those of Haydn and Mozart and exploit the improved piano of his time, drawing many new effects from it. In these sonatas, he experimented with compositional techniques which he later expanded in the symphonies and string quartets. The sixteen string quartets are among the greatest music composed; and each of the five superb piano concertos is remarkable for its individuality.

While most of Beethoven's important works are for instruments, his sense of drama was also expressed in vocal music, including two masses and his only opera, *Fidelio*.

Beethoven's work is usually divided into three periods: early (up to 1802), middle (1803–1814), and late (1815–1827). Some works of the early period show the influence of Haydn and Mozart, but others clearly show Beethoven's personal style. The works of the middle period tend to be longer and more heroic; the sublime works of the late period often contain fugues as well as passages that sound surprisingly harsh and "modern." When a violinist complained that the music was very difficult to play, Beethoven reportedly replied, "Do you believe that I think of a wretched fiddle when the spirit speaks to me?"

PIANO SONATA IN C MINOR, OP. 13 (PATHÉTIQUE; 1798)

The title *Pathétique*, coined by Beethoven, suggests the tragically passionate character of his famous Piano Sonata in C Minor, Op. 13 (we'll focus on the first of its three movements). Beethoven's impetuous playing and masterful improvisational powers are mirrored in the sonata's extreme dynamic contrasts, explosive accents, and crashing chords. At the age of twenty-seven, during his early period, Beethoven had already created a powerful and original piano style that foreshadowed nineteenth-century romanticism.

[*8-record/cassette set:*
  Side 7, bands 1–3]

[8-record/cassette set:
  Side 7, band 1]

First Movement:

Grave (solemn, slow introduction);
Allegro di molto e con brio (very fast and brilliant allegro)

The *Pathétique* begins in C minor with an intense, slow introduction, dominated by an opening motive in dotted rhythm: long-short-long-short-long-long.

This six-note idea seems to pose a series of unresolved questions as it is repeated on higher and higher pitch levels. The tragic mood is intensified by dissonant chords, sudden contrasts of dynamics and register, and pauses filled with expectancy. The slow introduction is integrated into the allegro that follows it in imaginative and dramatic ways.

The tension of the introduction is maintained in the allegro con brio, a breathless, fast movement in sonata form. The opening theme, in C minor, begins with a staccato idea that rapidly rises up a 2-octave scale. It is accompanied by low broken octaves, the rapid alternation of two tones an octave apart.

Growing directly out of the opening theme is a bridge that is also built from a climbing staccato motive.

This bridge motive has an important role later in the movement.

The contrasting second theme, which enters without a pause, is spun out of a short motive that is repeatedly shifted between low and high registers.

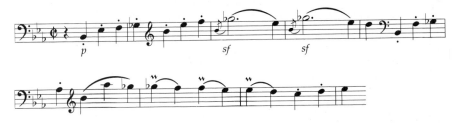

This restless idea begins in E flat minor but then moves through different keys. The exposition is rounded off by several themes, including a high running passage and a return of the opening staccato idea in E flat major. (The exposition is sometimes repeated.)

The development section begins with a dramatic surprise: Beethoven brings back the opening bars of the slow introduction. This reappearance creates an enormous contrast of tempo, rhythm, and mood. After four bars of slow music, the fast tempo resumes as Beethoven combines two different ideas: the staccato bridge motive and a quickened version of the introduction motive. The introduction motive is presented in a rhythmically altered form: short-short-short-long-long.

The bridge motive is then developed in the bass, played by the pianist's left hand while the right hand has high broken octaves. After several high accented notes, the brief development concludes with a running passage that leads down to the recapitulation.

For a while, the recapitulation runs its usual course as themes from the exposition are presented in the tonic key of C minor. But Beethoven has one more surprise for the coda—after a loud dissonant chord and a brief pause, he again brings back the opening of the slow introduction. This time the slow music is even more moving, as it is punctuated by moments of silence. Then the fast tempo resumes, and the opening staccato idea and powerful chords bring the movement to a decisive close.

SYMPHONY NO. 5 IN C MINOR, OP. 67 (1808)

The Fifth Symphony opens with one of the most famous rhythmic ideas in all music, a short-short-short-long motive. Beethoven reportedly interpreted this four-note motive as "fate knocking at the door." It dominates the first movement and plays an important role later in the symphony, too. The entire work can be seen as an emotional progression from the conflict and struggle of the first movement, in C minor, to the exultation and victory of the final movement, in C major. The finale is the climax of the symphony; it is longer than the first movement and more powerful in sound.

Through several different techniques, Beethoven brilliantly welds four contrasting movements into a unified work. The basic rhythmic motive of the first movement (short-short-short-long) is used in a marchlike theme in the third movement. And this third-movement theme is later quoted dramatically within the finale. The last two movements are also connected by a bridge passage.

Beethoven jotted down a few themes for the Fifth Symphony in 1804, but mainly worked on it during 1807 and 1808, an amazingly productive period when he also composed the Mass in C Major; the Sonata for Cello and Piano, Op. 69; and the Sixth Symphony.

First Movement:

Allegro con brio (allegro with vigor)

Side B, band 6

[*8-record/cassette set:*
  Side 6, band 1]

The allegro con brio is an enormously powerful and concentrated movement in sonata form. Its character is determined by a single rhythmic motive, short-short-short-long, from which Beethoven creates an astonishing variety of musical ideas. Tension and expectation are generated from the very beginning of the movement. Three rapid notes of the same pitch are followed by a downward leap to a held, suspenseful tone. This powerful idea is hammered out twice by all the strings in unison; the second time, it is a step lower in pitch.

As the opening theme continues in C minor, Beethoven maintains excitement by quickly developing his basic idea. He crowds varied repetitions of the motive together and rapidly shifts the motive to different pitches and instruments.

The second theme, in E flat major, dramatically combines different ideas. It begins with an unaccompanied horn call that asserts the basic motive in a varied form (short-short-short-long-long-long).

This horn-call motive announces a new legato melody which is calm and contrasts with the preceding agitation. Yet even during this lyrical moment, we are not allowed to forget the basic motive; now it is muttered in the background by cellos and double basses.

Beethoven generates tension in the development section by breaking the horn-call motive into smaller and smaller fragments until it is represented by only a single tone. Supported by a chord, this tone is echoed between woodwinds and strings in a breathtaking decrescendo. The recapitulation comes as a tremendous climax as the full orchestra thunders the basic motive. The recapitulation also brings a new expressive oboe solo at the end of the first theme. The heroic closing section of the recapitulation, in C major, moves without a break into a long and exciting coda in C minor. This coda is like a second development section in which the basic motive creates still greater power and energy.

Listening Outline   To be read while music is heard

*SYMPHONY NO. 5 IN C MINOR, OP. 67 (1808),
BY LUDWIG VAN BEETHOVEN*

First Movement: Allegro con brio

Sonata form, duple meter ($\frac{2}{4}$), C minor

2 flutes, 2 oboes, 2 clarinets, 2 bassoons, 2 French horns, 2 trumpets, timpani, 1st violins, 2d violins, violas, cellos, double basses

(About 6½ minutes)

EXPOSITION

First theme   1. *a.* Basic motive, *ff*, repeated a step lower, strings in unison.

          b. Sudden *p,* strings quickly develop basic motive, minor key, powerful chords, high held tone.

Bridge   2. *a.* Basic motive, *ff*, orchestra in unison.

          b. Sudden *p,* strings quickly develop basic motive, crescendo, *ff,* powerful chords.

Second theme   3. *a.* Solo French horns, *ff*, horn-call motive.

          b. Violins, *p,* lyrical melody in major. Basic motive accompanies in low strings.

       Crescendo to

4. *a.* Triumphant melody, *ff,* violins.

       b. Woodwinds and horns, basic motive rushes downward. Cadences in basic
          rhythm. Pause.
       (Exposition may be repeated.)

DEVELOPMENT
     1. *a.* Basic motive, *ff,* horns, strings.
       b. Sudden *p,* strings and woodwinds, basic motive quickly developed. Motive
          climbs to rapidly repeated chords, *ff.*
     2. *a.* Violins, *ff,* horn-call motive, low strings, descending line.

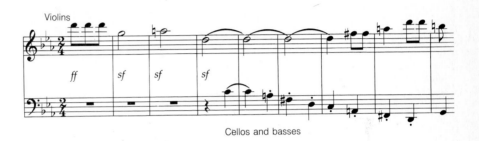

       b. High woodwinds, *ff,* in dialogue with lower strings, *ff.* Horn-call motive
          broken into tiny fragments. Decrescendo to *pp.*

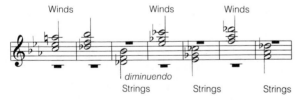

       c. Sudden *ff,* horn-call rhythm.
       d. Sudden *pp,* woodwinds echoed by strings.
       e. Sudden *ff,* repeated motive drives into

RECAPITULATION
First theme
     1. *a.* Climactic basic motive, full orchestra, *ff,* repeated a step lower.
       b. Sudden *p,* strings quickly develop basic motive, minor key, chords lead to
       c. Oboe solo.
Bridge
     2. Basic motive quickly developed in strings, crescendo to *ff,* full orchestra.
Second theme
     3. *a.* Horn-call motive, solo bassoons, *ff* (horns sometimes added).
       b. Lyrical major melody, *p,* violins and flutes alternate. Basic motive
         accompanies in timpani, *p.* Crescendo to

4. *a.* Triumphant melody, *ff,* violins.
   b. Woodwinds, basic motive rushes downward.
      Cadences in basic rhythm.

CODA
1. *a.* Rapidly repeated chords, *ff.*
   b. Horn-call motive, lower strings, *f,* with higher violin melody, minor.

Descending violin melody, staccato, leads to
2. *a.* New, rising theme in strings, legato and staccato.

   b. High woodwinds, *ff,* answered by lower strings in powerful interchange.
      Rapidly repeated notes lead to
3. *a.* Basic motive, *ff,* repeated a step lower, full orchestra.
   b. Sudden *p,* basic motive quickly developed in strings and woodwinds.
   c. Sudden *ff,* powerful concluding chords.

Second Movement:

Andante con moto (moderately slow, with movement)

[8-record/cassette set:
Side 6, band 2] The second movement, in A flat major, is mostly relaxed and lyrical, but it includes moments of tension and heroism. It is an extended set of variations based on two themes. The main theme (A), softly introduced by the cellos and violas, is a long, legato melody of great nobility. The second theme (B) begins very gently in the clarinets but soon brings a startling contrast of mood. The full orchestra suddenly bursts in, and the clarinet melody is transformed into a triumphant trumpet fanfare. A hushed transitional passage then leads back to the main theme, presented now in quicker notes.

After several variations, there is a middle section in which fragments of the themes are treated in new ways. Woodwind instruments are featured, and there is a brief episode in minor. The movement concludes with a final variation of the main melody—now majestically proclaimed by the full orchestra—and a coda that poetically recalls what has come before.

160

Listening Outline
To be read while music is heard

SYMPHONY NO. 5 IN C MINOR, OP. 67 (1808),
BY LUDWIG VAN BEETHOVEN

Second Movement: Andante con moto

Theme and variations, triple meter ($\frac{3}{8}$), A flat major

2 flutes, 2 oboes, 2 clarinets, 2 bassoons, 2 French horns, 2 trumpets, timpani, 1st violins, 2d violins, violas, cellos, double basses

(About 10 minutes)

THEME A   1. Lyrical melody, violas and cellos, *p*.

Melody continues in higher register, violins alternate with flute.

THEME B   2. *a.* Clarinets, *p*, rising phrases.

Violins, *pp*, sudden *ff*, full orchestra.
     b. Trumpets, *ff*, rising phrases.

Violins, *pp*, sustained notes.

161

VARIATION A¹   3. Violas and cellos, *p*, lyrical melody in even-flowing rhythm.

p

Melody continues in higher register, violins alternate with flute.

VARIATION B¹   4. *a.* Clarinets, *p*, rising phrases. Violins, *pp*, sudden *ff*, full orchestra.
     b. Trumpets, *ff*, rising phrases. Violins, *pp*, sustained notes, cellos, low repeated notes.

VARIATION A²   5. *a.* Violas and cellos, *p*, lyrical melody decorated by quick, even-flowing notes.

p

     b. Violins, *pp*, repeat decorated melody in higher register.
     c. Loud repeated chords, decorated melody in cellos and double basses. Upward scales lead to high held tone.

MIDDLE SECTION   6. Sudden *pp*, repeated string chords, clarinet phrase passed to bassoon and flute. High woodwind interlude leads to

     7. *a.* Full orchestra, *ff*, rising phrases, timpani rolls.
     b. Strings, *p*, repeated short figure.
     8. *a.* Woodwinds, *p*, staccato variation of lyrical melody, minor key.
     b. Rising scales in flute, strings. Crescendo.

VARIATION A³   9. Full orchestra, *ff*, lyrical melody in high register, major key, rising scales. Flute and violins, *p*, continue melody.

CODA   10. *a.* Più mosso (faster tempo), bassoon, *p*, variation of lyrical phrase. Violins, crescendo.
     b. Original tempo, flute and strings, *p*, conclusion of lyrical melody.
     c. Clarinets, *p*, variation of lyrical phrase, low strings, crescendo. Cadence in full orchestra, *ff*.

Third Movement:

Allegro (scherzo)

[8-record/cassette set:
   Side 6, band 3]
The rapid third movement is a scherzo, in C minor, composed of three sections: A (scherzo) B (trio) A′ (scherzo). The scherzo opens with a hushed, mysterious theme played by cellos and double basses in a low register.

Allegro

pp

162

Soon, in sharp contrast, a bold repeated-note theme is hammered out loudly by the horns.

This theme is dominated by the rhythmic pattern short-short-short-long and recalls the basic motive of the first movement.

The B section (trio), in major, brings a gruff, hurried theme, played by cellos and double basses.

This theme is imitated, in the style of a fugue, by each of the higher strings. The bustling rhythmic motion of the B section has a feeling of energy and rough humor.

When the scherzo section (A') returns, it is hushed and ominous throughout, sounding like a ghost of its former self. The mysterious opening theme is now played pizzicato rather than legato. The repeated-note theme is completely transformed in mood; it is no longer proclaimed by horns but is whispered by clarinets, plucked violins, and oboe.

One of the most extraordinary passages in the symphony follows the scherzo section (A'): a bridge leading from the dark, mysterious world of the scherzo to the bright sunlight of the finale. It opens with a feeling of suspended animation as the timpani softly repeat a single tone against a sustained chord in the strings. Over the timpani pulsation, the violins hesitantly play a fragment of the mysterious scherzo theme. Tension mounts as this fragment is carried higher and higher, until a sudden crescendo climaxes with the heroic opening of the finale.

Fourth Movement:

Allegro

The fourth movement, in sonata form, is the climax of the symphony. It brings the victory of C major over C minor, of optimism and exultation over struggle and uncertainty. For greater power and brilliance, Beethoven enlarged the orchestra in the finale to include three trombones, a piccolo, and a contrabassoon. Brass instruments are especially prominent and give a marchlike character to much of the movement.

[8-record/cassette set: Side 6, band 3 cont.]

The exposition is rich in melodic ideas; even the bridge has a theme of its own, and there is also a distinctive closing theme. The triumphant opening

theme begins with the three tones of the C major triad, brilliantly proclaimed by the trumpets.

A bridge theme, similar in mood to the opening theme, is announced by
the horns and continued by the violins.

Triplets lend a joyous quality to the second theme, which contrasts loud
and soft phrases.

Two powerful chords and a brief pause announce the closing theme of the
exposition. This melody, composed of descending phrases, is first played
by the strings and woodwinds and then forcefully repeated by the entire
orchestra.

The development focuses mainly on the second theme and its triplet
rhythm. A huge climax at the end of the development is followed by one of

the most marvelous surprises in all music. Beethoven dramatically quotes the whispered repeated-note theme (short-short-short-long) of the preceding scherzo movement. This ominous quotation is like a sudden recollection of past anxiety, and it creates a connection between the last two movements. Leading into the powerful recapitulation of the fourth movement, it prepares the renewal of the victory over uncertainty.

During the long coda of the finale, earlier themes are heard in altered and quickened versions. Several times, the music keeps going even though the listener thinks it's coming to an end. Over and over, Beethoven affirms the tonic key and resolves the frenzied tensions built up during the symphony. Such control over tension is an essential element of Beethoven's genius.

THE ROMANTIC PERIOD

V

Two Men Contemplating the Moon (1819), by the German painter Caspar David Friedrich. The romantics were especially drawn to the realm of fantasy: the unconscious, the irrational, the world of dreams.

[**1**] ROMANTICISM IN MUSIC (1820–1900)

The early nineteenth century brought the flowering of romanticism, a cultural movement that stressed emotion, imagination, and individualism. In part, romanticism was a rebellion against the neoclassicism of the eighteenth century and the age of reason. Romantic writers broke away from time-honored conventions and emphasized freedom of expression. Painters used bolder, more brilliant colors and preferred dynamic motion to gracefully balanced poses.

But romanticism was too diverse and complex to be defined by any single formula. It aimed to broaden all human horizons and encompass the totality of our experience. The romantic movement was international in scope and influenced all the arts.

Emotional subjectivity was a basic quality of romanticism in art. "All good poetry is the spontaneous overflow of powerful feelings," wrote William Wordsworth, the English romantic poet. And "spontaneous overflow" made much romantic literature autobiographical; authors projected their personalities in their work. Walt Whitman, the American poet, expressed this subjective attitude beautifully when he began a poem, "I celebrate myself, and sing myself."

In exploring their inner lives, the romantics were especially drawn to the realm of fantasy: the unconscious, the irrational, the world of dreams. Romantic literature includes tales of horror and the supernatural such as Edgar Allan Poe's stories and Mary Wollstonecraft Shelley's *Frankenstein*, and Thomas de Quincy's descriptions of his drug-induced dreams. The visual arts include the nightmarish etchings of the Spanish painter Francisco Goya.

The romantic fascination with fantasy was paired with interest in exoticism and the past—the far-away and the long-ago. For example, the French artist Eugène Delacroix often depicted violent scenes in far-off lands; and the romantics cherished the Middle Ages and found inspiration in medieval folk ballads and tales. (In contrast, the neoclassicists had considered the medieval period the "dark ages.") Romantic novels set in the Middle Ages include Sir Walter Scott's *Ivanhoe* (1819) and Victor Hugo's *Hunchback of Notre Dame* (1831). There was a "gothic revival" in architecture, and a new appreciation of the gothic cathedrals.

Of all the inspirations for romantic art, none was more important than nature, which was seen as a source of consolation and a mirror of the human heart—Wordsworth, for instance, thought of nature as "the nurse,/the guide, the guardian of my heart and soul."

THE ROMANTIC PERIOD

(Ghent, Museum of Fine Arts)

Portrait of an Insane Man ("Kleptomaniac"), *by Théodore Géricault (1822–1823). Romanticism aimed to broaden horizons—indeed, to encompass the totality of human experience. The French artist Géricault movingly documented human suffering and insanity.*

(Scala/Art Resource)

Liberty Leading the People, by Eugène Delacroix (1830). Romantic painters and musicians often saw political revolution as a reflection of their own struggle for artistic freedom. Delacroix combined a realistic description of street fighting in Paris in the July Revolution of 1830 with a symbolic representation of liberty.

(Museum of Fine Arts, Boston)

Slave Ship, *by Joseph Turner (1839). Romantic sensitivity to nature was revealed in landscape painting, which attained new importance. In the seascapes of the English painter Turner, the sweep of waves expressed not only the power of nature but human passion as well.*

(Scala/Art Resource)

The Gleaners, *by Jean-François Millet (1857). The industrial revolution spurred interest in the working class and the poor. The French painter Millet realistically portrayed the labor of peasant women picking up leftover grain in the fields.*

(Lauros-Giraudon/Art Resource)

The Death of Sardanapalus (1827), by Eugène Delacroix, shows a defeated Assyrian tyrant who has his wives killed before taking his own life. The violent and sensuous painting reflects the romantic preoccupation with the exotic.

This romantic sensitivity to nature is also revealed in landscape painting, which attained new importance; artists like John Constable and William Turner in England were masters at conveying the movement of nature—rippling brooks, drifting clouds, stormy seas.

However, romanticism also coincided with the industrial revolution, and many writers and artists recorded its new social realities. The novels of Charles Dickens and the paintings of Gustave Courbet reflect an interest in the working class and the poor.

THE ROMANTIC PERIOD IN MUSIC

The romantic period in music extended from about 1820 to 1900. Among the most important romantic composers were Franz Schubert, Robert Schumann, Frédéric Chopin, Felix Mendelssohn, Hector Berlioz, Bedřich Smetana, Peter Ilyich Tchaikovsky, Johannes Brahms, Giuseppe Verdi, Giacomo Puccini, and Richard Wagner. The length of this list—even

(National Gallery, London)

The Hay Wain (1821), by John Constable. Of all the sources of inspiration for romantic art, none was more important than nature.

though some important composers have been omitted from it—testifies to the richness, variety, and continuing importance of romantic music.

Romantic musicians, inspired by the image of Beethoven as a "free artist," often composed to fulfill an inner need rather than to execute a commission or meet the demands of an aristocratic or church patron; and they also thought in terms of creating something for posterity. Sometimes, however, they were "free artists" by necessity rather than choice, since most aristocrats could no longer afford private opera houses, orchestras, and "composers in residence." Romantic composers came from the middle class, wrote primarily for a middle-class audience, and had to sell their wares in the marketplace. Because few could support themselves through composition alone, they also worked as conductors (like Mendelssohn), music teachers (like Chopin), and music critics (like Berlioz). Some were touring virtuosos, like the Hungarian Franz Liszt (1811–1886). Liszt, the composer who invented the tone poem, was one of the most dazzling and charismatic pianists of all time.

The rise of the urban middle class led to the formation of many orchestras and opera groups, and the development of regular subscription concerts. Private music making increased, too—the piano became a fixture in every middle-class home. The nineteenth century also saw the founding of music conservatories in Europe and the United States.

Another influence on romantic music was audiences' fascination with virtuosity. Liszt and the violinist Niccolò Paganini were musical heroes; and following Liszt's example, performers like the pianist Clara Schumann began to give solo recitals in addition to their customary appearances with orchestras.

CHARACTERISTICS OF ROMANTIC MUSIC

Composers of the romantic period continued to use the musical forms of the preceding classical era. The emotional intensity associated with romanticism was present in the work of Mozart and particularly in that of Beethoven, who greatly influenced composers after him. The romantic preference for expressive, songlike melody also grew out of the classical style.

Nonetheless, there are many differences between romantic and classical music. Romantic works tend to have greater ranges of tone color, dynamics, and pitch. Also, the romantic harmonic vocabulary is broader, with more emphasis on colorful, unstable chords. Romantic music is linked more closely to the other arts, particularly to literature. New forms developed, and in all forms there was greater tension and less emphasis on balance and resolution. But romantic music is so diverse that generalizations are apt to mislead. Some romantic composers, such as Mendelssohn and Brahms, created works that were deeply rooted in classical tradition; others, such as Berlioz, Liszt, and Wagner, were more revolutionary.

Romantic composers wrote primarily for a middle-class audience. In this picture by Moritz von Schwind, Franz Schubert is shown at the piano accompanying the singer Johann Michael Vogl.

(Bettmann Archive)

Individuality of Style

Romantic music puts unprecedented emphasis on self-expression and indi-viduality of style. There is "not a bar which I have not truly felt and which is not an echo of my innermost feelings," wrote Tchaikovsky of his Fourth Symphony. "A new world of music" was the goal of the young Chopin. Many romantics created music that sounds unique and reflects their per-sonalities. Robert Schumann observed that "Chopin will soon be unable to write anything without people crying out at the seventh or eighth bar, 'That is indeed by him.'" And today, with some listening experience, a music lover can tell within a few minutes—sometimes within a few sec-onds—whether a piece is by Schumann or Chopin, Tchaikovsky or Brahms.

Expressive Aims and Subjects

The romantics explored a universe of feeling that included flamboyance and intimacy, unpredictability and melancholy, rapture and longing. Countless songs and operas glorify romantic love. Often the lovers are unhappy and face overwhelming obstacles. Fascination with the fantastic and diabolical is expressed in music like the *Dream of a Witches' Sabbath* from Berlioz's *Symphonie fantastique (Fantastic Symphony)*. All aspects of nature attracted romantic musicians. In different sections of Part V we'll study music that depicts a wild horseback ride on a stormy night (Schu-bert's *Erlkönig,* or *Erlking*), the flow of a river (Smetana's *Moldau*), and a spectacular fire and flood (Wagner's *Götterdämmerung,* or *Twilight of the Gods*). Romantic composers also dealt with subjects drawn from the Middle Ages and from Shakespeare's plays.

Nationalism and Exoticism

Nationalism was an important political movement that influenced nine-teenth-century music. Musical *nationalism* was expressed when romantic composers deliberately created music with a specific national identity, using the folk songs, dances, legends, and history of their homelands. This national flavor of romantic music—whether Polish, Russian, Bohemian (Czech), or German—contrasts with the more universal character of classi-cal music.

Fascination with national identity also led composers to draw on colorful materials from foreign lands, a trend known as musical *exoticism.* For instance, some wrote melodies in an Asian style or used rhythms and instruments associated with distant lands. The French composer Georges Bizet wrote *Carmen,* an opera set in Spain; the Italian Giacomo Puccini evoked Japan in *Madame Butterfly;* and the Russian Rimsky-Korsakov sug-gested an Arabian atmosphere in his orchestral work *Scheherazade*. Musical exoticism was in keeping with the romantics' attraction to things remote, picturesque, and mysterious.

Program Music

The nineteenth century was the great age of **_program music,_** instrumental music associated with a story, poem, idea, or scene. Usually the nonmusical element is specified by a title or by explanatory comments called a **_program._** A programmatic instrumental piece can represent the emotions, characters, and events of a particular story, or it can evoke the sounds and motions of nature. For example, in Tchaikovsky's _Romeo and Juliet,_ an orchestral work inspired by Shakespeare's play, agitated music depicts the feud between the rival families, a tender melody conveys young love, and a funeral-march rhythm suggests the lovers' tragic fate. And in _The Moldau_, an orchestral work glorifying the main river of Bohemia, Smetana uses musical effects that call to mind a flowing stream, a hunting scene, a peasant wedding, and the crash of waves.

Program music in some form or another has existed for centuries, but it became particularly prominent in the romantic period, when music was closely associated with literature. Many composers—Berlioz, Schumann, Liszt, and Wagner, for example—were prolific authors as well. Artists in all fields were intoxicated by the idea of a "union of the arts." Poets wanted their poetry to be musical, and musicians wanted their music to be poetic.

Expressive Tone Color

Romantic composers reveled in rich and sensuous sound, using tone color to obtain variety of mood and atmosphere. Never before had timbre been so important.

In both symphonic and operatic works, the romantic orchestra was larger and more varied in tone color than the classical orchestra. Toward the end of the romantic era, an orchestra might include close to 100 musicians. (There were twenty to sixty players in the classical ensemble.) The constant expansion of the orchestra reflected composers' changing needs as well as the growing size of concert halls and opera houses. The brass, woodwind, and percussion sections of the orchestra took on a more active role. Romantic composers increased the power of the brass section to something spectacular, calling for trombones, tubas, and more horns and trumpets. In 1824, Beethoven broke precedent by asking for nine brasses in the Ninth Symphony; and in 1894, the Austrian composer Gustav Mahler (1860–1911) demanded twenty-five brass instruments for his Second Symphony. The addition of valves had made it easier for horns and trumpets to cope with intricate melodies.

The woodwind section took on new tone colors as the contrabassoon, bass clarinet, English horn, and piccolo became regular members of the orchestra. Improvements in the construction of instruments allowed woodwind players to perform more flexibly and accurately. Orchestral sounds became more brilliant and sensuously appealing through increased use of cymbals, the triangle, and the harp.

New sounds were drawn from all instruments of the nineteenth-century orchestra. Flutists were asked to play in the breathy low register, and violinists to strike the strings with the wood of their bows. These demands compelled performers to attain a higher level of technical virtuosity.

New ways of blending and combining tone colors were sought to achieve the most poignant and intense sound. In 1844, Hector Berlioz's *Treatise on Modern Instrumentation and Orchestration* signaled the recognition of orchestration as an art in itself.

The piano, the favorite instrument of the romantic age, was improved vastly during the 1820s and 1830s. A cast-iron frame was introduced to hold the strings under greater tension, and the hammers were covered with felt. Thus the piano's tone became more "singing." Its range was also extended. With a stronger instrument, the pianist could produce more sound. And use of the damper ("loud") pedal allowed a sonorous blend of tones from all registers of the piano.

Colorful Harmony

In addition to exploiting new tone colors, the romantics explored new chords and novel ways of using familiar chords. Seeking greater emotional intensity, composers emphasized rich, colorful, and complex harmonies. There was more prominent use of *chromatic harmony,* which employs chords containing tones not found in the prevailing major or minor scale. Such chord tones come from the chromatic scale (which has twelve tones), rather than from the major or minor scales (which have seven different tones). Chromatic chords add color and motion to romantic music. Dissonant, or unstable, chords were also used more freely than during the classical era. By deliberately delaying the resolution of dissonance to a consonant, or stable, chord, romantic composers created feelings of yearning, tension, and mystery.

A romantic piece tends to have a wide variety of keys and rapid modulations, or changes from one key to another. Because of the nature and frequency of these key shifts, the tonic key is somewhat less clear than in classical works. The feeling of tonal gravity tends to be less strong. By the end of the romantic period, even more emphasis was given to harmonic instability and less to stability and resolution.

Expanded Range of Dynamics, Pitch, and Tempo

Romantic music also calls for a wide range of dynamics. It includes sharp contrasts between faint whispers and sonorities of unprecedented power.

The classical dynamic extremes of *ff* and *pp* didn't meet the needs of romantics, who sometimes demanded *ffff* and *pppp*. Seeking more and more expressiveness, nineteenth-century composers used frequent crescendos and decrescendos, as well as sudden dynamic changes.

The range of pitch was expanded, too, as composers reached for extremely high or low sounds. In search of increased brilliance and depth of sound, the romantics exploited instruments like the piccolo and contrabassoon, as well as the expanded keyboard of the piano.

Mood changes in romantic music are often underlined by accelerandos, ritardandos, and subtle variations of pace: there are many more fluctuations in tempo than there are in classical music. To intensify the expression of the music, romantic performers made use of *rubato*, the slight holding back or pressing forward of tempo.

Form: Miniature and Monumental

The nineteenth century was very much an age of contradictions. Romantic composers characteristically expressed themselves both in musical miniatures and in monumental compositions. On the one hand are piano pieces by Chopin and songs by Schubert that last but a few minutes. Such short forms were meant to be heard in the intimate surroundings of a home; they met the needs of the growing number of people who owned pianos. These miniatures were a perfect outlet for the romantic genius at creating an intense mood through a melody, a few chords, or an unusual tone color. On the other hand, there are gigantic works by Berlioz and Wagner that call for a huge number of performers and last several hours. Mammoth compositions, of course, were designed for large opera houses or concert halls.

Romantic composers continued to write symphonies, sonatas, string quartets, concertos, operas, and choral works, but their individual movements tended to be longer than Haydn's and Mozart's. For example, a typical nineteenth-century symphony might last about 45 minutes, as opposed to 25 minutes for an eighteenth-century symphony. And as the romantic period drew to a close, compositions tended to become even longer, more richly orchestrated, and more complex in harmony. For example, Mahler's Eighth Symphony (*Symphony of a Thousand*, 1907) lasts about an hour and a half and calls for eight vocal soloists, a boys' choir, two choruses, and a gigantic orchestra.

New techniques were used to unify such long works. Following the example of Beethoven's Fifth Symphony, the same theme or themes might occur in several movements. When a melody returns in a later movement or section of a romantic work, its character may be changed by use of different dynamics, orchestration, or rhythm—a technique known as *thematic transformation.* A striking use of thematic transformation occurs in Berlioz's *Symphonie fantastique* (*Fantastic Symphony*, 1830), where a lyrical melody from the opening movement becomes a grotesque dance tune in the finale.

Different movements or sections of a romantic work can also be linked through transitional passages; one movement of a symphony or concerto may lead directly into the next. Here, again, Beethoven was the pioneer. And nineteenth-century operas are unified by melodic ideas that reappear in different acts or scenes, some of which may be tied together by connecting passages.

In dealing with an age that so prized individuality, generalizations are especially difficult. The great diversity found in romantic music can best be appreciated, perhaps, by approaching each piece as its composer did—with an open mind and heart.

[ROMANTIC **2**]

THE ART SONG

One of the most distinctive forms in romantic music is the *art song,* a composition for solo voice and piano. Here, the accompaniment is an integral part of the composer's conception, and it serves as an interpretive partner to the voice. Although they are now performed in concert halls, romantic songs were written to be sung and enjoyed at home.

Poetry and music are intimately fused in the art song. It is no accident that this form flowered with the emergence of a rich body of romantic poetry in the early nineteenth century. Many of the finest song composers—Schubert, Schumann, and Brahms, for example—were German or Austrian and set poems in their native language. Among the poets favored by these composers were Johann Wolfgang von Goethe (1749–1832) and Heinrich Heine (1797–1856). The German word *Lied (song)* is commonly used for a song with German text. (*Lied* is pronounced *leet;* its plural, *Lieder,* is pronounced *leader.*)

Yearning—inspired by a lost love, nature, legend, or other times and places—haunted the imagination of romantic poets. Thus art songs are filled with the despair of unrequited love, the beauty of flowers, trees, and brooks, and the supernatural happenings of folk tales. There are also songs of joy, wit, and humor. But by and large, romantic song was a reaching out of the soul.

Song composers interpreted a poem, translating its mood, atmosphere, and imagery into music. They created a vocal melody that was musically satisfying and perfectly molded to the text. Important words were emphasized by stressed tones or melodic climaxes.

The voice shares the interpretive task with the piano. Emotions and images of the text get added dimension from the keyboard commentary. Arpeggios in the piano might suggest the splashing of oars or the motion of a mill wheel. Chords in a low register might depict darkness or a lover's torment. The mood is often set by a brief piano introduction and summed up at the end by a piano section called a *postlude.*

STROPHIC AND THROUGH-COMPOSED FORM

When a poem has several stanzas, the musical setting must accommodate their total emotional impact. Composers can use *strophic form,* repeating the same music for each stanza of the poem. This makes the song easy to remember. Strophic form is used in almost all folk songs. Or composers might use *through-composed form,* writing new music for each stanza. (*Through-composed* is a translation of the German term *durchkomponiert.*) Through-composed form allows music to reflect a poem's changing moods.

The art song is not restricted to strophic or through-composed form. There are many ways that music can be molded to the structure and feeling of a poem. A three-stanza poem is frequently set as follows: A (stanza 1) B (stanza 2) A (stanza 3). This might be called a *modified strophic form,* since two of the three stanzas are set to the same music.

THE SONG CYCLE

Romantic art songs are sometimes grouped in a set, or *song cycle.* A cycle may be unified by a story line that runs through the poems, or by musical ideas linking the songs. Among the great romantic song cycles are *Die Winterreise* (*The Winter Journey,* 1827), by Schubert, and *Dichterliebe* (*Poet's Love,* 1840), by Schumann.

In their art songs, romantic composers achieved a perfect union of music and poetry. They created an intensely personal world with a tremendous variety of moods. These miniatures contain some of the most haunting melodies and harmonies in all music.

FRANZ SCHUBERT [ROMANTIC 3]

Franz Schubert (1797–1828), the earliest master of the romantic art song, was unlike any great composer before him: he never held an official musical position and was neither a conductor nor a virtuoso; his income came

(Omikron/Photo Researchers)

Franz Schubert.

entirely from composition. "I have come into the world for no other purpose than to compose," he said. The full measure of his genius was recognized only years after his tragically early death.

Schubert was born in Vienna, the son of a schoolmaster. Even as a child, he had astounding musical gifts. "If I wanted to instruct him in anything new," recalled his amazed teacher, "he knew it already." At eleven, he became a choirboy in the court chapel and won a scholarship to the Imperial Seminary.

Schubert managed to compose an extraordinary number of masterpieces in his late teens while teaching at his father's school, a job he hated. His love of poetry led him to the art song; he composed his first great song, *Gretchen am Spinnrade (Gretchen at the Spinning Wheel)*, when he was seventeen, and the next year he composed 143 songs, including *The Erlking*.

When he was nineteen, Schubert's productivity rose to a peak; he composed 179 works, including two symphonies, an opera, and a mass. At twenty-one, he gave up teaching school to devote himself to music. He associated with a group of Viennese poets and artists who led a bohemian existence; often, he lived with friends because he had no money to rent a room of his own. Working incredibly fast, from seven in the morning until early afternoon, he turned out one piece after another. He spent his afternoons in cafes and many of his evenings at "Schubertiads," parties where only his music was played. Most of his works were composed for performances in the homes of Vienna's cultivated middle class; unlike Beethoven, he did not mingle with the aristocracy. The publication and performance of his songs brought him some recognition, but his two most important symphonies—the *Unfinished* and the *Great* C Major—were not performed in public during his lifetime.

Schubert died in 1828, age thirty-one. His reputation was mainly that of a fine song composer, until the *Unfinished* Symphony was performed nearly forty years later and the world could recognize his comprehensive greatness.

SCHUBERT'S MUSIC

Along with over 600 songs, Schubert composed symphonies, string quartets and other chamber music, sonatas and short pieces for piano, masses, and operas. The songs embrace an enormous variety of moods and types; their melodies range from simple, folklike tunes to complex lines that suggest impassioned speech, and their piano accompaniments are equally rich and evocative. Schubert's imaginative harmonies and dissonances provide some of the most poetic moments in music.

The spirit of song pervades his instrumental music, too, and his longer works often include variation movements based on his own songs; his famous *Trout* Quintet in A Major (1819) is an example. Many of the sym-

[*8-record/cassette set:*]
[*Side 7, band 4*]

178

phonies and chamber works have long, lyrical melodies, and a number of them—especially the *Unfinished* Symphony (1822) and the *Great* C Major Symphony (1825–1826)—are comparable in power and emotional intensity to Beethoven's. The *Unfinished* was written six years before Schubert's death; no one knows why it has only two (rather than four) movements. The *Great* C Major was discovered ten years after his death by Robert Schumann.

ERLKÖNIG (THE ERLKING; 1815)

Schubert's song *Erlkönig (The Erlking)* is one of the earliest and finest examples of musical romanticism. A friend of Schubert's tells how he saw the eighteen-year-old composer reading Goethe's narrative ballad of the supernatural. "He paced up and down several times with the book; suddenly he sat down, and in no time at all (just as quickly as he could write) there was the glorious ballad finished on the paper." Goethe's ballad, in dialogue almost throughout, tells of a father riding on horseback through a storm with his sick child in his arms. The delirious boy has visions of the legendary Erlking, the king of the elves who symbolizes death.

Side B, band 7

[8-record/cassette set:
   Side 7, band 5]

Schubert employs a through-composed setting to capture the mounting excitement of the poem. The piano part, with its rapid octaves and menacing bass motive, conveys the tension of the wild ride.

The piano's relentless triplet rhythm unifies the episodes of the song and suggests the horse's gallop.

By imaginatively varying the music, Schubert makes one singer sound like several characters in a miniature drama. The terrified boy sings in a high register in minor. Three times during the poem, he cries out, "My father, my father." Each time, the boy sings a musical outcry that is intensified through dissonant harmonies.

Mein Va - ter, mein Va - ter,

To convey mounting fear, Schubert pitches the boy's outcry higher and higher each time. The reassuring father sings in a low register that contrasts with the high-pitched outcries of his child. The Erlking, who tries to entice the boy, has coy melodies in major keys.

"Du lie - bes Kind, komm, geh mit mir! gar schö - ne Spie - le spiel' - ich mit dir;

The deeply moving climax of *The Erlking* comes when father and son arrive home and the galloping accompaniment gradually comes to a halt. In a bleak, heartbreaking recitative that allows every word to make its impact, the narrator tells us, "In his arms the child was dead!"

Piano
introduction, rapid
octaves, *f*, bass
motive, minor key.

Narrator

Wer reitet so spät durch Nacht und Wind?	Who rides so late through the night and the wind?
Es ist der Vater mit seinem Kind;	It is the father with his child;
Er hat den Knaben wohl in dem Arm,	he folds the boy close in his arms,
Er fasst ihn sicher, er hält ihn warm.	he clasps him securely, he holds him warmly.

Father

Low register.

"Mein Sohn, was birgst du so bang dein Gesicht?"	"My son, why do you hide your face so anxiously?"

Son

Higher register.

"Siehst, Vater, du den Erlkönig nicht?	"Father, don't you see the Erlking?
Den Erlenkönig mit Kron' und Schweif?"	The Erlking with his crown and his train?"

"Mein Sohn, es ist ein Nebelstreif."	"My son, it is a streak of mist."	Low register.

Erlking

"Du liebes Kind, komm, geh mit mir!	"Dear child, come, go with me!	Coaxing tune, *pp*, higher register, major.
Gar schöne Spiele spiel' ich mit dir,	I'll play the prettiest games with you.	
Manch bunte Blumen sind an dem Strand,	Many colored flowers grow along the shore;	
Meine Mutter hat manch gülden Gewand."	my mother has many golden garments."	

Son

"Mein Vater, mein Vater, und hörest du nicht,	"My father, my father, and don't you hear	Outcry, *f*, minor.
Was Erlenkönig mir leise verspricht?"	the Erlking whispering promises to me?"	

Father

"Sei ruhig, bleibe ruhig, mein Kind:	"Be quiet, stay quiet, my child;	Low register.
In dürren Blättern säuselt der Wind."	the wind is rustling in the dead leaves."	

Erlking

"Willst, feiner Knabe, du mit mir gehn?	"My handsome boy, will you come with me?	Playful tune, *pp*, major.
Meine Töchter sollen dich warten schön;	My daughters shall wait upon you;	
Meine Töchter führen den nächtlichen Reihn	my daughters lead off in the dance every night,	
Und wiegen und tanzen und singen dich ein."	and cradle and dance and sing you to sleep."	

Son

"Mein Vater, mein Vater, und siehst du nicht dort	"My father, my father, and don't you see there	Outcry, *f*, higher than before, minor.
Erlkönigs Töchter am düstern Ort?"	the Erlking's daughters in the shadows?"	

Father

"Mein Sohn, mein Sohn, ich seh' es genau:	"My son, my son, I see it clearly;	Lower register.
Es scheinen die alten Weiden so grau."	the old willows look so gray."	

Erlking

"Ich liebe dich, mich reizt deine schöne Gestalt;	"I love you, your beautiful figure delights me!
Und bist du nicht willig, so brauch' ich Gewalt."	And if you are not willing, then I shall use force!"

Son

Outcry, *f*, highest yet.

"Mein Vater, mein Vater, jetzt fasst er mich an!	"My father, my father, now he is taking hold of me!
Erlkönig hat mir ein Leids getan!"	The Erlking has hurt me!"

Narrator

Dem Vater grauset's, er reitet geschwind,	The father shudders, he rides swiftly on;
Er hält in Armen das ächzende Kind,	he holds in his arms the groaning child,
Erreicht den Hof mit Mühe und Not;	he reaches the courtyard weary and anxious:
In seinen Armen das Kind war tot.	in his arms the child was dead.

Piano stops.

Recitative.

[ROMANTIC 4] ROBERT SCHUMANN

Robert Schumann (1810–1856) in many ways embodied musical romanticism. His works are intensely autobiographical and usually have descriptive titles, texts, or programs. He expressed his essentially lyrical nature in startlingly original piano pieces and songs. And as a writer and critic, he discovered and made famous some of the leading composers of his day.

Schumann was born in Zwickau, Germany. He studied law at Leipzig University but actually devoted himself to literature and music. At twenty, he decided to become a piano virtuoso, but this goal became impossible when he developed serious problems with his right hand which were not helped by medical treatments or by a gadget he used to stretch and strengthen the fingers. "Don't worry about my finger," he wrote to his mother; "I can compose without it"—and in his twenties he did compose many piano works which remain a basic part of the repertory, although at the time they were often considered too unconventional and personal. During his twenties, too, he founded and edited the influential *New Journal of Music*, which contained his appreciative reviews of young "radical" composers like Chopin and Berlioz.

While studying piano, Schumann met his teacher's daughter and pupil,

(Omikron/Photo Researchers)

Clara and Robert Schumann. Clara Wieck Schumann was an ideal interpreter of her husband's piano works and introduced many of them to the public.

Clara Wieck, then a nine-year-old prodigy. The two were engaged when Clara was seventeen; but her father was bitterly opposed, and the couple had to fight against him in court before they could be married. Their marriage was a happy one that produced eight children; Clara—herself a composer—was also the ideal interpreter of Robert's works and introduced many of them to the public.

Schumann held some musical positions but was temperamentally unsuited for them, and during his later years, his mental and physical health deteriorated. In 1854 he tried to drown himself and was committed to an asylum, where he died two years later.

SCHUMANN'S MUSIC

During his first ten years as a composer, Schumann published only piano pieces, and his musical style seemed to grow out of piano improvisation. His short pieces often express a single mood through a sensitive melody; dance rhythms, dotted rhythms, and syncopations are also prominent.

In 1840, the year of his marriage, he composed many art songs which also reveal his gift for melody. Both the songs and the short piano pieces are usually organized in sets or cycles, whose titles—*Carnaval (Carnival)*, *Kinderscenen (Scenes of Childhood)*, *Nachtstücke (Night Pieces)*, *Dichterliebe*

(*Poet's Love*), *Fantasiestücke (Fantasy Pieces)*—give insight into his imagination. Schumann thought of music in emotional, literary, and autobiographical terms; his work is full of extramusical references.

After 1840, possibly as a result of Clara's influence, he turned to symphonies and chamber music. The symphonies are romantic in their emphasis on lyrical second themes, use of thematic transformation, and connections between movements.

AUFSCHWUNG (SOARING),
FROM FANTASIESTÜCKE (FANTASY PIECES), OP. 12 (1837)

[*8-record/cassette set:*
Side 8, band 1]

Aufschwung (Soaring) is one of the *Fantasiestücke (Fantasy Pieces)*, a set of eight short piano pieces with titles like *Des Abends (Evening)*, *Grillen (Whims)*, *In der Nacht (In the Night)*, and *Traümes Wirren (Dream Visions)*. Like many other romantics, Schumann was especially drawn to the world of fantasy and linked his works with definite images or poetic ideas.

Soaring is passionate and impulsive, with a very fast tempo, driving rhythms, and rapid changes of musical ideas. It may be outlined A B A C A B A. The restless main theme, A, is loud, with powerful accents and dotted rhythms. Theme B is lyrical and continuously flowing. Both a melody and a rapid accompanying figure are played by the pianist's right hand. The extended middle section, C, brings a more relaxed mood and flexible tempo. Near the end of section C, a crescendo creates tension and prepares for the return of the impulsive main theme. *Soaring* vividly expresses the outgoing side of Schumann's musical personality.

FRÉDÉRIC CHOPIN

Frédéric Chopin (1810–1849) was the only great composer who wrote almost exclusively for the piano. The son of a Polish mother and a French father, he was brought up in Warsaw and graduated from the Warsaw Conservatory. At twenty-one, he arrived in Paris, then the center of romanticism and the artistic capital of Europe.

In Paris, he met such writers as Victor Hugo, Balzac, and Heine and became close friends with the painter Delacroix and with Liszt and Berlioz. His playing soon gained him access to aristocratic salons; he was a shy, reserved man who preferred salons to concert halls, and it was for such intimate gatherings that he conceived his short pieces like the nocturnes, waltzes, and preludes. He earned a good living teaching piano to the daughters of the rich and lived in luxury.

Chopin had a well-known love affair with Aurore Dudevant, a novelist whose pen name was George Sand; a frail man, he thrived on her care and composed many of his greatest works during the years they lived together. After they separated, his health declined rapidly and he composed very little. He died of tuberculosis at thirty-nine.

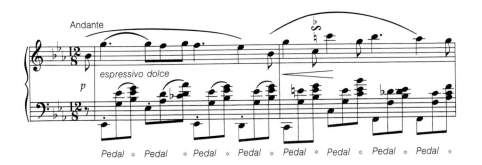

(Giraudon/Art Resource)

Frédéric Chopin, in a portrait by Eugène Delacroix.

CHOPIN'S MUSIC

By the age of eighteen, Chopin had evolved an utterly personal and original style. Most of his pieces are exquisite miniatures; they evoke an infinite variety of moods and are always elegant, graceful, and melodic. Unlike Schumann's works, they do not have literary programs or titles. The mazurkas and polonaises—stylized dances—capture a Polish spirit without actually using folk tunes.

No other composer has made the piano sound as beautiful as Chopin, who creates the illusion that the piano sings. He uses graceful and delicate ornamentation and exploits the pedals sensitively. His colorful treatment of harmony was highly original and influenced later composers.

NOCTURNE IN E FLAT MAJOR, OP. 9, NO. 2 (1830–1831)

Chopin composed his popular Nocturne in E Flat Major, Op. 9, No. 2, when he was about twenty. A **nocturne,** or *night piece,* is a slow, lyrical, and intimate composition for piano. Like much of Chopin's music, the Nocturne in E Flat Major is tinged with melancholy. It opens with a legato melody containing graceful upward leaps which become increasingly wide as the line unfolds.

Side B, band 8

[*8-record/cassette set:* *Side 8, band 4*]

185

Pedal ⁕ Pedal ⁕ Pedal ⁕ Pedal ⁕ Pedal ⁕ Pedal ⁕ Pedal ⁕

This melody is heard again three times during the piece. With each repetition, it is varied by ever more elaborate decorative tones and trills.

A sonorous foundation for the melody is provided by the widely spaced notes in the accompaniment that are connected by the damper ("loud") pedal.

The music is reflective in mood until near the end, when it suddenly becomes passionate. The melody rises to a high register and is played forcefully in octaves. Then, after a brilliant trill-like passage, the excitement subsides, and the nocturne ends calmly.

ÉTUDE IN C MINOR, OP. 10, NO. 12 (REVOLUTIONARY; 1831?)

[8-record/cassette set: Side 8, band 5]

The Russian takeover of Warsaw in 1831 may have inspired Chopin to compose the blazing and furious *Revolutionary* Étude in C Minor, Op. 10, No. 12. An *étude* is a study piece designed to help a performer master specific technical difficulties. The *Revolutionary* Étude, for example, develops speed and endurance in a pianist's left hand, which must play rapid passages throughout. Chopin's études reach beyond mere exercises in technique to become masterpieces of music, exciting to hear as well as to master.

The *Revolutionary* Étude begins with a dramatic outburst. High, disso-

Nationalism

nant chords and downward-rushing passages lead to the main melody, marked *appassionato (impassioned)*, which is played in octaves by the right hand. Tension mounts because of the melody's dotted rhythms and its tempestuous accompaniment. Toward the end of the piece, after a climax, the tension momentarily subsides. Then a torrential passage sweeps down the keyboard to come to rest in powerful closing chords.

POLONAISE IN A FLAT MAJOR, OP. 53 (1842)

The *polonaise,* a piece in triple meter, originated as a stately processional dance for the Polish nobility. Chopin's heroic polonaises evoke the ancient splendor of the Polish people.

   The Polonaise in A Flat Major is majestic and powerful, with moments of lyrical contrast. It may be outlined as follows: introduction–A B A'–coda. Its main theme makes a grand entrance. The majesty of this theme is enhanced by intervals of thirds in the right hand and by the resonant, wide-ranging accompaniment. After the main theme is repeated twice with an even richer texture, Chopin offers the contrasting middle section (B). This is a marchlike melody accompanied by relentlessly repeated rapid octaves in the left hand. This section tests a pianist's strength and endurance. Powerful crescendos bring mounting excitement. Then Chopin gradually relaxes the mood to prepare for the final return of the heroic main theme (A').

FELIX MENDELSSOHN [ROMANTIC 6]

Felix Mendelssohn (1809–1847), a romantic whose music was rooted in classicism, was born in Hamburg, Germany, to a wealthy and distinguished Jewish family. (He was, however, raised as a Protestant.) By the age of nine, he was a brilliant pianist; by thirteen, he had written symphonies, concertos, sonatas, and vocal works of astounding quality. As a teenager, he performed his works at home with a private orchestra for the intellectual and artistic elite of Berlin, where the Mendelssohns had settled.

   In 1829, at age twenty, he conducted Bach's *St. Matthew Passion* in its first performance since the composer's death. This historic concert rekindled interest in Bach and earned Mendelssohn an international reputation. He performed as a pianist, organist, and conductor in Germany and in England, where his music was especially popular. He often visited and played for Queen Victoria, and the high point of his career was the triumphant premiere of his oratorio *Elijah* in Birmingham in 1846. When only

(Metropolitan Museum of Art,
Crosby Brown Collection
of Musical Instruments, 1901)

Felix Mendelssohn.

twenty-six, he became conductor of the Leipzig Gewandhaus Orchestra; and he founded the Leipzig Conservatory at age thirty-three.

Mendelssohn's personal life was more conventional than that of many romantics; he was happily married and had four children. But constant travel and work sapped his strength, and he died, after a stroke, at the age of thirty-eight.

MENDELSSOHN'S MUSIC

Mendelssohn's music radiates the elegance and balance of his personality; it evokes many moods but avoids emotional extremes and typically conveys an elfin quality through rapid movement, lightness, and transparent orchestral texture. He wrote an enormous amount of music in all the forms of his day except opera; today, only a few of his works are in the concert repertory, but these are very popular. They include the Violin Concerto—which we'll study—the *Midsummer Night's Dream* and *Hebrides* overtures; the *Italian* (1833) and *Scotch* (1842) symphonies; the oratorio *Elijah*; and a number of chamber works.

CONCERTO FOR VIOLIN AND ORCHESTRA IN E MINOR, OP. 64

The Violin Concerto in E Minor, Op. 64, was inspired by Mendelssohn's friendship with the concertmaster of his orchestra, the famous violinist Ferdinand David. "I should like to make a violin concerto for you next winter," Mendelssohn wrote. "One in E minor runs in my head and its beginning gives me no rest." With David as soloist, Mendelssohn's Violin Concerto met great success at its premiere in 1845, and its unique fusion of lyricism and virtuosity has made it one of the best-loved concertos.

The concerto's three movements are played without pause, in a characteristic linking technique used by romantic composers. Mendelssohn's love of balance is reflected in the cooperation and interplay between soloist and orchestra. Themes pass from one to another, producing a beautiful contrast of tone color and expression. At one moment, the violinist plays a melody while the orchestra discreetly accompanies; at another, the woodwinds present thematic fragments while the soloist has dazzling running passages. We'll now consider the first movement.

First Movement:

Side C, band 1

[*8-record/cassette set:*
Side 8, band 6]

Allegro molto appassionato (very impassioned allegro)

Though Mendelssohn is usually considered a conservative composer, a "classical romantic," his opening movement departs from classical con-

188

certo form. Traditionally, the opening movement of a concerto began with an extended section for orchestra. But Mendelssohn's first movement begins with the soloist, who presents the main theme. This ardent, expansive melody is heard high above a murmuring string accompaniment. The orchestra then expands the violin's theme and introduces a new, flowing melody that begins the bridge section of this sonata-form movement. Toward the end of the bridge the excitement is gradually relaxed to prepare for the second theme, a tranquil woodwind melody which the soloist accompanies with a single sustained tone. This unusual combination of instruments produces a delicate, intimate sound. Following this, the violin reclaims the spotlight and sings the tranquil theme while the woodwinds support.

The cadenza has a new function in this movement. In classical concertos, the cadenza was improvised by the soloist and played near the end of the movement. Here, the composer has written it out and placed it at the end of the development section as a transition to the recapitulation. Mendelssohn wanted the cadenza to be an integral part of the movement, not merely something tacked on to display the soloist's virtuosity. Listen for the magical moment when the violinist's rapid arpeggios are joined by the orchestra softly playing the first theme of the recapitulation.

Listening Outline   To be read while music is heard

CONCERTO FOR VIOLIN AND ORCHESTRA IN E MINOR, OP. 64 (1844), BY FELIX MENDELSSOHN

First Movement: Allegro molto appassionato

Sonata form, duple meter ($\frac{2}{2}$), E minor

Solo violin, 2 flutes, 2 oboes, 2 clarinets, 2 bassoons, 2 French horns, 2 trumpets, timpani, 1st violins, 2d violins, violas, cellos, double basses

(About 13 minutes)

EXPOSITION
First theme   1. *a.* Strings, *p*, introduce solo violin. Main melody in minor, high register, legato.

        b. Running notes in solo violin. Crescendo, climbing phrases.

        c. Orchestra, *ff,* main melody. Increased rhythmic motion leads to cadence.

Bridge   2. *a.* Violins, flowing bridge theme. Solo violin repeats bridge theme an octave higher.

        b. Solo violin phrases sweep downward and upward through wide range. Flute joins. Crescendo. Running passage rises and falls. Decrescendo, mood calms.

Second theme 3. *a.* Clarinets and flutes, *pp,* calm melody in major. Solo violin accompanies with sustained tone.

        b. Solo violin, *pp,* calm theme expanded. Woodwinds, then strings accompany.

        4. *a.* Main melody in solo violin, major. Brilliant running passages, pizzicato accompaniment. Crescendo.

        b. Climactic orchestral trills alternate with solo violin, opening of main melody. Decrescendo.

DEVELOPMENT

        1. *a.* Solo violin, *p,* flowing bridge theme. Violins, *f.*

        b. Running passage in solo violin and fragments of main melody in orchestra.

        2. Solo violin, *p,* main melody varied. Decrescendo. Violin melody slowly descends. Orchestral crescendo to *ff.*

CADENZA   3. Unaccompanied solo violin, broken chords. Ascents to high tones, trills, fragment of main melody. Rapid broken chords lead into

RECAPITULATION

First theme 1. Main melody in orchestra, *p.* Broken chords continue in solo violin. Crescendo.

Bridge   2. *a.* Orchestra, *ff,* bridge theme.

        b. Solo violin, *mf,* bridge theme carried downward. Decrescendo.

Second theme 3. *a.* Woodwinds, *pp,* calm melody in major. Solo violin accompanies with sustained tone.

        b. Solo violin, *pp,* calm theme expanded. Woodwinds, then strings accompany.

4. *a.* Brilliant running passages in solo violin. Pizzicato accompaniment. Crescendo.
   b. Climactic orchestral trills alternate with solo violin, opening of main melody. Decrescendo.

CODA   5. Solo violin, bridge theme. Tempo becomes faster. Crescendo. Brilliant running passages. Full orchestra, *ff.* Sustained tone in bassoon connects with second movement.

PROGRAM MUSIC [ROMANTIC 7]

Romantic composers were particularly attracted to *program music*—instrumental music associated with a story, poem, idea, or scene. Programmatic orchestral works such as Berlioz's *Fantastic Symphony*, Tchaikovsky's *Romeo and Juliet*, and Smetana's *Moldau* depict emotions, characters, and events, or the sounds and motions of nature; these nonmusical ideas are usually specified by the title or by the composer's explanatory comments (the *program*).

Program compositions draw on music's capacity to suggest and evoke. Music can, of course, imitate certain sounds (bird songs, bells, thunder, wind), and composers sometimes exploit the correspondence between musical rhythm and objects in motion (continuous rapid notes, for example, can evoke waves or a stream). Most important is the ability of music to create mood, emotion, and atmosphere: an agitated theme may represent conflict; a lyrical melody may symbolize love. However, music alone makes no definite reference to ideas, emotions, and objects; it cannot identify anything. What lets us fully grasp a composer's source or inspiration is the title or a verbal explanation.

The aim of most program music is expression more than mere description; Beethoven, for example, referred to his Sixth Symphony (the *Pastoral*) as "an expression of feeling rather than painting." Even the most "realistic" episodes in program music can also serve a purely musical function; and one can generally appreciate a descriptive piece as pure music, without knowing its title or program. (We can enjoy the lyrical theme of Tchaikovsky's *Romeo and Juliet* without associating it with young love.) The forms used for program music are similar to those used for nonprogram music, or *absolute music*; thus a programmatic work can be heard simply as a rondo, fugue, sonata form, or theme and variations. But our pleasure may be greater when we can relate music to literary or pictorial ideas, and romantic composers were well aware of this. Occasionally, they even added programs or titles to finished works; and both musicians and audiences in the romantic era liked to read stories into all music, whether intended by the composer or not.

Most romantic program music was written for piano or orchestra. The main forms of orchestral program music are the program symphony, the concert overture, the symphonic poem (tone poem), and incidental music.

A *program symphony* is a composition in several movements—as its name implies, a symphony with a program. Each movement usually has a descriptive title. For example, Berlioz's *Fantastic Symphony* has five movements: (1) *Reveries, Passions,* (2) *A Ball,* (3) *Scene in the Country,* (4) *March to the Scaffold,* and (5) *Dream of a Witches' Sabbath.* (This work is discussed in Section 8.)

A *concert overture* has one movement, usually in sonata form. The romantic concert overture was modeled after the opera overture, a one-movement composition that establishes the mood of an opera. But the concert overture is *not* intended to usher in a stage work; it is an independent composition. Well-known concert overtures include Mendelssohn's *Hebrides* Overture and Tchaikovsky's *Overture 1812* and *Romeo and Juliet* Overture, which is studied in Section 10.

A *symphonic poem,* or *tone poem,* is also a one-movement composition. Symphonic poems take many traditional forms—sonata form, rondo, or theme and variations—as well as irregular forms. This flexibility of form separates the symphonic poem from the concert overture, which usually is in sonata form. Franz Liszt developed the symphonic poem in the late 1840s and 1850s, and it became the most important type of program music after 1860. Well-known tone poems include *Les Préludes* (1854), by Liszt; *Don Juan* (1888) and *Till Eulenspiegel* (1895), by Richard Strauss (1864–1949); and *The Sorcerer's Apprentice* (1897), by Paul Dukas. During the late nineteenth century, symphonic poems became an important means of expression for nationalism in music. In Section 9, we'll consider a nationalistic tone poem, Smetana's *Moldau,* which depicts the longest river of Bohemia (in Czechoslovakia) as it winds through the countryside.

Incidental music is music that is intended to be performed before and during a play. It is "incidental" to the staged drama, but it sets the mood for certain scenes. Interludes, background music, marches, and dances are all incidental music (as are today's movie scores). Mendelssohn's incidental music for *A Midsummer Night's Dream* includes his famous *Wedding March.*

[*8-record/cassette set:* Side 9, band 1]

[ROMANTIC 8] HECTOR BERLIOZ

Hector Berlioz (1803–1869), one of the first French romantic composers and a daring creator of new orchestral sounds, was born in a small town near Grenoble. His father, a physician, sent him to Paris to study medicine, but he was "filled with horror" by the dissecting room and shocked his parents by abandoning medicine to pursue a career in music. He studied at the Paris Conservatory, haunted the opera house, and composed.

When he was twenty-three, Berlioz was overwhelmed with the works of Shakespeare and also fell madly in love with a Shakespearean actress, Harriet Smithson, to whom he wrote such wild, impassioned letters that she considered him a lunatic and refused to see him. To depict his "endless and unquenchable passion," Berlioz wrote the *Symphonie fantastique* (*Fantastic Symphony*) in 1830, which startled Parisians by its sensationally autobiographical program, its amazingly novel orchestration, and its vivid depiction of the weird and diabolical.

In 1830, too, Berlioz won the Prix de Rome (the Rome Prize), subsidizing two years' study in Rome; when he returned to Paris, he finally met and married Harriet Smithson—after she had attended a performance of the *Fantastic Symphony* and realized that it depicted her. (They separated, however, after only a few years.)

Berlioz's unconventional music irritated the opera and concert establishment. To get a hearing for his works, he had to arrange concerts at his own expense—an enormous undertaking which drained him financially, physically, and emotionally. Although he had a following of about 1,200 who faithfully bought tickets to his concerts, this was not enough support for a composer of difficult, monumental works requiring hundreds of performers. Berlioz turned to musical journalism, becoming a brilliant and witty music critic who tried to convince the Parisians that music was not merely entertainment but a dramatic emotional expression.

Outside France, Berlioz's stock was higher. After 1840, he was in demand throughout Europe, conducting his own and others' music. As one of the first great conductors, he influenced a whole generation of musicians. But his last years were bitter; he was passed over for important positions and honors and composed very little during the six years before his death at sixty-five.

BERLIOZ'S MUSIC

"The prevailing qualities of my music," Berlioz wrote, "are passionate expressiveness, inner fire, rhythmic drive, and unexpectedness." Above all, Berlioz's music sounds unique. It includes abrupt contrasts, fluctuating dynamics, and many changes in tempo.

As an orchestrator, Berlioz was extraordinarily imaginative and innovative. At a time when the average orchestra had about sixty players, he often assembled hundreds of musicians to achieve new power, tone colors, and timbres. His melodies are often long, irregular, and asymmetrical, taking unexpected turns. Most of his works are for orchestra, or orchestra with chorus and vocal soloists; all are dramatic and programmatic. He invented new forms: his "dramatic symphony" *Romeo and Juliet* (1839) is for orchestra, chorus, and vocal soloists; and his "dramatic legend" *The Damnation of Faust* combines opera and oratorio. He also wrote three operas and a grandiose, monumental Requiem.

Berlioz knew he was a pioneer; he wrote of the Requiem, "I have seen one man listening in terror, shaken to the depths of his soul, while his next neighbor could not catch an idea, though trying with all his might to do so."

SYMPHONIE FANTASTIQUE (FANTASTIC SYMPHONY; 1830)

The astonishing *Symphonie fantastique (Fantastic Symphony)*, a five-movement program symphony (we'll study its fourth and fifth movements), is a romantic manifesto. Both the music and Berlioz's program reflect the twenty-six-year-old composer's unrequited passion for the actress Harriet Smithson:

A young musician of extraordinary sensibility and abundant imagination, in the depths of despair because of hopeless love, has poisoned himself with opium. The drug is too feeble to kill him but plunges him into a heavy sleep accompanied by weird visions. His sensations, emotions, and memories, as they pass through his affected mind, are transformed into musical images and ideas. The beloved one herself becomes to him a melody, a recurrent theme *(idée fixe)* which haunts him continually.

A single melody, which Berlioz called the *idée fixe*, or *fixed idea*, is used to represent the beloved. When introduced in the first movement, it sounds, in Berlioz's description, "passionate but at the same time noble and shy."

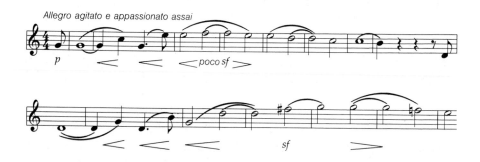

It appears in all five movements and unifies the contrasting episodes of the symphony. This recurrence of the same theme in every movement of a symphony was a striking novelty in Berlioz's day. The theme changes in character during the work, sounding, in turn, exultant, waltzlike, and vulgar.

Another innovation in the symphony is its requirement of a very large and colorful orchestra: piccolo, 2 flutes, 2 oboes, English horn, 2 clarinets, 4 bassoons, 4 French horns, 2 cornets, 2 trumpets, 3 trombones, 2 tubas, 4 timpani, bass drum, snare drum, cymbals, bells, 2 harps, and strings. Beethoven had not used the English horn, tuba, bells, cornet, or harp in his symphonies. Berlioz saves the heaviest orchestration for the last two movements, where he depicts the fantastic and diabolical. Though the macabre and supernatural had long been dealt with in opera (in Mozart's *Don Giovanni*, for example), this is its first expression in an important symphony.

Fourth Movement: March to the Scaffold
Allegretto non troppo

> He dreams that he has murdered his beloved, that he has been condemned to death and is being led to execution. A march that is alternately somber and wild, brilliant and solemn, accompanies the procession. . . . The tumultuous outbursts are followed without transition by the muffled sound of heavy steps. At the end, the fixed idea returns for a moment, like a last thought of love interrupted by the death blow.

Side B, band 9

[*8-record/cassette set:*]
[*Side 10, band 1*]

idee fix

"The March to the Scaffold is fifty times more frightening than I expected," Berlioz gleefully observed after the first rehearsals of the *Fantastic Symphony*. It is not until this fiendish fourth movement that all the brass and percussion instruments enter the action. Berlioz creates a menacing atmosphere with the opening orchestral sound, a unique combination of muted French horns, timpani tuned a third apart, and basses playing pizzicato chords. The first theme, stated by the cellos and basses, moves steadily downward for two octaves.

This idea is repeated several times with countermelodies in the bassoons. Then we hear a syncopated march tune blared by the brasses and woodwinds.

At the end of the march a solo clarinet begins to play the *idée fixe* but is savagely interrupted by a very loud chord representing the fall of the guillotine's blade.

Fifth Movement: Dream of a Witches' Sabbath
Larghetto; Allegro

[*Instructor's records:*]
[*Side 2, band 1*]

He sees himself at a witches' sabbath in the midst of a hideous crowd of ghouls, sorcerers, and monsters of every description, united for his funeral. Strange noises, groans, shrieks of laughter, distant cries, which other cries seem to answer. The melody of the loved one is heard, but it has lost its character of nobleness and timidity; it is no more than a dance tune, ignoble, trivial, and grotesque. It is she who comes to the sabbath! . . . A howl of joy greets her arrival. . . . She participates in the diabolical orgy. . . . The funeral knell, burlesque of the *Dies irae*. Witches' dance. The dance and the *Dies irae* combined.

The *Dream of a Witches' Sabbath* is the most "fantastic" movement of the symphony; it depicts a series of grotesque events. Its slow, hushed introduction (larghetto) immediately draws the listener into the realm of the macabre and supernatural, evoking "strange noises, groans, shrieks of laughter" and "distant cries." Eerie tremolos in high muted strings and menacing low tones of cellos and basses begin a succession of fragmentary ideas in starkly contrasting tone colors, registers, and dynamics. In the exploratory spirit of his romantic age, Berlioz dared to create sounds that are weird rather than conventionally pleasing.

In the allegro section, the beloved is revealed to be a witch. Her theme, the once "noble and timid" *idée fixe*, is transformed into a dance tune that is "trivial and grotesque." Played shrilly by a high-pitched clarinet, the tune moves in quick notes decorated by trills.

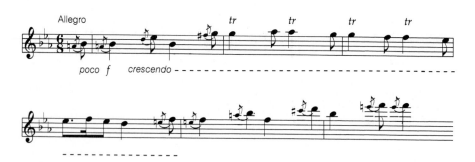

A "funeral knell" of sonorous bells lends an awesome atmosphere to the next part of the movement. Tubas and bassoons intone a solemn low melody in long, even notes.

This melody is the medieval chant *Dies irae (Day of wrath)*, traditionally sung in the mass for the dead. Berlioz quotes it here as a symbol of eternal damnation. Soon the chant melody is shifted up to a high register and played by woodwinds and pizzicato strings in a quick dancelike rhythm.

Thus Berlioz dared to parody a sacred chant by transforming it into a trivial tune, as he had just done moments earlier with the *idée fixe*.

Berlioz conveys the frenzy of a witches' dance in a fuguelike section. The fugue subject (the witches' dance) is introduced by the lower strings and then imitated by other instruments.

A crescendo builds to a powerful climax in which the rapid witches' dance, played in the strings, is set against the slower-moving *Dies irae*, proclaimed by the brasses and woodwinds. This musical nightmare ends in an orgy of orchestral power.

[9] NATIONALISM IN NINETEENTH-CENTURY MUSIC

During the nineteenth century, nationalism—awakened partly by resistance to Napoleon's invading armies—was a dominant force in Europe. Patriotic feelings and common bonds of language, culture, and history were also strengthened by romanticism, which glorified love for one's national heritage. As a revolutionary political movement, nationalism led to the unification of some countries (like Germany and Italy) that had been divided into tiny states and spurred revolts in countries under foreign rule (like Poland and Bohemia). As a potent cultural movement, it led to the revival of national languages (such as Czech) and to a new interest in the peasantry and folk art—songs, dances, poetry, legends.

Nationalism also influenced romantic music, as composers deliberately gave their works a distinctive national identity. They used folk songs and dances, created original melodies with a folk flavor, and wrote operas and program music inspired by their countries' history, legends, and landscapes. Their works bear titles like *Russian Easter* Overture (by Rimsky-Korsakov), *Finlandia* (by Sibelius), and *Slavonic Dances* (by Dvořák). But, beyond their use of folk songs and patriotic elements, their music often sounds Scandinavian, Slavic, or Russian because its rhythm, tone color, and melody spring from national tradition.

The strongest impact of nationalism was felt in countries whose own musical heritage had been dominated by the music of Italy, France, Germany, or Austria. Early in the nineteenth century, Chopin transformed the dances of his native Poland into great art. After about 1860, groups or "schools" of composers consciously declared their musical independence and established national styles. The Scandinavian countries produced Edvard Grieg (Norwegian, 1843–1907) and Jean Sibelius (Finnish, 1865–1957). Bohemia (which is now part of Czechoslovakia) produced Bedřich Smetana (1824–1887; we'll study his symphonic poem *The Moldau*) and Antonin Dvořák (1841–1904). Dvořák's Symphony No. 9 (*From the New World*; 1893)—his most famous work, written while he was living in the United States—glorifies both the Czech and the American folk spirit. An important national school is the Russian, which created highly distinctive music. Mikhail Glinka's opera *A Life for the Tsar* (1836) laid the groundwork for a national style, and in the 1860s five young men—now known as the *Russian five*—formed a true national school. They were Mily Balakirev (1837–1910), César Cui (1835–1918), Alexander Borodin (1833–1887), Nikolai

[Instructor's records: Side 3, band 1]

Rimsky-Korsakov (1844–1908), and Modest Mussorgsky (1839–1881). Remarkably, all but Balakirev began as amateurs, and most of them held nonmusical jobs. Mussorgsky was the most original and probably the greatest of the Russian five, and his opera *Boris Godunov* is a masterpiece of musical nationalism.

[*Instructor's records:*
Side 2, band 2]

We'll turn now to a famous nationalistic work, *The Moldau*.

THE MOLDAU (1847), BY BEDŘICH SMETANA

Bedřich Smetana (1824–1884) was the founder of Czech national music. His works are steeped in the folk music and legends of his native Bohemia (now part of Czechoslovakia). But he grew up when Bohemia was under Austrian domination, and in this repressive atmosphere his musical nationalism could make little headway; he emigrated to Sweden in 1856.

[*8-record/cassette set:*
Side 9, band 2]

In 1862, when Austria had made some liberal concessions, Smetana returned to Prague. He was active as a composer, pianist, conductor, and teacher and wrote *The Bartered Bride*, his most famous opera. At age fifty, he became completely deaf, but some of his finest works followed, including *Má Vlast* (*My Country*, 1874–1879), a cycle of six symphonic poems. His last years were blighted by syphilis, and he died at sixty in an asylum.

"Today I took an excursion to the St. John Rapids where I sailed in a boat through huge waves. . . . The view of the landscape was both beautiful and grand." Smetana's trip inspired his symphonic poem *The Moldau*, which depicts Bohemia's main river as it flows through the countryside. This orchestral work, part of the cycle *Má Vlast* (*My Country*), is both a romantic representation of nature and a display of Czech nationalism. It was written in three weeks shortly after Smetana became deaf. *The Moldau*'s fresh, optimistic mood gives no hint of the composer's anguish and despair. Smetana wrote the following program to preface his score:

> The composition depicts the course of the river, beginning from its two small sources, one cold the other warm, the joining of both streams into one, then the flow of the Moldau through forests and across meadows, through the countryside where merry feasts are celebrated; water nymphs dance in the moonlight; on nearby rocks can be seen the outline of ruined castles, proudly soaring into the sky. The Moldau swirls through the St. John Rapids and flows in a broad stream toward Prague. It passes Vyšehrad [where an ancient royal castle once stood] and finally the river disappears in the distance as it flows majestically into the Elbe.

The Moldau falls into contrasting musical sections that represent different scenes and episodes described in the program. Hunting at the river bank is suggested by horn fanfares, a peasant wedding by a rustic polka—the Bohemian dance; and a moonlit night is represented by shimmering woodwinds and a serene melody in high muted strings. An expansive folklike

199

theme that recurs several times symbolizes the river. Smetana unifies the symphonic poem by running notes evoking the movement of water, sometimes rippling, sometimes turbulent.

Listening Outline   To be read while music is heard

THE MOLDAU (1874), BY BEDŘICH SMETANA

Allegro comodo non agitato (unhurried allegro, not agitated), sextuple meter ($\frac{6}{8}$), E minor

Piccolo, 2 flutes, 2 oboes, 2 clarinets, 2 bassoons, 4 French horns, 2 trumpets, 3 trombones, tuba, timpani, bass drum, triangle, cymbals, harp, 1st violins, 2d violins, violas, cellos, double basses

(About 11½ minutes)

Two springs   1. *a.* Flutes, *p*, running notes. Harp, pizzicato violins.

	Clarinets, *p*, join, running notes.
	b. Lower strings, *p*, running notes lead to

The river   2. Violins, songlike river theme, minor key. Running-note accompaniment in strings.

River theme extended.

Forest hunt   3. *a.* French horns and trumpets, *f*, hunting calls. Strings, running notes. Crescendo to *ff*.
      b. Decrescendo to *ppp*.

Peasant
wedding   4. *a.* Strings, *p*, polka.

Crescendo to *f*, triangle strokes.
      b. Decrescendo to *ppp*, melody descends.

Moonlight:
dance of
water nymphs
	5. *a.* Woodwinds, *pp*, sustained tones. Flutes, *p*, running notes lead to
	   b. High muted violins, *pp*, serene legato melody. Harp, *p*.
	   c. Brasses, *pp*. Staccato chords join accompaniment to violin melody.
	   d. Crescendo. Woodwinds, running notes lead to

The river The rapids	6. Violins, river theme. Running-note accompaniment in strings. 7. *a.* Full orchestra, *ff*. Brasses, timpani roll, piccolo, cymbal crashes. *b.* Strings, *pp*. Quick crescendo.
The river at its widest point	8. Full orchestra, *ff*, river theme in major key. Faster tempo.
Vyšehrad, the ancient castle	9. *a.* Brasses and woodwinds, *ff*, hymnlike melody. Cymbal crashes. *b.* Decrescendo. Violins, *ppp*. Full orchestra, *ff*, closing chords.

PETER ILYICH TCHAIKOVSKY

Peter Ilyich Tchaikovsky (1840–1893), the most famous Russian composer, started his career as a government clerk and began to study music theory at the relatively late age of twenty-one. His progress in music was rapid, however. After graduating from the St. Petersburg Conservatory, he became a professor of harmony at the Moscow Conservatory and composed furiously: a symphony, an opera, a tone poem, and—by the age of thirty—his first great orchestral work, *Romeo and Juliet*.

The year 1877 was dramatic for Tchaikovsky. He married, disastrously and apparently only to conceal his homosexuality, attempted suicide two weeks after the wedding, and had a nervous collapse. (He and his wife separated and never saw each other again.) But in 1877 he also acquired a wealthy benefactress, Nadezhda von Meck, with whom he had a curious but intimate friendship—they corresponded but did not meet. Madame von Meck gave him an annuity that allowed him to leave the conservatory and devote himself to composition; fourteen years later, he was deeply hurt when she cut off the annuity and stopped writing to him.

During these years, Tchaikovsky achieved success conducting his own works throughout Europe (and, in 1891, in the United States), but he remained a spiritually troubled man. In 1893, nine days after conducting the premiere of his Symphony No. 6 (*Pathétique*), which ends unconventionally with a slow, despairing finale, he died at the age of fifty-three.

(Granger Collection)

*Peter Ilyich
Tchaikovsky.*

TCHAIKOVSKY'S MUSIC

Tchaikovsky thought of himself as *"Russian* in the fullest sense of the word," but his style was influenced by French, Italian, and German music as well as Russian folk song. His works are much more in the western tradition than those of his contemporaries, the "Russian five." He fused national and international elements to produce intensely subjective and passionate music.

Among his most popular orchestral compositions are Symphonies No. 4 (1877), No. 5 (1888), and No. 6 (*Pathétique*, 1893); the Piano Concerto No. 1 in B Flat Minor (1875); the Violin Concerto (1878); and the overture-fantasy *Romeo and Juliet*, which we'll study. He wrote some of the best scores for ballet—*Swan Lake* (1876), *The Sleeping Beauty* (1889), and *The Nutcracker* (1892)—and the spirit of ballet permeates much of his music. He also wrote eight operas and the orchestral showpieces *Marche slave* and *Overture 1812*.

All of Tchaikovsky's music has beautiful melodies that stretch and leap widely. He treats the orchestra colorfully and uses sharp contrasts of themes, tempos, and dynamics to create emotion.

ROMEO AND JULIET, OVERTURE-FANTASY

[8-record/cassette set:
Side 10, band 2]

Romantic composers felt an artistic kinship to Shakespeare because of his passionate poetry, dramatic contrast, and profound knowledge of the human heart. Some of Shakespeare's plays inspired many of the finest nineteenth-century compositions. Among these were *Macbeth* and *Othello*, set as operas by Verdi, and *A Midsummer Night's Dream*, depicted in incidental music by Mendelssohn. *Romeo and Juliet* inspired both a "dramatic symphony" by Berlioz and a concert overture by Tchaikovsky.

Tchaikovsky composed *Romeo and Juliet* at twenty-nine, near the beginning of his musical career. Now one of the best-loved orchestral works, *Romeo and Juliet* was a dismal failure at its premiere in 1870. "After the concert we dined. . . . No one said a single word to me about the overture the whole evening. And yet I yearned so for appreciation and kindness." Tchaikovsky decided to revise the overture. He composed a new theme to represent Friar Laurence, adopting the suggestion of his friend Balakirev. Despite this, the work remained unappreciated. Only about twenty years later, after further revisions, did *Romeo and Juliet* achieve worldwide popularity.

Like Shakespeare's play, Tchaikovsky's *Romeo and Juliet* glorifies a romantic love powerful enough to triumph over death. He captures the essential emotions of Shakespeare's play without defining each character or the exact course of events. Highly contrasted themes are used to express the conflict between family hatred and youthful love. Tchaikovsky also

202

depicts the gentle and philosophical Friar Laurence, intermediary between the lovers and the harsh outside world.

Romeo and Juliet is a concert overture consisting of a slow introduction and a fast movement in sonata form. (Tchaikovsky's title, *Overture-Fantasy,* implies that he treated the musical material in a free and imaginative way.) We can enjoy *Romeo and Juliet* as an exciting orchestral piece without knowing the play. However, a new dimension is added to our listening experience when we associate the music with the drama.

Tchaikovsky opens the overture with the Friar Laurence theme, a solemn, hymnlike melody. As the slow introduction unfolds, brooding strings set an atmosphere of impending tragedy. The clash of swords and the anger of the feud between the Montagues and the Capulets is suggested by the violent first theme of the allegro. Syncopations, rushing strings, and massive sounds create enormous excitement. The second theme of the exposition, a tender love theme, is expressively scored for English horn and muted violas. When the love theme returns in the recapitulation, it has a new exultant character, as Tchaikovsky envelops the listener in opulent sound. There are long crescendos as the melody is led higher and higher to ever more passionate orchestral climaxes.

In the coda, Tchaikovsky transforms the love theme into a song of mourning, while timpani softly beat the rhythm of a funeral march. Then, a new hymn and a tender reminiscence of the love theme suggest that Romeo and Juliet are reunited in death.

Listening Outline To be read while music is heard

ROMEO AND JULIET, OVERTURE-FANTASY (1869),
BY PETER ILYICH TCHAIKOVSKY

Andante non tanto quasi moderato (andante, almost a moderate tempo, slow introduction); Allegro giusto (moderate allegro)

Sonata form, quadruple meter ($\frac{4}{4}$), B minor

Piccolo, 2 flutes, 2 oboes, English horn, 2 clarinets, 2 bassoons, 4 French horns, 2 trumpets, 3 trombones, tuba, timpani, cymbals, bass drum, harp, 1st violins, 2d violins, violas, cellos, double basses

(About 18½ minutes)

INTRODUCTION
Andante non
tanto quasi
moderato   1. *a.* Low clarinets and bassoons, *p*, hymnlike Friar Laurence theme.

b. Strings and French horns, *p*, sustained tones. Basses.
c. Woodwinds and strings, crescendo. Harp, *mf*, flutes, *p*.
2. a. Pizzicato strings accompany high woodwinds, *p*, Friar Laurence theme.
   b. Strings and French horns, *p*, sustained tones. Basses.
   c. Strings and woodwinds, crescendo. Harp, *mf*, violins, *p*.
3. a. Strings answered by high woodwinds, *mf*. Crescendo to *ff*, full orchestra, accelerando. Timpani roll, decrescendo, much slower tempo.
   b. Strings, *p*, answered by woodwind chords, *pp*. Crescendo and accelerando to

Allegro giusto
EXPOSITION
First theme   1. a. Orchestra, *f*, feud theme, minor.

b. Cellos imitated by piccolo, *f*, feud motive.
c. Cymbal crashes against rushing notes in strings. Crescendo to *ff*.
d. Full orchestra, *ff*, feud theme. Cymbal crashes.

Bridge   2. Suddenly soft, woodwinds. Basses and French horns, *pp*, rhythm slows.
Second theme   3. a. English horn and muted violas, love theme, major.

b. Muted violins, *pp*, gently pulsating melody.

Crescendo.
c. High woodwinds, *p*, love theme extended.

Closing section 4. Harp, *p*, accompanies muted strings, bassoon, English horn, *p*.

204

DEVELOPMENT

1. Strings, woodwinds, *p*, feud motive. Crescendo, rushing notes in strings, *f*.
2. *a.* French horns, *p*, Friar Laurence theme, strings accompany. Violins, *pp*, high repeated notes, brass, woodwind chords, *pp*.
   b. Horns, *p*, Friar Laurence theme. Crescendo, rushing notes in strings, *f*.
   c. Horns, *p*, Friar Laurence theme, strings accompany. Violins, *pp*, high repeated notes, brass, woodwind chords, *pp*.
   d. Horns, *p*, Friar Laurence theme.
3. Low strings, *f*, answered by woodwinds, *f*, feud motive. Crescendo to *ff*, cymbal crashes.
4. *a.* Trumpets, *ff*, Friar Laurence theme.
   b. Strings, *ff*, rushing notes, cymbal crashes.

RECAPITULATION

First theme
1. Full orchestra, *ff*, feud theme, minor, cymbal crashes. Downward-rushing notes in strings.

Second theme
2. Oboes, *p*, gently pulsating melody, major. Violins accompany *pp*. Crescendo.
3. *a.* Strings, *f*, love theme extended. Crescendo to *ff*. Love theme repeated. Decrescendo.
   b. Cellos, woodwinds, *mf*, love-theme phrases. French horn. Crescendo.
   c. Strings, *ff*, love theme. Feud motive, cymbal crashes.
4. *a.* Full orchestra, *ff*, feud theme, cymbal crashes.
   b. Brasses, *ff*, Friar Laurence theme.
   c. Full orchestra, *ff*, feud theme, cymbal crashes.
   d. Brasses, *ff*, Friar Laurence theme.
   e. Full orchestra, *ff*, cymbal crashes. Cellos and basses, timpani roll, decrescendo to *p*.

CODA

1. Timpani, *p*, funeral-march rhythm. Strings, *mf*, love theme transformed into song of mourning. Very moderate tempo.

2. Woodwinds, *pp*, hymnlike melody. Harp.
3. Violins, *mf*, love theme varied. Timpani roll, crescendo.
4. Full orchestra, *ff*, repeated chords.

JOHANNES BRAHMS

Johannes Brahms (1833–1897) was a romantic who breathed new life into classical forms. He was born in Hamburg, Germany, where his father made a precarious living as a bass player. At thirteen, Brahms led a double life: during the day he studied piano, music theory, and composition; at

conservative

piano & art songs

(Bettmann Archive)

Johannes Brahms.

night, he played dance music for prostitutes and their clients in waterfront bars.

On his first concert tour, when he was twenty, Brahms met Robert Schumann and Schumann's wife Clara, who were to shape the course of his artistic and personal life. The Schumanns listened enthusiastically to Brahms's music, and Robert published an article hailing Brahms as a musical messiah.

As Brahms was preparing new works for an eager publisher, Schumann had a nervous collapse and tried to drown himself. When Schumann was committed to an asylum, leaving Clara with seven children to support, Brahms came to live in the Schumann home. He stayed there for two years, helping to care for the children when Clara was on tour and becoming increasingly involved with Clara, who was fourteen years older than he. It is not known what passed between them (they destroyed many of their letters). Afterward, they remained lifelong friends, and Brahms never married.

Brahms desperately wanted to become conductor of the Philharmonic Orchestra in Hamburg. When he was passed over for the post in 1862, he left Hamburg for Vienna, where he spent the rest of his life. He conducted a Viennese musical society and introduced many forgotten works of Bach, Handel, and Mozart. He had a wide knowledge of older music (which made him extremely critical of his own work), edited baroque and classical compositions, and collected music manuscripts.

Brahms always lived frugally, though he earned a good income from publishers and from playing and conducting his works. He hid a shy, sensitive nature behind a mask of sarcasm and rudeness; yet he could be very generous to talented young musicians (Dvořák was one).

When Clara Schumann lay dying in 1896, his grief found expression in the haunting *Four Serious Songs*; not long after, it was discovered that he had cancer. On March 7, 1897, he dragged himself to hear a performance of his Fourth Symphony; the audience and orchestra gave him a tremendous ovation. Less than a month later, at age sixty-four, he died.

BRAHMS'S MUSIC

Brahms created masterpieces in all the traditional forms (except opera): four symphonies; two concertos for piano, one for violin, and one for violin and cello; piano pieces; over 200 songs; some magnificent choral music, such as the *German Requiem* (1868); and numerous chamber pieces. His work is personal in style but rooted in the music of Haydn, Mozart, and Beethoven. Brahms reinterpreted classical forms using the harmonic and instrumental resources of his own time. We'll study his masterful treatment of theme and variations in the last movement of his Fourth Symphony.

Brahms's music has a range of moods, but particularly an autumnal feeling and lyrical warmth. Lyricism pervades even the rich polyphonic textures he was so fond of, and he was always able to make them sound natural and spontaneous. One scholar has observed, "It is possible to sing every Brahms movement from beginning to end as though it were a single, uninterrupted melody." His music is rhythmically exciting, with contrasting patterns and syncopations (the use of "2 against 3"—one instrument playing two even notes to a beat while another plays three—is one of his trademarks). It also has a special quality of sound: rich, dark tone colors and, in the orchestral works, a blending of the instrumental choirs that favors mellow instruments like the viola, clarinet, and French horn.

All of his music radiates the security and solidity of a complete master who fully justified Schumann's prediction of greatness.

SYMPHONY NO. 4 IN E MINOR, OP. 98

Brahms composed his Fourth Symphony during the summers of 1884 and 1885 in the tiny Austrian town of Mürzzuschlag. At its Vienna premiere in 1886, the Fourth Symphony bewildered the audience; some even hissed. Yet this work grew on the Viennese and was responsible for Brahms's greatest triumph in Vienna, less than a month before his death. At a concert of the Vienna Philharmonic Orchestra on March 7, 1897, tremendous applause broke out after every movement of the symphony. "Tears ran down his cheeks," a biographer of Brahms writes, "as he stood there, shrunken in form, with lined countenance, strained expression, white hair hanging lank, and through the audience there was a feeling as of a stifled sob, for each knew that he was saying farewell. Another outburst of applause and yet another; one more acknowledgment from the master; and Brahms and his Vienna had parted forever."

The Fourth Symphony combines strength and lyricism with the autumnal melancholy that is so typical of Brahms's music. The first movement, in sonata form, is dominated by its expansive opening theme. Listen for the magical moment when the first two phrases of the theme are presented in long notes to usher in the recapitulation. The slow second movement is based upon a pair of songlike themes that are stated and then recapitulated with imaginative changes in orchestration. The rapid third movement is· a scherzo in sonata form. Let's now examine the fourth movement.

Fourth Movement

Side C, band 4

[*8-record/cassette set:*
Side 12, band 2]

The monumental fourth movement, marked *allegro energico e passionato (energetic and impassioned allegro),* is the climax of the symphony. It is a type of theme and variations related to the baroque ground-bass form (also called *passacaglia).* Brahms's use of a baroque variation form is unique in the romantic symphonic literature and reflects his strong attachment to the musical past.

The movement, in E minor, consists of a theme, thirty variations, and an extended coda. Brasses and woodwinds introduce the theme, a solemn eight-note melody that steadily ascends by step before coming to a cadence.

Brahms borrowed the theme from Bach's Cantata No. 150, *Unto Thee, O Lord, I Lift Up My Soul,* but enhanced it harmonically and dramatically by inserting a new chromatic note into the original melody.

The variations embrace a wide range of moods: some are impassioned, others are lyrical or playful. Like the baroque masters he revered, Brahms focuses the listener's attention on the ever-changing melodic and rhythmic ideas rather than on the repeated theme. Some variations sound completely new, even though most tones of the theme are retained. Brahms's delight in disguising a theme was noted by his contemporaries. When he grew a beard one summer, a friend joked that Brahms's face was now as hard to recognize under the beard as the theme in his variations.

The variations are connected to each other and maintain the theme's 8-bar form and triple meter. In variations 1 to 3, the theme is heard in the top or middle part, but from variation 4 to variation 11, the theme is presented in the bass, with countermelodies above it. From variation 12 on, the theme appears either in the top, middle, or bass part.

The movement is composed of three large sections and a coda:

A	B	A'	Coda
Theme, Variations 1–11	Variations 12–15	Variations 16–30	

The rapid A section, in minor, is mostly forceful and intense. The B section brings a more relaxed mood, a slower tempo, and a major key in three of its four variations. Section A' returns to the quick tempo, minor key, and energetic mood of the opening section and is treated somewhat like a recapitulation. The opening variation of A', variation 16, is very similar to the original theme, and variations 24 and 25 are based upon variations 1 and 2. Sections A, B, and A' all contain subgroups of variations that belong together because of similarities in melody, rhythm, texture, or orchestration. In the listening outline, these subgroups are indicated by brackets.

The impassioned coda begins with a climactic reappearance of the main theme in the woodwinds and brasses. Then Brahms abandons the strict succession of 8-bar units and treats the theme more freely, presenting it in accelerated transformations in the trombones, woodwinds, and full orchestra.

Listening Outline To be read while music is heard

SYMPHONY NO. 4 IN E MINOR (1885),
BY JOHANNES BRAHMS

Fourth Movement: Allegro energico e passionato

Theme and variations (ground-bass or passacaglia form), triple meter ($\frac{3}{4}$ and $\frac{3}{2}$), E minor

2 flutes, 2 oboes, 2 clarinets, 2 bassoons, contrabassoon, 4 French horns, 2 trumpets, 3 trombones, timpani, 1st violins, 2d violins, violas, cellos, double basses

(About 10½ minutes)

A
   THEME   Brasses and woodwinds, *f*, ascending theme, minor key.

VARIATION 1	Timpani rolls and horns, *f*, answered by syncopated theme in pizzicato violins, decrescendo.
VARIATION 2	Oboe, *mp*, legato melody, against theme in pizzicato cellos, *mp*, flutes join, crescendo.
VARIATION 3	Woodwinds, *f*, staccato melody, brasses, *f*, timpani roll.
VARIATION 4	Violins, *f*, lyrical melody, against theme in cellos and basses.

VARIATION 5	Violins, varied lyrical melody, against theme in pizzicato basses.
VARIATION 6	Violins continue melody against legato theme in basses, melody rises, crescendo to
VARIATION 7	High violin melody, *f*, forceful dotted rhythm (short-long, short-long), melody descends.
VARIATION 8	Rushing notes in violins, *f*, against theme in bass, decrescendo.
VARIATION 9	Suddenly loud, faster rushing notes in strings, suddenly soft, woodwinds, descending chromatic scale.
VARIATION 10	Sustained chords, *p*, strings answered by woodwinds.
VARIATION 11	Violins, *p*, staccato phrases, flutes, *pp*, descending chromatic scale.

B

VARIATION 12	Extended legato flute solo, slower tempo, strings accompany, *p*, melody descends, decrescendo.
VARIATION 13	Clarinet phrases, *p*, answered by oboe, low strings, *pp*, major key, flute, descending oboe phrase introduces
VARIATION 14	Trombones, *pp*, slow chords, strings accompany, descending horn phrase introduces
VARIATION 15	Oboe and brasses, *pp*, slow chords, strings accompany, descending flute phrase, ritardando, pause.

A′

VARIATION 16	Brasses and woodwinds, *ff*, original theme and tempo, minor key, high violins, *ff*, descending scale.
VARIATION 17	String tremolo, *p*, woodwinds, *mf*.
VARIATION 18	Horns and high woodwinds, *f*, ascending melody, crescendo.
VARIATION 19	Violins, *f*, staccato phrases, answered by woodwinds, *f*.
VARIATION 20	Violins and brasses, *f*, rapid staccato notes.
VARIATION 21	Timpani rolls, upward rushes in violins, *ff*, answered by trombones, *ff*.
VARIATION 22	Suddenly soft, woodwinds, staccato phrases, staccato strings, *pp*.
VARIATION 23	Suddenly loud, horns, ascending theme.
VARIATION 24	Timpani and brasses, *ff*, answered by high violins, *ff*, theme.
VARIATION 25	High violin tremolo, *ff*, legato melody punctuated by repeated chords in orchestra, *ff*.

210

	VARIATION 26	Suddenly soft, melody in horns, *p*, oboes and violas continue, *p*.
	VARIATION 27	Woodwind sighs, *p*, accompanied by flowing phrases in strings.
	VARIATION 28	High woodwinds, lilting melody, strings accompany, *p*.
	VARIATION 29	Flute, *p*, rising phrases, pizzicato strings, violins, legato phrase.
	VARIATION 30	Suddenly loud, cellos and violins, downward phrase in imitation, crescendo timpani rolls, tempo slows.
CODA		*a.* Brasses and woodwinds, *ff,* theme, faster tempo, woodwinds answered by brass chords.
		b. Trombones, *ff,* accelerated ascending theme, staccato, timpani rolls.

marcato

c. Violins, *p*, crescendo.
d. Woodwinds, *f*, accelerated ascending theme answered by orchestra, *ff.*
e. Orchestra, *ff*, accelerated ascending theme, powerful ending chords.

GIUSEPPE VERDI [ROMANTIC **12**]

Opera

Giuseppe Verdi (1813–1901), the most popular of all opera composers, was born to a poor family in a tiny Italian village. He began studying music in a nearby town, Busseto, where he was taken into the home of a wealthy patron who later also supported his education in Milan. When he completed his studies, he became municipal music director in Busseto and married his patron's daughter; three years later he returned to Milan with the score of his first opera, *Oberto*.

Oberto was produced at La Scala in 1839, had a modest success, and brought Verdi a contract for more operas. Then disaster struck: his wife and their two children died. Verdi managed to complete his next opera, but it was a failure and, in despair, he vowed to compose no more.

What changed his mind was a libretto about the ancient Jews exiled from their homeland. Verdi was an ardent nationalist who yearned for a free and united Italy and saw the Jews as a symbol of the enslaved Italians. He quickly composed *Nabucco* (*Nebuchadnezzar*, king of Babylon, 1842), which was a huge success. From then on, Verdi and his operas came to symbolize Italian independence. (The cry *Viva Verdi* also stood for the patriotic slogan "Vittorio Emmanuele, Re D'Italia"—*Victor Emmanuel, king of Italy.*)

In his late thirties, Verdi composed *Rigoletto* (1851), *Il Trovatore* (1853), and *La Traviata* (1853). Although the public loved them, critics were often scandalized by their subject matter—they seemed to condone rape, sui-

211

(Brown Brothers)

Giuseppe Verdi.

cide, and free love. But Verdi was fiercely independent and himself lived openly with his second wife for ten years before marrying her.

After these successes had made him wealthy, Verdi bought an estate in Busseto; and in 1861 he was elected to the first parliament that convened after Italy had become a nation. In his later years he wrote *Aïda* (1871), *Otello* (1887), and—at the age of seventy-nine—*Falstaff* (1893).

VERDI'S MUSIC

Verdi composed not for the musical elite but for a mass public whose main entertainment was opera. He wanted subjects that were "original, interesting, . . . and passionate; passions above all!" Almost all his mature works are serious and end unhappily; they move quickly and involve extremes of hatred, love, jealousy, and fear, and his powerful music underlines the dramatic situations.

Expressive vocal melody is the soul of a Verdi opera. There are many duets, trios, and quartets; and the chorus plays an important role. Verdi's style became less conventional as he grew older; his later works have greater musical continuity, less difference between aria and recitative, more imaginative orchestration, and richer accompaniments. His last three operas—*Aïda*, *Otello*, and *Falstaff*—are perhaps his greatest. *Falstaff*, his final work, is a comic masterpiece which ends with a carefree fugue to the words *All the world's a joke!*

RIGOLETTO (1851)

Verdi dared to create an operatic hero out of a hunchback, a court jester named Rigoletto, whose only redeeming quality is an intense love for his daughter Gilda. Rigoletto's master, the licentious Duke of Mantua, has won Gilda's love while posing as a poor student. He seduces the innocent girl, causing Rigoletto to plot his death. Gilda loves the Duke even after learning about his dissolute character, and she ultimately sacrifices her own life to save his. Vice triumphs in this powerful drama.

Act III: La donna è mobile (Woman is fickle)

[8-record/cassette set:
  Side 11, band 1]

Act III of *Rigoletto* contains one of the most famous and popular pieces in opera, the Duke's aria *La donna è mobile*. The scene is an inn where the Duke has come to meet Maddalena, the voluptuous sister of Sparafucile, a cutthroat whom Rigoletto has hired to kill the Duke. *La donna è mobile* (*Woman is fickle*), carefree and tuneful, expresses the Duke's pleasure-loving personality. Even before the premiere of *Rigoletto*, which was to take place in Venice, Verdi knew this aria would be a hit; so that it would not leak out during rehearsals and be sung by every Venetian gondolier, he waited until the last possible moment before giving the manuscript to the tenor who was to sing it.

Aria. Orchestra introduces Duke's melody.

La donna è mobile	Woman is fickle
Qual piuma al vento,	Like a feather in the wind,
Muta d'accento	She changes her words
E di pensiero.	And her thoughts.
Sempre un amabile	Always a lovable
Leggiadro viso,	And lovely face,
In pianto o in riso,	Weeping or laughing,
È menzognero.	Is lying.
La donna è mobile, ecc.	Woman is fickle, etc.

Orchestra. Duke's melody repeated with different words.

È sempre misero	The man's always wretched
Chi a lei s'affida,	Who believes in her,
Chi le confida	Who recklessly entrusts
Mal cauto il core!	His heart to her!
Pur mai non sentesi	And yet one who never
Felice appieno	Drinks love on that breast
Chi su quel seno	Never feels
Non liba amore!	Entirely happy!
La donna è mobile, ecc.	Woman is fickle, etc.

GIACOMO PUCCINI [ROMANTIC **13**]

Giacomo Puccini (1858–1924), who created some of the best-loved operas, came from a long line of composers and church organists. During his student years at Milan University, he lived a hand-to-mouth existence; but the success of his first opera, shortly after his graduation, brought him commissions and an annual income from Italy's leading music publisher. In 1893, he became known throughout Italy for his opera *Manon Lescaut*; after 1896, he was wealthy and world-famous from the enormous success of *La Bohème*. *Tosca* (1900) and *Madame Butterfly* (1904) were also very popular; he died before finishing his last opera, *Turandot*, which was completed by a friend.

Puccini's marvelous sense of theater has given his operas lasting appeal. His melodies have short, memorable phrases and are intensely emotional; he used the orchestra to reinforce the vocal melody and to suggest mood.

opera

To achieve unity and continuity, he minimized the difference between aria and recitative and used the same material in different acts. Puccini was very much concerned with the literary and dramatic qualities of his librettos; he spent as much time polishing them as composing the music and often demanded endless changes from the librettists. Some of his operas (notably *Tosca*) reflect an artistic trend of the 1890s known as *verismo*—that is, *realism*, or the quality of being "true to life." But they also feature exoticism: *Madame Butterfly* is set in Japan and *Turandot* in China, and both have melodic and rhythmic elements derived from the music of these countries.

LA BOHÈME (1896)

La Bohème (Bohemian Life) takes place in the Latin Quarter of Paris around 1830. Its hero is Rodolfo, a young poet who shares a garret with Marcello, a painter, Colline, a philosopher, and Schaunard, a musician. Mimi, the heroine, is a poor, tubercular seamstress who lives in the same building. The simple, touching plot has been aptly summarized as "boy meets girl, boy loses girl, boy and girl are reunited as girl dies of consumption in boy's arms and curtain falls." Everyone can relate to the characters and emotions of this enchanting opera. Though there are many realistic touches in this picture of bohemian life, it is seen through a romantic haze.

Act I:

Scene between Rodolfo and Mimi

Side D, band 1

[*8-record/cassette set:*
Side 11, band 2]

Toward the end of Act I, Mimi and Rodolfo meet and fall in love. Her candle has blown out, and she knocks on his door asking for a light. After a short musical conversation, Mimi realizes she has lost her key, and they both search for it in the dark. When their hands touch, Rodolfo sings the aria *Che gelida manina (What a cold little hand)*. He sings about himself, his dreams and his fantasies. Mimi responds with a poetic description of her simple life in the aria *Mi chiamano Mimì (They call me Mimi)*.

Puccini's sensuous melody casts a glow over the entire scene. His music has an improvisatory quality that is due to the many fluctuations of tempo. When Mimi enters, the orchestra murmurs a touching phrase, Mimi's theme, which suggests her fragility and tenderness. Each of the two arias begins simply, almost in conversation. Then the melody grows warmer until it reaches a climax in a broad, passionate phrase. The climactic phrase of Rodolfo's aria, sung to the words *Talor dal mio forziere (My hoard of treasure is robbed by two thieves: a pair of beautiful eyes)*, is the love theme of the whole opera. Mimi's emotional high point is reached when she dreams about the end of winter (*Ma quando vien la sgelo*), when "the first kiss of April" is hers. Returning to reality at the end of her aria, she sings in conversational repeated tones.

(Rodolfo closes the door, sets his light on the table, and tries to write. But he tears up the paper and throws the pen down.)

Flute melody.

Rodolfo

Non sono in vena.

I'm not in the mood.

(A timid knock at the door.)

Chi è la?

Who's there?

Speechlike.

Mimi

Scusi.

Excuse me . . .

Rodolfo

Una donna!

A woman!

Mimi

Di grazia, mi si è spento

I'm sorry . . . my light

Mimi's theme, *pp,* in orchestra.

Il lume.

Has gone out.

Rodolfo

Ecco.

(opens) Here.

Mimi

(in the doorway, with a candlestick and a key)

Vorrebbe . . .?

Would you . . .?

Rodolfo

S'accomodi un momento.

Come in for a moment.

Mimi

Non occorre.

There's no need.

Rodolfo

La prego, entri.

Please . . . come in.

(Mimi enters, has a fit of coughing.)

Rodolfo

Si sente male?

You're not well?

Mimi

No . . . nulla.

No . . . it's nothing.

Rodolfo

Impallidisce!

You're pale!

Mimi

È il respir . . . quelle scale . . .   I'm out of breath . . . the stairs . . .

(She faints, and Rodolfo is just in time to support her and help her to a chair. The key and the candlestick fall from her hands.)

Rodolfo

Ed ora come faccio?   Now what shall I do?

(He gets some water and sprinkles her face.)
Così.   So.
Che viso d'ammalata!   How ill she looks!

(Mimi comes to.)

Si sente meglio?   Are you better now?

Mimi

Sì.   Yes.

Rodolfo

Qui c'è tanto freddo.   It's so cold here.
Segga vicino al fuoco.   Come and sit by the fire.

(He helps her to a chair by the stove.)
Aspetti . . . un po' di vino.   Wait . . . some wine.

Mimi

Grazie.   Thank you.

Rodolfo

A lei.   Here.

Mimi

Poco, poco.   Just a little.

Rodolfo

Così.   There.

Mimi

Grazie.   Thank you.

Rodolfo

Che bella bambina!   What a lovely creature!

216

Mimi

Ora permetta
Che accenda il lume.
È tutto passato.

Now, please,
Relight my candle.
I'm better now.

Rodolfo

Tanta fretta.

Such a hurry.

Mimi

Sì.

Yes.

(Rodolfo lights her candle for her.)
Grazie. Buona sera.

Thank you. Good evening.

Rodolfo

Buona sera.

Good evening.

(Mimi goes out, then reappears at the door.)

Mimi

Oh! sventata, sventata,
La chiave della stanza
Dove l'ho lasciata?

Oh! foolish me! . . .
Where have I left
The key to my room?

A little faster.
Tuneful vocal
melody.

Rodolfo

Non stia sull'uscio:
Il lume vacilla al vento.

Don't stand in the door:
The wind makes your light flicker.

(Her candle goes out.)

Mimi

Oh Dio! Torni ad accenderlo.

Heavens! Will you relight it?

(Rodolfo rushes to her with his light, but when he reaches the door, his candle goes out, too. The room is dark.)

Rodolfo

Oh Dio! Anche il mio s'è spento.

There . . . Now mine's out, too.

Mimi

Ah! E la chiave ove sarà?

Ah! And where can my key be?

Rodolfo

Buio pesto!

Pitch dark!

Mimi

Disgraziata!
Unlucky me!

Rodolfo

Ove sarà?
Where can it be?

Mimi

Importuna è la vicina . . .
You've a bothersome neighbor . . .

Rodolfo

Ma le pare!
Not at all.

Mimi

Importuna è la vicina . . .
You've a bothersome neighbor . . .

Rodolfo

Cosa dice, ma le pare!
What do you mean? Not at all.

Mimi

Cerchi.
Search.

Rodolfo

Cerco.
I'm searching.

(They both grope on the floor for the key.)

Mimi

Ove sarà?
Where can it be?

Rodolfo

Ah!
Ah! (finds the key, pockets it)

Mimi

L'ha trovata?
Did you find it?

Rodolfo

No.
No.

Mimi

Mi parve . . .
I thought . . .

Rodolfo

In verità!
Truthfully!

Mimi

Cerca?   Are you hunting?

Rodolfo

Cerco.   I'm hunting for it.

(Guided by her voice, Rodolfo pretends to search as he draws closer to   Orchestra alone,
her. Then his hand meets hers, and he holds it.)   tempo slows.

Mimi

Ah!   (Surprised) Ah!

(They rise. Rodolfo continues to hold Mimi's hand.)

Rodolfo

Che gelida manina,   What a cold little hand,   Rodolfo's aria.
Se la lasci riscaldar.   Let me warm it.

Che ge - li - da ma - ni - na,   se la la - sci   ri - scal - dar.

Cercar che giova? Al buio   What's the use of searching?
Non si trova. Ma per fortuna   We'll never find it now.
È una notte di luna,   But luckily there's a moon,   Harp.
E qui la luna l'abbiamo vicina.   And she's our neighbor here.
Aspetti, signorina,   Just wait, my dear young lady,
Le dirò con due parole chi son,   And meanwhile I'll tell you
Chi son, e che faccio, come vivo. In a word who and what I am.
Vuole?   Shall I?

(Mimi is silent.)

Chi son? Chi son? Son un poeta.   Who am I? I'm a poet.
Che cosa faccio? Scrivo.   My business? Writing.
E come vivo? Vivo.   How do I live? I live.
In povertà mia lieta   In my happy poverty
Scialo da gran signore   I squander like a prince
Rima ed inni d'amore.   My poems and songs of love.
Per sogni e per chimere   In hopes and dreams
E per castelli in aria   And castles in air,
L'anima ho milionaria.   I'm a millionaire in spirit.
Talor dal mio forziere   My hoard of treasure   Love theme.
Ruban tutti i gioielli   Is robbed by two thieves:
Due ladri: gli occhi belli.   A pair of beautiful eyes.

Ta - lor dal mio for - zie - re___ ru-ban tut-ti j gio-

iel - li due la - dri: gli oc - chi bel - li.

Ventrar con voi pur ora	They came in now with you
Ed i miei sogni usati,	And all my lovely dreams,
Ed i bei sogni miei	My dreams of the past,
Tosto si dileguar!	Were soon stolen away.
Ma il furto non m'accora	But the theft doesn't upset me,
Poichè, poichè v'ha preso stanza	Since the empty place was filled
La speranza.	With hope.
Or che mi conoscete	Now that you know me,
Parlate voi. Deh parlate.	It's your turn to speak.
Chi siete? Vi piaccia dir?	Tell me, please, who are you?

Mimi

Mimi's aria.

Sì.	Yes.
Mi chiamano Mimì,	They call me Mimi,
Ma il mio nome è Lucia.	But my real name is Lucia.

Andante lento

Mi chia - ma - no Mi - mì, ma il mio no - me è Lu - ci - a___

La storia mia è breve.	My story is brief.
A tela o a seta	I embroider silk and satin
Ricamo in casa e fuori.	At home or outside.
Son tranquilla e lieta,	I'm tranquil and happy,
Ed è mio svago	And my pastime
Far gigli e rose.	Is making lilies and roses.
Mi piaccion quelle cose	I love all things
Che han si dolce malia,	That have a gentle magic,
Che parlano d'amor, di primavere,	That talk of love, of spring,
Che parlano di sogni e di chimere,	That talk of dreams and fancies—
Quelle cose che han nome poesia . . .	The things called poetry . . .
Lei m'intende?	Do you understand me?

Rodolfo

Sì.	Yes.

Mimi

Mi chiamano Mimì.	They call me Mimi—
Il perchè non so.	I don't know why.
Sola, mi fo il pranzo	I live all by myself
Da me stessa.	And I eat all alone.
Non vado sempre a messa,	I don't often go to church,
Ma prego assai il Signor.	But I like to pray.
Vivo sola, soletta,	I stay all alone
Là in una bianca cameretta;	In my tiny white room,
Guardo sui tetti e in cielo.	I look at the roofs and the sky.
Ma quando vien lo sgelo	But when the thaw comes
Il primo sole è mio,	The first sunshine is mine,
Il primo bacio	The first kiss
Dell'aprile è mio!	Of April is mine!
Il primo sole è mio!	The first sunshine is mine!
Germoglia in un vaso una rosa.	A rose blossoms in my vase,
Foglia a foglia l'aspiro.	I breathe in its perfume,
Così gentil è il profumo d'un fior.	Petal by petal. So lovely,
Ma i fior ch'io faccio, ahimè,	So sweet is the flower's perfume.
I fior ch'io faccio,	But the flowers I make,
Ahimè non hanno odore.	Alas, have no scent.
Altro di me non le saprei narrare.	What else can I say?
Sono la sua vicina	I'm your neighbor,
Che la vien fuori d'ora a	Disturbing you at this impossible
importunare.	hour.

RICHARD WAGNER [ROMANTIC **14**]

Few composers have had so powerful an impact on their time as Richard Wagner (1813–1883). His operas and artistic philosophy influenced not only musicians but poets, painters, and playwrights. Such was his preeminence that an opera house of his own design was built in Bayreuth, Germany, solely for performances of his music dramas.

Wagner was born in Leipzig in a theatrical family. His boyhood dream was to be a poet and playwright, but at fifteen he was overwhelmed by Beethoven's music and decided to become a composer. He taught himself by studying scores, had only six months of formal training in music theory, and never mastered an instrument. As a student at Leipzig University he dueled, drank, and gambled; and a similar pattern persisted later—he always lived shamelessly off other people and ran up debts he could not repay.

During his early twenties, Wagner conducted in small German theaters

Richard Wagner.

and wrote several operas. In 1839, he decided to try his luck in Paris, then the center of grand opera; he and his wife spent two miserable years there, during which he was unable to get an opera performed and was reduced to musical hackwork. But he returned to Germany in 1842 for the production of his opera *Rienzi* in Dresden; the work was immensely successful, and he was appointed conductor of the Dresden Opera. Wagner spent six years at this post, becoming famous as both an opera composer and a conductor.

When the revolutions of 1848 were sweeping across Europe, Wagner's life in Dresden had become difficult because of accumulated debts. Hoping that a new society would wipe these out and produce conditions favorable to his art, he participated in an insurrection and then had to flee to Switzerland. For several years he did no composing; instead, he worked out his theories of art in several essays and completed the librettos to *Der Ring des Nibelungen* (*The Ring of the Nibelung*), a set of four operas based on Nordic mythology which was to occupy him for twenty-five years. He interrupted his work on the music for *The Ring* to compose *Tristan and Isolde* (1857–1859).

Wagner had several bad years after finishing *Tristan*. His opera *Tannhäuser* was a failure at the Paris Opera; *Tristan* was abandoned by the Vienna Opera; and he was hounded by creditors. In 1864, however, he was rescued by King Ludwig of Bavaria, an eighteen-year-old fanatical Wagnerite who put all the resources of the Munich Opera at his disposal. At this time, Wagner fell in love with Cosima von Bülow, who was Liszt's daughter and the wife of Hans von Bülow, Wagner's close friend and favorite conductor; she gave birth to two of Wagner's children while still married to von Bülow. Shortly after Wagner's first wife died, he married Cosima.

In Wagner, musical genius was allied with selfishness, ruthlessness, rabid German nationalism, and absolute self-conviction. He forged an audience for his complex music dramas from a public accustomed to conventional opera. The performance of the *Ring* cycle at Bayreuth in 1876 was perhaps the single most important musical event of the century; and—though some critics still found his music too dissonant, heavily orchestrated, and long-winded—he was generally acclaimed the greatest composer of his time. A year after completing *Parsifal* (1877–1882), his last opera, he died in Venice at age sixty-nine.

WAGNER'S MUSIC

For Wagner, an opera house was a temple in which the spectator was to be overwhelmed by music and drama. He wrote his own librettos, based on medieval Germanic legends and myths and with characters that are usually larger than life—heroes, gods, demigods. He called his works *music dramas* rather than operas, but today many people find his music more exciting than his rather static drama.

222

Within each act, there is a continuous musical flow (Wagner called this "unending melody") instead of traditional arias, recitatives, and ensembles, and there are no breaks where applause can interrupt. His vocal line, which he conceived as "speech song," is inspired by the rhythms and pitches of the German text. Wagner revolutionized opera by shifting the focus from voice to orchestra and treating the orchestra symphonically. His expanded and colorful orchestration expresses the drama and constantly develops, transforms, and intertwines musical ideas. (And the orchestral sound is so full that only very powerful voices can cut through it.) In the orchestra—and sometimes in the vocal parts—he uses brief, recurrent musical themes called *leitmotifs* (*leading motives*). A **leitmotif** is a short musical idea associated with a person, an object, or a thought in the drama.

The tension of Wagner's music is heightened by chromatic and dissonant harmonies—ultimately, these led to the breakdown of tonality and to the new musical language of the twentieth century.

GÖTTERDÄMMERUNG (THE TWILIGHT OF THE GODS, 1874)

Götterdämmerung (*The Twilight of the Gods*) is the fourth and concluding music drama in Wagner's gigantic cycle *Der Ring des Nibelungen* (*The Ring of the Nibelung*). With all its gods, giants, dwarfs, and magic fire, the *Ring* is really about Wagner's view of nineteenth-century society. He uses Nordic mythology to warn that society destroys itself through lust for money and power. It is fitting that Wagner first sketched the plot of the *Ring* in 1848, a year that brought Marx's *Communist Manifesto* and revolutions throughout Europe.

Act III: Immolation Scene

Wagner builds an overwhelming climax at the end of the *Ring* as human beings and gods are punished for their crimes by an all-consuming fire and flood. To grasp this scene fully, it's helpful to know what has taken place in the three preceding music dramas.

[8-record/cassette set: Side 12, band 1]

A Nibelung dwarf has stolen gold belonging to the Rhinemaidens, mermaids in the Rhine River. From this gold, the dwarf fashions a ring that can bestow world power on anyone who wears it and is willing to renounce love. The dwarf, in turn, is robbed of his prize by Wotan, king of the gods. (*Wednesday* comes from *Wotan's day*.) Furious, the dwarf casts a curse on the ring and anyone who wears it. Soon Wotan is forced to give up the ring; he lives in fear that someone will use it to destroy him. Hoping to protect himself, he surrounds his castle, Valhalla, with a bodyguard of heroes. His daughters, goddesses called *Valkyries*, swoop over battlefields on horseback bearing away the dead bodies of the bravest warriors.

Brünnhilde, one of the Valkyries, is Wotan's favorite daughter. Thinking she is following Wotan's inner feelings, Brünnhilde disobeys her father by saving Siegmund, a hero fated to die. She is punished by being turned into a mortal. Cast into a deep sleep by Wotan, she lies on a mountain surrounded by magic fire. The hero Siegfried, son of Siegmund, penetrates the fire, awakens Brünnhilde, and becomes her husband.

In the course of his adventures, Siegfried has gained possession of the ring, but he is unaware of its power. Shortly before the *Immolation* Scene, Siegfried is murdered through the treachery of Hagen, who wants the ring.

The *Immolation* Scene occurs in front of a castle on the Rhine. Brünnhilde sings an exalted farewell before sacrificing herself to join Siegfried in death. At her command, warriors build a huge funeral pyre of logs. As Siegfried's body is lifted onto the pyre, Brünnhilde takes the magic ring from him and puts it on, bequeathing it to the Rhinemaidens. The following excerpt begins as Brünnhilde addresses a pair of ravens, Wotan's messengers.

In this glorious conclusion to *The Twilight of the Gods*, Brünnhilde's soaring vocal line is matched by the powerful orchestra. Various leitmotifs are heard, sometimes together. After Brünnhilde rides into the funeral pyre, the orchestra magnificently depicts the flames and the overflowing of the Rhine. The opera ends as Valhalla, the castle of the gods, is engulfed in flames to the accompaniment of the leitmotif "redemption by love." Wagner seems to be expressing the feeling that despite the destruction of mortals and gods, a new world will be reborn through love. (In the following libretto excerpt, words in quotation marks—like "Law" and "Magic fire"— refer to specific leitmotifs. These leitmotifs are indicated where they can be most clearly heard.)

Trumpets and trombones, *f*, "Law."

(Brünnhilde has put the Ring on her finger and now takes a firebrand from one of the men.)

Brünnhilde

Fliegt heim, ihr Raben! — Fly home, you ravens!

raunt es eurem Herren, — Whisper to your ruler

was hier am Rhein ihr gehört! — the things you heard by the Rhine.

Full orchestra, *f*, "Magic fire," "Loge, god of fire."

An Brünnhildes Felsen fliegt vorbei: — And go by the way of Brunnhild's rock!

der dort noch lodert,
weiset Loge nach Walhall!

The place still blazes.
Send the fire-god
to Valhall,

Denn der Götter Ende
dämmert nun auf:

For the final dusk
has come to all gods!

so—werf' ich den Brand
in Walhalls prangende Burg.

So—now hurl the brand
at Valhall's glittering pomp.

Cymbal crash.

(She hurls the torch onto the pyre. Two ravens fly up and disappear in
the background. She turns to her horse.)

Strings surge
upward as pyre
bursts into flames.

Grane, mein Ross,
sei mir gegrüsst!

Grane, my horse!
We meet once more!

Horns, "Ride of the
Valkyries."

"Ride of the Valkyries"

Weisst du auch, mein Freund,
wohin ich dich führe?

Im Feuer leuchtend

Do you know, my friend,
just where we are faring?

In radiant fires

Flute and voice,
"Redemption by
love."

"Redemption by love"

liegt dort dein Herr,
Siegfried, mein seliger Held.

there lies your lord,
Siegfried, the lord of my life.

Dem Freunde zu folgen,
wieherst du freudig?

You're joyfully neighing
just to be with him?

Lockt dich zu ihm
die lachende Lohe?

Laughter of flames
allures you to follow?

Fühl' meine Brust auch,
wie sie entbrennt;
helles Feuer
das Herz mir erfasst.

Feel how my bosom
so hotly burns.
Radiant fire
takes hold of my heart.

Trumpet, "Siegfried."	*Ihn zu umschlingen,* *umschlossen, von ihm,* *in mächtigster Minne* *vermählt ihm zu sein!*

On to embrace him,
to live in his arms,
thus yoked to him ever
in mightiest love!

Hei-a-ja-ho! Grane!
Grüss deinen Herren!
Siegfried! Siegfried! Sieh!
selig grüsst dich dein Weib!

Heiajaho! Grane!
Give your lord greeting!
Siegfried! Siegfried! See!
Brunnhild hails you with joy!

Brasses, "Ride of the Valkyries."	(She swings herself onto the horse and makes it leap into the burning pyre.)
Full orchestra, *ff*, "Magic fire."	(Flames fill the whole space in front of the castle, which itself catches fire. Men and women press to the front of the stage in terror.)

"Magic fire"

Decrescendo, descending chromatic scale, "Magic sleep." Strings, upward running notes. Crescendo.	(When all seems wrapped in flames, the glow is suddenly extinguished, so that only a cloud of smoke is seen.)

(At the same time, the Rhine upswells mightily and pours its waters over the pyre. The three Rhinemaidens ride the waves and appear by the pyre. At their appearance, Hagen—Siegfried's murderer—is seized with alarm. He flings away his spear, shield, and helmet, and madly plunges into the flood, crying:) |

Hagen

(Omitted from our recording.)	*Zurück vom Ring!*

The ring is mine!

Downward strings and decrescendo depict drowning. Oboes, and clarinets, lilting "Rhinemaidens."	(Two Rhinemaidens grab Hagen around the neck and drag him down into the water. A Rhinemaiden exultantly holds up the recovered Ring.)

p

crescendo -

"Rhinemaidens"

(Through the bank of clouds which lie on the horizon, a red glow breaks forth with increasing brightness.)

Brasses, solemn, "Valhalla."

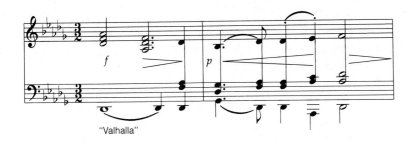

"Valhalla"

(In its light, the Rhine is observed to have returned to its bed, and the Rhinemaidens are circling and playing with the Ring in the calm water.)

Interweaving of leitmotifs: Oboes and clarinets, "Rhinemaidens"; violins, "Redemption by love"; brasses, "Valhalla."

(From the ruins of the half-burned castle, the men and women perceive the red glow in the heavens, in which appears the castle of Valhalla, where the gods and heroes are sitting together.)

Crescendo. Trumpets and trombones, *f,* "Siegfried."

"Siegfried"

(Bright flames seize Valhalla. The curtain falls as the gods become entirely hidden by the flames.)

Violins, *p,* "Redemption by love."

THE TWENTIETH CENTURY

VI

*Piano Lesson (1916), by Henri Matisse. The early twentieth
century brought radical new developments in the arts.*
(Museum of Modern Art, New York)

[1] MUSICAL STYLES: 1900–1950

The years 1900 to 1913 brought radical new developments in science and art. During the period preceding World War I, discoveries were made that overturned long-held beliefs. Sigmund Freud explored the unconscious and developed psychoanalysis, and Albert Einstein revolutionized the view of the universe with his special theory of relativity. Pablo Picasso's painting and sculpture distorted human figures and objects with unprecedented daring, showing them from several angles at one time; Wassily Kandinsky's abstract paintings no longer tried to represent the visual world.

In music, too, the early twentieth century was a time of revolt. The years following 1900 saw more fundamental changes in the language of music than any time since the beginning of the baroque era. There were entirely new approaches to the organization of pitch and rhythm and a vast expansion in the vocabulary of sounds used, especially percussive sounds. Some compositions so broke with tradition that they were met with violent hostility. The most famous riot in music history occurred in Paris on May 29, 1913, at the premiere of Igor Stravinsky's ballet *Le Sacre du printemps (The Rite of Spring)*. Police had to be called in as hecklers booed, laughed, made animal noises, and actually fought with those in the audience who wanted to hear Stravinsky's evocation of primitive rites. One music critic complained that *The Rite of Spring* produced the "sensation of acute and almost cruel dissonance" and that "from the first measure to the last, whatever note one expects is never the one that comes. . . ." Another wrote, "To say that much of it is hideous in sound is a mild description. . . . It has no relation to music at all as most of us understand the word."

Today, we are amused by the initial failure of some music critics to understand this composition, now recognized to be a masterpiece. Chords, rhythms, and percussive sounds that were baffling in 1913 are now commonly heard in jazz, rock, and music for movies and television. But the hostile critics of the early 1900s were right in seeing that a great transformation in musical language was taking place.

From the late 1600s to about 1900, musical structure was governed by certain general principles. As different as the works of Bach, Beethoven, and Brahms may be, they share fundamental techniques of organizing pitches around a central tone. After 1900, however, no single system governs the organization of pitch in all musical compositions. Each piece is more likely to have a system of pitch relationships unique to that particular piece.

In the past, composers depended on the listener's awareness—conscious or unconscious—of the general principles underlying the inter-

(Museum of Modern Art, New York)

Girl before a Mirror (1932), by Pablo Picasso. Twentieth-century artists distorted human figures with unprecedented daring.

relationship of tones and chords. For example, they relied on the listener's expectation that a dominant chord would normally be followed by a tonic chord. By substituting another chord for the expected one, the composer could create a feeling of suspense, drama, or surprise. Twentieth-century music relies less on preestablished relationships and expectations. Listeners are guided by musical cues contained only within an individual composition. This new approach to the organization of sound makes twentieth-century music fascinating. When we listen openly, with no assumptions about how tones "should" relate, modern music is an adventure.

1900–1950: AN AGE OF MUSICAL DIVERSITY

The range of musical styles during the first half of the twentieth century was vast. The stylistic diversity in the works of Claude Debussy, Igor Stravinsky, Arnold Schoenberg, Alban Berg, Anton Webern, Béla Bartók, Charles Ives, George Gershwin, and Aaron Copland—to name only the composers studied here—is a continuation and an intensification of the diversity of romantic music. Not only do twentieth-century composers seem to be using different languages, but radical changes of style occur even within the works of individual composers.

Such great variety of musical styles reflected the diversity of modern life and an expansion of musical sources. Through the work of scholars and performers, a wider range of music became available, and composers drew inspiration from folk and popular music, Asian and African music, and European art music from the Middle Ages through the nineteenth century.

Composers were especially attracted to unconventional rhythms, sounds, and melodic patterns in folk and popular music. Folk music was studied more systematically than before, partly because scholars could now record peasant songs; and one of the greatest twentieth-century composers, Béla Bartók, was also a leading authority on peasant music. Bartók's imagination was fired by the music of his native Hungary and other parts of eastern Europe; he considered it "the ideal starting point for a musical renaissance." Igor Stravinsky drew upon Russian folk songs; Charles Ives used American revival hymns, ragtime, and patriotic songs.

Non-European music was also an important influence. Western composers were more receptive and sympathetic to Asian and African cultures than they had been earlier. Echoes of the gamelan—the Indonesian orchestra—can be heard in some of Debussy's works; and the novel rhythmic procedures of another Frenchman, Olivier Messiaen (b. 1908), grew out of his study of Indian music.

Another non-European influence was American jazz; musicians were fascinated by its syncopated rhythms, improvisational quality, and unique tone colors (unlike a string-dominated symphony orchestra, a jazz band emphasizes woodwinds, brasses, and percussion). Jazz elements were used as early as 1908 by Debussy (in *Golliwogg's Cakewalk* from the suite *Children's Corner*) and 1918 by Stravinsky (in *The Soldier's Tale*), but the peak of jazz influence came during the "jazz age" of the 1920s. To American composers, jazz represented a kind of musical nationalism, the search for an "American sound"; for Europeans, it represented musical exoticism. During the 1920s and 1930s, composers such as George Gershwin used jazz and popular elements within "classical" forms.

Modern composers could also draw inspiration from a wider historical range of music. During the twentieth century, music from remote times has been unearthed by scholars, published, performed, and recorded. Early masters have been rediscovered—for example, Perotin and Machaut from the medieval period, Josquin Desprez and Gesualdo from the Renaissance, and Purcell and Vivaldi from the baroque. And some important modern composers have been music historians, like Anton Webern, or performers of early music, like Paul Hindemith. Music from the past has been a fruitful source of forms, rhythms, tone colors, textures, and compositional techniques. Baroque dances, and forms like the passacaglia and concerto grosso, are being used again; and the long-forgotten harpsichord has been put to new use in works such as Elliott Carter's Sonata for Flute, Oboe, Cello, and Harpsichord, which we'll study. Occasionally, modern composers use themes of earlier composers—Benjamin Britten (English, 1913–1976) based his *Young Person's Guide to the Orchestra* on a theme by Henry Purcell (about 1659–1695).

[*Instructor's records:*
  Side 4, band 3]

IMPRESSIONISM

(Photo by George Routhier/Musée Marmottan)

Impression, Sunrise, *by Claude Monet (1874). At an exhibition in Paris in 1874, this painting annoyed a critic who viewed it as a formless collection of tiny colored patches. Using Monet's own title, he mockingly called the entire show the "exhibition of the impressionists." The term "impressionist" stuck but eventually lost its negative implications. Like the impressionist painters, the French composer Claude Debussy was a master at evoking a fleeting mood and misty atmosphere.*

THE TWENTIETH CENTURY

(Collection, Museum of Modern Art, New York, Purchase)

Street Scene, Dresden, *by Ernst Ludwig Kirchner (1908). German expressionist painters used deliberate distortion and violent colors to communicate the tension and anguish of the human psyche. Expressionist composers include Arnold Schoenberg, Alban Berg, and Anton Webern.*

(Collection, Museum of Modern Art, New York, Mrs. Simon Guggenheim Fund)

(Collection, Museum of Modern Art, New York, Mrs. Simon Guggenheim Fund)

Painting No. 198 (above) and **Painting No. 200** (right), by Wassily Kandinsky (1914). Kandinsky stated that his abstract paintings were a "graphic representation of a mood and not of objects."

(Collection, Museum of Modern Art, New York. Mrs. Simon Guggenheim Fund)

Three Musicians, by Pablo Picasso (1921). In Picasso's cubist paintings, three-dimensional objects and human figures are distorted into planes. In 1920, Picasso designed the costumes for Pulcinella, a ballet with music by his friend Igor Stravinsky; Picasso's portrait of Stravinsky is shown in the text.

Rhapsody, by Hans Hofmann (1965). Hofmann's abstract expressionist painting is animated by dynamic tension of form and color.

(Metropolitan Museum of Art, Gift of Renate Hofmann, 1975)

(Collections, Museum of Modern Art, New York, Gift of David Whitney)

*Untitled, from the portfolio **Marilyn**, by Andy Warhol (1967). Pop artists like Warhol use ordinary subjects from everyday life and the mass media.*

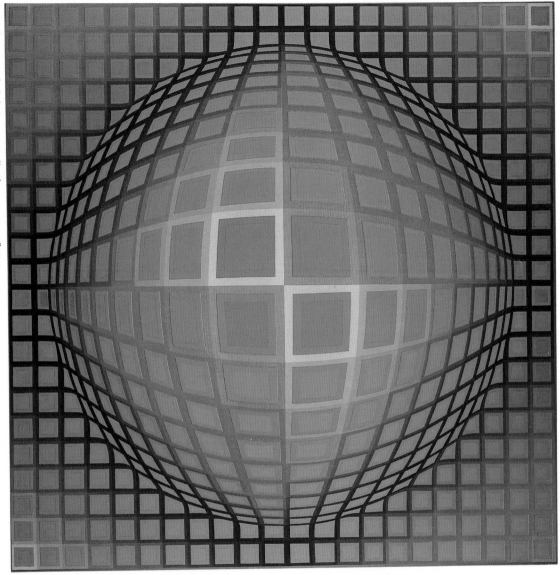

(Albright-Knox Art Gallery, Buffalo, New York, Gift of Seymour H. Knox, 1969.)

Vega-Nor, by Victor Vasarely (1969). Op or "optical" artists such as Vaserely exploit optical illusions and other visual effects.

(Robert and Ryda Levi Foundation)

Hundred-Yard Dash, by Alexander Calder (1969). Calder created stabiles—large, stationary sculptures. He was also the originator of the mobile—a sculpture that moves with the aid of air currents.

However, all this does not imply that past styles are simply imitated: they are used with harmonies, rhythms, melodies, and tone colors that would have been inconceivable before the twentieth century.

Modern composers were also influenced by the music of the immediate past. Wagner, especially, was as potent an influence as Beethoven had been for the romantics; composers took Wagner's style as a departure point or else reacted violently against all he stood for.

In addition, of course, composers have been affected by technological and social trends. For example, the twentieth century has seen dramatic changes in how music reaches its listeners: radio, television, and recordings have brought music to a much larger audience and vastly increased the amount and scope of music available. More women have been active as composers, music educators, virtuoso soloists, orchestra musicians, and conductors. (Ellen Taaffe Zwilich, whose *Passages* we'll study, is only one example of noted American women composers.) Another trend is the vital role of American colleges and universities in our musical culture. They have reached countless students through music courses, housed most of the electronic studios, sponsored many performing groups, and trained and employed many composers, performers, and scholars. Thus, colleges and universities have indirectly become patrons of music, as the church and the aristocracy once were.

Finally, there has been a very significant change in the musical tastes of audiences. In the twentieth century, the concert and operatic repertory has been dominated by music from the past. This is a new situation in music history: before the nineteenth century, audiences demanded and got the latest music; and even during the romantic period, when interest in earlier music was high, concert programs consisted mainly of recent works. After 1900, however, listeners and performers were often baffled by the dissonances, percussive sounds, and irregular rhythms of some new music; conductors therefore tended to rely on traditional music and to favor contemporary works that were relatively accessible in style. During the 1950s and 1960s, more effort was made by individuals and organizations to present contemporary music, and to commission it. Yet few serious composers can live on commissions alone; most composers today are also teachers, conductors, or performers.

Let's now examine some of the characteristics of twentieth-century music.

CHARACTERISTICS OF TWENTIETH-CENTURY MUSIC

Tone Color

During the twentieth century, tone color has become a more important element of music than it ever was before. It often has a major role, creating variety, continuity, and mood. In Webern's Orchestral Piece, Op. 10, No. 3

(1913), for example, the use of eerie, bell-like sounds at the beginning and end is vital to the form. If this composition were altered in tone color by being played on a piano, it would lose much. An orchestral work from an earlier period, say, Beethoven's Fifth Symphony, suffers less in a piano arrangement.

In modern music, noiselike and percussive sounds are often used, and instruments are played at the very top or bottom of their ranges. Uncommon playing techniques have become normal. For example, the *glissando,* a rapid slide up or down a scale, is more widely used. Woodwind and brass players are often asked to produce a fluttery sound by rapidly rolling their tongues while they play. And string players frequently strike the strings with the stick of the bow, rather than draw the bow across the strings.

Percussion instruments have become prominent and numerous, reflecting the twentieth-century interest in unusual rhythms and tone colors. Instruments that have become standard during the 1900s include the xylophone, celesta, and wood block, to name a few. Composers occasionally call for noisemakers—typewriters, sirens, and automobile brake drums. A piano is often used to add a percussive edge to the sound of an orchestra. Modern composers often draw hard, drumlike sounds from the piano, in contrast to the romantics, who wanted the instrument to "sing." Besides expanding the percussion section of the orchestra, early twentieth-century composers wrote works for unconventional performing groups in which percussion plays a major role. Well-known examples are Stravinsky's *Les Noces* (*The Wedding*, 1914–1923), for vocal soloists, chorus, four pianos, and percussion; Bartók's Music for Strings, Percussion, and Celesta (1936); and Varèse's *Ionisation* (1931), one of the first works for percussion ensemble.

Modern orchestral and chamber works often sound transparent; individual tone colors are heard clearly. To bring out the individuality of different melodic lines that are played simultaneously, a composer will often assign each line to a different timbre. In general, there is less emphasis on blended sound than during the romantic period. Many twentieth-century works are written for nonstandard chamber groups made up of instruments with sharply contrasting tone colors. Stravinsky's *L'Histoire du soldat* (*The Soldier's Tale*, 1918), for example, is scored for violin, double bass, clarinet, bassoon, cornet, trombone, and percussion. Even orchestral works often sound as though they are scored for a group of soloists.

Harmony

Consonance and dissonance

The twentieth century brought fundamental changes in the way chords are treated. Up to about 1900, chords were divided into two opposing types: consonant and dissonant. A consonant chord was stable; it functioned as a point of rest or arrival. A dissonant chord was unstable; its tension demanded onward motion, or resolution to a stable, consonant chord. Traditionally, only the triad, a three-tone chord, could be consonant. All others were considered dissonant. In the nineteenth century, composers came to use ever more dissonant chords, and they treated dissonances with increasing freedom. By the early twentieth century, the traditional distinction between consonance and dissonance was abandoned in much music. A combination of tones that earlier would have been used to generate instability and expectation might now be treated as a stable chord, a point of arrival. In Stravinsky's words, dissonance "is no longer tied down to its former function. Having become an entity in itself, it frequently happens that dissonance neither prepares nor anticipates anything. Dissonance is thus no more an agent of disorder than consonance is a guarantee of security."

This "emancipation of the dissonance" does not prevent composers from differentiating between chords of greater or lesser tension. Relatively mild-sounding chords may be goals of motion, while harsher chords are used for transitional sounds. But no longer is there a general principle that determines whether a chord is stable or not. It is now entirely up to the composer's discretion. "We find ourself confronted with a new logic of music that would have appeared unthinkable to the masters of the past," wrote Stravinsky. "This new logic has opened our eyes to riches whose existence we never suspected."

New chord structures

Before 1900, there were general principles governing chord construction: certain combinations of tones were considered chords, while others were not. At the core of traditional harmony is the triad. A triad might be made up of alternate tones of a major scale, such as the first *(do)*, third *(mi)*, and fifth *(sol)*. Within a triad, there are two intervals of a third.

Although the triad often appears in twentieth-century music, it no longer is so fundamental.

Some twentieth-century composers create fresh harmonies by placing one traditional chord against another. Such a combination of two chords heard at the same time is called a *polychord.*

Copland, Appalachian Spring

A polychord can be heard either as a single block of sound or as two distinct layers, depending on whether the two combined chords contrast in tone color and register.

Another development in twentieth-century music is the use of chordal structures *not* based on triads. One used commonly is the *fourth chord,* in which the tones are a fourth apart, instead of a third. (From *do* to *fa,* or from *re* to *sol,* is an interval of a fourth.)

Ives, The Cage

Harmonic resources have been extended also through the *tone cluster,* a chord made up of tones only a half step or a whole step apart. A tone cluster can be produced on a piano by striking a group of adjacent keys with the fist or forearm.

Ives, The Majority

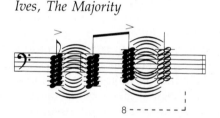

Alternatives to the Traditional Tonal System

Twentieth-century composers also explored alternatives to tonality, which had governed the organization of pitch since the 1600s. After 1900, the traditional tonal system was modified in many different ways, and some composers discarded it entirely. The new techniques of pitch organization are so varied as to resist easy generalization.

Some compositions have a central tone but are missing other traditional elements, such as the central major or minor scale, the tonic triad, or the dominant-tonic relationship. For instance, Stravinsky's *Serenade in A,* as its title suggests, revolves around the tone A but is not in a major or minor key; and some composers have used the ancient church modes, or scales borrowed from nonwestern countries, or scales they themselves invented. Twentieth-century pieces are often organized around a central chord other than the triad, and this basic chord may well be one that was considered a dissonance earlier. Melodies, sections, and entire compositions are rounded off not by a dominant-tonic cadence but by other chord progressions.

Another twentieth-century approach to pitch organization is **polytonality,** the use of two or more keys at one time. When only two different keys are used at once—as is most common—the technique is called **bitonality.** A famous bitonal passage occurs in Stravinsky's ballet *Petrushka,* when one clarinet plays in C major and another plays in F sharp major:

In general, the greater the contrast of tone color, register, and rhythm between the different layers of sound, the more we can hear the different keys.

A further departure from tradition is *atonality,* the absence of tonality or key. Atonality was foreshadowed in nineteenth-century works such as Wagner's *Tristan and Isolde,* where the pull of a central key is weakened by frequent modulations and by liberal use of all twelve tones in the chromatic scale. Arnold Schoenberg wrote the first significant atonal pieces around 1908. He avoided traditional chord progressions in these works and used all twelve tones without regard to their traditional relationship to major or minor scales. But atonality is not a specific technique of composition; each atonal work is structured according to its needs. (Though the word *atonality* is imprecise and negative, no other term has yet come into general use.)

Before long, Schoenberg felt the need for a more systematic approach to atonal composition, and during the early 1920s he developed the *twelve-tone system,* a new technique of pitch organization. This system gives equal prominence to each of the twelve chromatic tones, rather than singling out one pitch, as the tonal system does. For about twenty years, only Schoenberg and a few disciples used the twelve-tone system, but during the 1950s it came to be used by composers all over the world.

Rhythm

The new techniques of pitch organization were accompanied by new ways to organize rhythm. The rhythmic vocabulary of music was expanded, with increased emphasis on irregularity and unpredictability. Rhythm is one of the most striking elements of twentieth-century music; it is used to generate power, drive, and excitement.

In the twentieth century, new rhythmic procedures are drawn from many sources, including folk music from all over the world, jazz, and European art music from the Middle Ages through the nineteenth century. Béla Bartók used the "free and varied rhythmic structures" of east European peasant music. The syncopations and complex rhythmic combinations of jazz fired the imagination of Stravinsky and Copland. And irregular phrase structures in Brahms's music inspired rhythmic innovations in Schoenberg's works.

Rapidly changing meters are characteristic of twentieth-century music, whereas baroque, classical, and romantic music maintain a single meter throughout a movement or section. Before the twentieth century, beats were organized into regularly recurring groups; the accented beat came at equal time intervals. Rhythmic irregularities such as syncopations or accents on weak beats were heard against a pervasive meter. But in many twentieth-century compositions, beats are grouped irregularly, and the accented beat comes at unequal time intervals. In some modern music the meter changes with almost every bar, so that we might count *1–2–3, 1–2–3–4–5, 1–2–3–4–5, 1–2–3, 1–2–3–4, 1–2–3–4–5, 1–2–3–4–5–6, 1–2–3–4–5, 1–2, 1–2–3–4–5–6*:

Stravinsky, Ritual of Abduction from The Rite of Spring

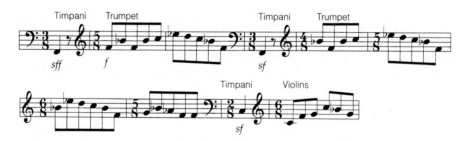

Count this again quickly and experience some of the rhythmic excitement of twentieth-century music, which often has a rapid and vigorous beat with jolting accents at unexpected times.

The rhythmic resources of twentieth-century music have also been expanded through the use of unconventional meters. Along with traditional meters such as duple and triple, modern composers use meters with five or seven beats to the measure. The pulses within a measure of any length may be grouped in irregular, asymmetrical ways. For example, eight quick pulses within a measure may be subdivided 3 + 3 + 2, or **1–2–3–4–5–6–**

7–8, **1**–2–3–4–5–6–7–8. This meter, common in east European folk music, is used by Bartók in one of his *Six Dances in Bulgarian Rhythm.*

Twentieth-century music often uses two or more contrasting and independent rhythms at the same time, a procedure called ***polyrhythm.*** Each part of the musical texture goes its own rhythmic way, often creating accents that are out of phase with accents in the other parts. Different meters are used at the same time. For example, one instrument may play in duple meter (*1–2, 1–2*) while another plays in triple meter (*1–2–3, 1–2–3*). Although polyrhythm occasionally occurs in classical and romantic music, it became both more common and more complex after 1900. The polyrhythms of jazz strongly influenced composers in the 1920s and 1930s.

Rhythmic repetition of a group of pitches is a widely used unifying technique in twentieth-century music. Many modern compositions contain an ***ostinato,*** a motive or phrase that is repeated persistently at the same pitch throughout a section. The ostinato may occur in the melody or in the accompaniment. (The accompaniment for the last music example has an eight-note ostinato: **1**–2–3–4–5–6–7–8.) Ostinatos can be found in music from various periods and cultures. In twentieth-century music, they usually serve to stabilize particular groups of pitches.

Melody

The new techniques of pitch and rhythmic organization that we've surveyed had a strong impact on twentieth-century melody. Melody no longer is necessarily tied to traditional chords or major and minor keys. It may be based on a wide variety of scales or freely use all twelve chromatic tones and not have a tonal center. Melody today often contains wide leaps that are difficult to sing. Rhythmic irregularity and changing meters tend to make twentieth-century melodies unpredictable. They often consist of a series of phrases that are irregular in length. In general, twentieth-century music relies less than classical and romantic music on melodies that are easy to sing and remember. Melody is as rich and varied as twentieth-century music itself; neither can be classified easily.

IMPRESSIONISM AND SYMBOLISM

[TWENTIETH CENTURY]

2

Many musical styles coexisted around the turn of the century. Among the most important was impressionism, best represented by the music of the French composer Claude Debussy (1862–1918). Musical impressionism is related to two slightly earlier artistic movements in France, which were catalysts for many developments during the twentieth century: impressionist painting and symbolist poetry.

La Grenouillère (1869), by Claude Monet. Impressionist painters were concerned primarily with effects of light, color, and atmosphere.

H. O. Havemeyer Collection, bequest of Mrs. H. O. Havemeyer, 1929)
(Metropolitan Museum of Art, New York,

240

In 1874, a group of French painters including Claude Monet (1840–1926), Auguste Renoir (1841–1919), and Camille Pissarro (1830–1903) had an exhibition in Paris. One Monet painting entitled *Impression: Sunrise* particularly annoyed an art critic, who mockingly called the entire show "the exhibition of the impressionists." The term *impressionist* stuck, but it eventually lost its derisive implication.

Today, most of us appreciate impressionist paintings, but during the 1870s they were seen as formless collections of tiny colored patches—which they are, when viewed closely, though from a distance the brush strokes become recognizable forms and shimmering colors. Impressionist painters were concerned primarily with effects of light, color, and atmosphere—with impermanence, change, and fluidity. Many of them worked outdoors rather than in a studio; they were fascinated by outdoor scenes from contemporary life (picnics in the woods, crowds on Parisian boulevards) and—most of all—by water. Using light, pastel colors, they depicted the ripples and waves of the ocean and the river Seine.

As the impressionists broke away from traditional techniques of painting, writers called *symbolists* rebelled against the conventions of French poetry. Like the painters, poets such as Stéphane Mallarmé (1842–1898), Paul Verlaine (1844–1896), and Arthur Rimbaud (1854–1891) emphasized fluidity, suggestion, and the purely musical, or sonorous, effects of words. Claude Debussy was a close friend of several symbolist poets; many of Verlaine's poems became texts for his songs, and Mallarmé's poem *L'Après-midi d'un faune (The Afternoon of a Faun)* inspired his most famous orchestral work.

CLAUDE DEBUSSY

TWENTIETH CENTURY

3

The French impressionist composer Claude Debussy (1862–1918) linked the romantic era with the twentieth century. From the early age of ten until he was twenty-two he studied at the Paris Conservatory, where his teachers regarded him as a talented rebel. In 1884 he won the prestigious Prix de Rome, which subsidized three years of study in Rome; but he left after two years because he lacked musical inspiration away from his beloved Paris.

Influences on Debussy's work included several visits to Russia, where he worked as a pianist for Tchaikovsky's patroness, Nadezhda von Meck, and formed a lifelong interest in Russian music. He was also influenced by the Asian music performed at the Paris International Exposition of 1889, and by the ideas and music of Richard Wagner, which were having a profound effect in France and both attracted and repelled him.

For years, Debussy led an unsettled life, earning a small income by

(Culver Pictures)

Claude Debussy.

teaching piano. His friends were mostly writers, like Stéphane Mallarmé, whose literary gatherings he attended regularly. He was little known to the musical public and not completely sure of himself, though he composed important works including his String Quartet (1893) and the tone poem *Prelude to "The Afternoon of a Faun"* (1894). But his opera *Pelléas and Mélisande* (1902) marked a turning point in his career: although the critics were sharply divided over it, it soon caught on, and he was recognized as the most important living French composer.

Debussy led a personal life filled with financial and emotional crises, constantly borrowing money (he had a craving for luxury) and having tempestuous love affairs. He was not gifted as a conductor and hated appearing in public, but to maintain his high standard of living he undertook concert tours and presented his music throughout Europe. He died in Paris in 1918.

DEBUSSY'S MUSIC

Like the French impressionist painters and symbolist poets, Debussy evoked fleeting moods and misty atmosphere, as the titles of his works suggest: *Reflets dans l'eau* (*Reflections in the Water*), *Nuages* (*Clouds*), and *Les Sons et les parfums tournent dans l'air du soir* (*Sounds and Perfumes Swirl in the Evening Air*). He was often inspired by literary and pictorial ideas, and his music sounds free and spontaneous, almost improvised. His stress on tone color, atmosphere, and fluidity is characteristic of *impressionism* in music.

Tone color truly gets unprecedented attention in his works; they have a sensuous, beautiful sound and subtle but crucial changes of timbre. The entire orchestra seldom plays together to produce massive sound; instead, there are brief but frequent solos. Woodwinds are prominent; strings and brasses are often muted. In his music for piano—which includes some of the finest piano works of the twentieth century—he creates hazy sonorities and uses a rich variety of bell- and gonglike sounds.

Debussy's treatment of harmony was a revolutionary aspect of musical impressionism. He tends to use a chord more for its special color and sensuous quality than for its function in a standard harmonic progression. He uses successions of dissonant chords that do not resolve. (When young, Debussy was asked which harmonic rules he followed; he replied, simply, "My pleasure.") He freely shifts a dissonant chord up or down the scale; the resulting parallel chords characterize his style.

Debussy, La Cathédrale engloutie (The Sunken Cathedral)*

Debussy's harmonic vocabulary is large. Along with traditional three- and four-note chords, he uses five-note chords with a lush, rich sound. Chord progressions that were highly unorthodox when Debussy wrote them soon came to seem mild and natural.

"One must drown the sense of tonality," he wrote. Although he never actually abandoned tonality, he weakened it by avoiding progressions that strongly affirm the key and by using scales in which the main tone is not emphasized. He turned to the medieval church modes and the pentatonic scales heard in Javanese music. A *pentatonic* scale is a five-tone scale, such as that produced by the five black keys of the piano in succession: F♯–G♯–A♯–C♯–D♯.

Debussy's most unusual and tonally vague scale is the *whole-tone scale,*

*Copyright 1910. Durand et Cie. Used by permission of the publisher Elkan-Vogel, Inc. Sole representative U.S.A.

made up of six different notes each a whole step away from the next (C–D–E–F♯–G♯–A♯–C). Unlike major and minor, the whole-tone scale has no special pull from *ti* to *do*, since its tones are all the same distance apart. And because no single tone stands out, the scale creates a blurred, indistinct effect.

Debussy, Voiles (Sails)*

The pulse in his music is sometimes as vague as the tonality. This rhythmic flexibility reflects the fluid, unaccented quality of the French language, and in fact he set French to music very sensitively. He composed fifty-nine art songs, many of which are set to symbolist poems. His only opera, *Pelléas and Mélisande*, is an almost word-for-word setting of a symbolist play by Maurice Maeterlinck. It is the essence of musical impressionism: nebulous, mysterious, dreamlike, with a discreet, understated orchestral accompaniment.

Although not large, Debussy's output is remarkably varied; in addition to his opera and art songs it includes works for piano, orchestra, and chamber ensembles. Echoes of his music can be heard in the works of many composers of the years 1900–1920; but no other musician can so fairly be described as an impressionist. Even the composer most similar to him, his younger French contemporary Maurice Ravel (1875–1937), wrote music with greater clarity of form. Debussy's style was both a final expression of romanticism and the beginning of a new era.

PRÉLUDE À "L'APRÈS-MIDI D'UN FAUNE" (PRELUDE TO "THE AFTERNOON OF A FAUN")

Side C, band 5

[*8-record/cassette set: Side 12, band 3*]

"The music of this Prelude," wrote Debussy regarding his *Prelude to "The Afternoon of a Faun,"* "is a very free illustration of the beautiful poem by Stéphane Mallarmé, *The Afternoon of a Faun.*" This poem evokes the dreams and erotic fantasies of a pagan forest creature who is half man, half goat. While playing "a long solo" on his flute, the intoxicated faun tries to recall whether he actually carried off two beautiful nymphs or only dreamed of doing so. Exhausted by the effort, he falls back to sleep in the warm sunshine.

*Copyright 1910. Durand et Cie. Used by permission of the publisher Elkan-Vogel, Inc. Sole representative U.S.A.

Debussy intended his music to suggest "the successive scenes through which pass the desires and dreams of the faun in the heat of this afternoon." The subtle, sensuous timbres of this miniature tone poem were new in Debussy's day. Woodwind solos, muted horn calls, and harp glissandos create a rich variety of delicate sounds. The dynamics are usually subdued, and the entire orchestra—from which trombones, trumpets, and timpani are excluded—rarely plays at one time. The music often swells sensuously, only to subside in voluptuous exhaustion.

The prelude begins with an unaccompanied flute melody; its vague pulse and tonality make it dreamlike and improvisatory. This flute melody is heard again and again, faster, slower, and against a variety of lush chords. Though the form of the prelude may be thought of as A B A', one section blends with the next. It has a continuous ebb and flow. The fluidity and weightlessness typical of impressionism are found in this music. We are never tempted to beat time to its subtle rhythms. The prelude ends magically with the main melody, played by muted horns, seeming to come from far off. The bell-like tones of antique cymbals finally evaporate into silence. With all its new sounds and musical techniques, the piece has aptly been described as a "quiet revolution" in the history of music.

Listening Outline   To be read while music is heard

PRÉLUDE À "L'APRÈS-MIDI D'UN FAUNE"
(PRELUDE TO "THE AFTERNOON OF A FAUN," 1894),
BY CLAUDE DEBUSSY

At a very moderate tempo, A B A' form, E major

3 flutes, 2 oboes, 1 English horn, 2 clarinets, 2 bassoons, 4 French horns, 2 harps, antique cymbals, 1st violins, 2d violins, violas, cellos, double basses

(About 10 minutes)

A   1. *a.* Solo flute, *p*, main melody.

Harp glissando; soft horn calls. Short pause. Harp glissando; soft horn calls.
b. Flute, *p*, main melody; tremolo strings in background. Oboe, *p*, continues melody. Orchestra swells to *f*. Solo clarinet fades into
c. Flute, *p*, main melody varied and expanded; harp and muted strings accompany. Flute melody comes to quiet close.
2. a. Clarinet; harp and cellos in background.
  b. New oboe melody.

Violins take up melody, crescendo and accelerando to climax. Excitement subsides. Ritardando. Clarinet, *p*, leads into

B

3. a. Woodwinds, *p*, legato melody in long notes. Crescendo.

b. Strings repeat melody; harps and pulsating woodwinds in background, crescendo. Decrescendo. Horns, *p*, solo violin, *p*, clarinet, oboe.

A'

4. a. Harp accompanies flute, *p*, main melody in longer notes. Oboe, staccato woodwinds.
  b. Harp accompanies oboe, *p*, main melody in longer notes. English horn, harp glissando.
5. a. Antique cymbals, bell-like tones. Flutes, *p*, main melody. Solo violins, *pp*, in high register.
  b. Flute and solo cello, main melody; harp in background.
  c. Oboe, *p*, brings melody to close. Harps, *p*.
  d. Muted horns and violins, *ppp*, beginning of main melody sounding far off. Flute, antique cymbals, and harp; delicate tones fade into silence.

TWENTIETH
CENTURY

4   NEOCLASSICISM

From about 1920 to 1950, the music of many composers, including Igor Stravinsky and Paul Hindemith (1895–1963), reflected an artistic movement known as *neoclassicism*. Neoclassicism is marked by emotional restraint, balance, and clarity; neoclassical compositions use musical forms and stylistic features of earlier periods (particularly the eighteenth century) to organize twentieth-century harmonies and rhythms.

Neoclassical composers—reacting against romanticism and impressionism—turned away from program music and the gigantic orchestras favored at the turn of the century; they preferred absolute music for chamber groups. The neoclassicists modeled many of their works after Bach's music, used clear polyphonic textures, and wrote fugues, concerti grossi, and baroque dance suites. (In fact, the term *neobaroque* might have been more appropriate for their work.) Most neoclassical music was tonal and used major and minor scales. Still, neoclassicism was more an attitude than a style, and neoclassical compositions sound completely modern—they play on the delightful tension between our expectations about old forms and their own novel harmonies and rhythms.

Neoclassicism was an important trend in other arts, too. The poet T. S. Eliot often quoted and alluded to earlier works; and Picasso (who designed sets for Stravinsky's first neoclassical work, *Pulcinella*, in 1920) went through a phase during which his paintings showed the influence of ancient Greek art.

IGOR STRAVINSKY [TWENTIETH CENTURY 5]

Even during his lifetime, Igor Stravinsky (1882–1971) was a legendary figure. His once revolutionary works were modern classics, and he influenced three generations of composers and other artists. Cultural giants like Picasso and T. S. Eliot were his friends. President John F. Kennedy honored him at a White House dinner in his eightieth year.

Stravinsky was born in Russia, near St. Petersburg (Leningrad), grew up in a musical atmosphere, and studied with Nikolai Rimsky-Korsakov. He had his first important opportunity in 1909, when the impresario Sergei Diaghilev heard his music. Diaghilev was the director of the Russian Ballet, an extremely influential troupe which employed great painters as well as important dancers, choreographers, and composers. Diaghilev first asked Stravinsky to orchestrate some piano pieces by Chopin as ballet music and then, in 1910, commissioned an original ballet, *The Firebird*, which was immensely successful. A year later (1911), Stravinsky's second ballet, *Petrushka*, was performed, and Stravinsky was hailed as a modern master. When his third ballet, *The Rite of Spring*, had its premiere in Paris in 1913, a riot erupted in the audience—spectators were shocked and outraged by its pagan primitivism, harsh dissonance, percussiveness, and pounding rhythms—but it too was recognized as a masterpiece and influenced composers all over the world.

[*8-record/cassette set: Side 13, band 1*]

During World War I, Stravinsky sought refuge in Switzerland; after the armistice, he moved to France, his home until the onset of World War II,

(Omikron/Photo Researchers)

Igor Stravinsky, in a sketch by Picasso.

when he came to the United States. In the 1920s and 1930s he was an international celebrity, constantly touring in Europe and the United States; and his compositions—which had originally been inspired by Russian folk music—became cooler and more objective. During his years in the United States (he lived outside Los Angeles), his young musical assistant, Robert Craft, familiarized him with the works of Schoenberg, Berg, and Webern, and in the 1950s Stravinsky astonished his followers by adopting Schoenberg's twelve-tone system.

Unlike Schoenberg and Bartók, Stravinsky got well-paying commissions for his work and was an astute businessman; he also loved order and discipline and said that he composed "every day, regularly, like a man with banking hours." In his seventies and eighties he was still touring, conducting his rich and intense late works.

STRAVINSKY'S MUSIC

Stravinsky's extensive output includes compositions of almost every kind, for voices, instruments, and the stage; and his innovations in rhythm, harmony, and tone color had an enormous influence on twentieth-century music.

His development shows dramatic changes of style. The three early ballets—*The Firebird* (1910), *Petrushka* (1911), and *The Rite of Spring* (1913)—call for very large orchestras and draw upon Russian folklore and folk tunes. During World War I, he wrote for chamber groups, using unconventional combinations of instruments and incorporating ragtime rhythms and popular dances (an example is *The Soldier's Tale*, 1918). From about 1920 to 1951 (the "neoclassical" era), he was inspired largely by eighteenth-century music; the ballet *Pulcinella* (1920) was based partly on the music of Giovanni Battista Pergolesi (1710–1736), and the opera *The Rake's Progress* (1951) was modeled on Mozart. His neoclassical works emphasize restraint, balance, and wit and are far removed from the violence of *The Rite of Spring*. But his shift to the twelve-tone system in the 1950s was an even more dramatic change of approach, since until then all his music had had a clear tonal center. Taking inspiration from Anton Webern (1883–1945), Stravinsky now wrote brief works in which melodic lines were "atomized" into short fragments in constantly changing tone colors and registers.

Despite such stylistic changes, however, all his music has an unmistakable "Stravinsky sound." Tone colors are dry and clear; the beat is strong. His work abounds in changing and irregular meters, and sometimes several meters are heard at once. Ostinatos—repeated rhythmic or melodic patterns—often unify sections of a piece. His treatment of musical form is also unique: rather than connecting themes with bridge passages, he makes abrupt shifts, but his music nevertheless sounds unified and continuous. The effectiveness of his rhythms, chords, and melodies often depends largely on his orchestration, in which highly contrasting tone colors are frequently combined. And his music has rich, novel harmonies—he makes even conventional chords sound unusual.

Stravinsky drew on a wide range of styles, from Russian folk songs to baroque melodies, from Renaissance madrigals to tango rhythms. He sometimes used existing music to create original compositions, but more often the music is entirely his own, while vaguely suggesting a past style.

LE SACRE DU PRINTEMPS (THE RITE OF SPRING, 1913)

Few compositions have had so powerful an impact on twentieth-century music as *Le Sacre du printemps (The Rite of Spring)*, Stravinsky's third ballet score for the Russian Ballet. Its harsh dissonances, percussive orchestration, rapidly changing meters, violent offbeat accents, and ostinatos fired the imaginations of many composers. The idea for *The Rite of Spring* came to Stravinsky as "a fleeting vision," while he was completing *The Firebird* in St. Petersburg in 1910. "I saw in imagination a solemn pagan rite: wise elders, seated in a circle, watching a young girl dance herself to death. They were sacrificing her to propitiate the god of spring." Later in life, Stravinsky revealed that "the most wonderful event" of every year of his

(Museum of Modern Art, New York)

Les Demoiselles d'Avignon (1907), by Picasso, reflects the influence of African sculpture.

childhood was "the violent Russian spring that seemed to begin in an hour and was like the whole earth cracking."

Stravinsky's interest in a so-called primitive or nonliterate culture was shared by many artists and scholars in the early 1900s. In 1907, Picasso's violent and path-breaking painting *Les Demoiselles d'Avignon* reflected the influence of African sculpture. In 1913—the same year as *The Rite of Spring*—Freud published *Totem and Taboo,* a study of the "resemblances between the psychic lives of savages and neurotics." But *primitivism*—the deliberate evocation of primitive power through insistent rhythms and percussive sounds—did not have a lasting impact on early twentieth-century music. Stravinsky never again wrote anything like *The Rite of Spring;* and with the exception of works like *Allegro barbaro* (1911), a piano piece by Bartók, few primitivistic compositions have entered the repertory.

The Rite of Spring consists of two large parts which are subdivided into sections with varying speeds. These subsections follow each other without pause. The titles of the dances suggest their primitive subject matter: Part I, *The Adoration of the Earth:* (1) *Introduction;* (2) *Omens of Spring: Dances of the Youths and Maidens;* (3) *Ritual of Abduction;* (4) *Spring Rounds;* (5) *Games of the Rival Tribes;* (6) *Procession of the Wise Elder;* (7) *Adoration of the Earth;* (8) *Dance of the Earth.* Part II, *The Sacrifice:* (1) *Introduction;* (2) *Mysterious Circles of the Young Girls;* (3) *Glorification of the Chosen Maiden;* (4) *Evocation of the Ancestors;* (5) *Ritual of the Ancestors;* (6) *Sacrificial Dance.* Each of the two large parts begins with a slow introduction and ends with a frenzied, climactic dance.

The Rite of Spring is written for an enormous orchestra including eight horns, four tubas, and a very important percussion section made up of five timpani, bass drum, tambourine, tam-tam, triangle, antique cymbals, and a guiro (a notched gourd scraped with a stick). The melodies of *The Rite of Spring* are folklike. They have narrow ranges like ancient Russian folk tunes and are made up of fragments that are repeated with slight changes in rhythm and pitch. Many individual chords are repeated, and each change of harmony produces a great impact. This melodic and harmonic repetition gives the music a ritualistic, hypnotic quality. Rhythm is a vital form-building element in *The Rite of Spring*; it has a life of its own, almost independent of melody and harmony. Today, *The Rite of Spring* is performed more frequently as a concert piece than as a ballet.

We shall now take a closer look at four sections of *The Rite of Spring:* the *Introduction, Dances of the Youths and Maidens,* and *Ritual of Abduction,* which open Part I; and the *Sacrificial Dance,* which concludes Part II.

Part I: Introduction

For Stravinsky, the *Introduction* to Part I represented "the awakening of nature, the scratching, gnawing, wiggling of birds and beasts." It begins with the strangely penetrating sound of a solo bassoon straining at the top of its register. As though improvising, the bassoon repeats a fragment of a Lithuanian folk tune in irregular ways.

Side D, band 2

[*8-record/cassette set:*]
[*Side 13, band 2*]

Soon other woodwind instruments join the bassoon with repeated fragments of their own. The impression of improvisation is strengthened by the absence of a clearly defined pulse or meter. Dissonant, unconventional chord structures are used. Toward the end of the *Introduction*, different layers of sounds—mostly from woodwinds and brasses—are piled on top of each other, and the music builds to a piercing climax. But suddenly, all sound is cut off; only the solo bassoon forlornly repeats its opening melody. Then the violins, playing pizzicato, introduce a repeated four-note figure.

This figure later serves as an ostinato in the *Dances of the Youths and Maidens*, which immediately follows the *Introduction*.

Side D, band 2

⎡ *8-record/cassette set:* ⎤
⎣ *Side 13, band 2 cont.* ⎦

Part I: Omens of Spring—Dances of the Youths and Maidens

Sounding almost like drums, the strings pound out a dissonant chord. There are unexpected and irregular accents whose violence is heightened by jabbing sounds from the eight horns. This is the way the passage might be counted (with a rapid pulse): 1–2–3–4, 1–2–3–4, 1–2–**3**–4, 1–2–3–4, 1–**2**–3–4, 1–2–3–4, 1–2–3–4, 1–**2**–3–4. The unchanging dissonant harmony is a polychord that combines two different traditional chords.

A succession of melodic fragments soon join the pounding chord and other repeated figures. The melodic fragments, played by brass and wood-wind instruments, are narrow in range and are repeated over and over with slight variations.

The rhythmic activity is constant and exciting, and gradually more and more instruments are added.

It's interesting to contrast Stravinsky's musical techniques in *Dances of the Youths and Maidens* with those of a classical movement in sonata form. A classical movement grows out of conflicts between different keys; this section of *The Rite of Spring* is based almost entirely on the repetition of a few chords. The themes in a classical movement are developed through different keys, varied, and broken into fragments that take on new emotional meanings. In *Dances of the Youths and Maidens*, Stravinsky simply repeats melodic fragments with relatively slight variation. His novel techniques grew out of the Russian musical tradition of the nineteenth century; like some of his Russian forebears, Stravinsky relies on variations of rhythm and tone color to create movement and growth.

Part I: Ritual of Abduction

The frenzied *Ritual of Abduction* grows out of the preceding section and is marked by violent strokes on the timpani and bass drum. Enormous tension is generated by powerful accents and rapid changes of meter (see the music example on page 238). This section of *The Rite of Spring* closes with high trills in the strings and flutes.

Side D, band 2

[*8-record/cassette set:* *Side 13, band 2 cont.*]

Part II: Sacrificial Dance

The *Sacrificial Dance* is the overwhelming climax of the whole work. It consists of sections that can be outlined as follows: A B A' C A" (very brief) C A'''. In the opening section (A), explosive, percussive chords fight brutal blows on the timpani. The time signature changes with almost every bar: $\frac{3}{16}$ $\frac{2}{16}$ $\frac{3}{16}$ $\frac{2}{8}$ $\frac{2}{16}$ $\frac{3}{16}$. The rapid pulse and irregular, jolting accents create intense excitement. The second section (B) begins with a sudden drop in dynamic level as a single chord is repeated obsessively. Brief silences between these repeated chords urge the listener to supply accents. Section C features brasses and percussive sounds from five timpani, a tam-tam (gong), and a bass drum. The *Sacrificial Dance* glorifies the power of rhythm, as does the entire *Rite of Spring*.

[*8-record/cassette set:* *Side 13, band 3*]

EXPRESSIONISM

Much twentieth-century music reflects an artistic movement called *expressionism*, which stressed intense, subjective emotion. It was largely centered in Germany and Austria from 1905 to 1925 and grew out of the emotional turbulence in the works of late romantics like Wagner, Richard Strauss, and Gustav Mahler. Expressionist painters, writers, and composers explored inner feelings rather than depicting outward appearances. They used deliberate distortions to assault and shock their audience, to communicate tension and anguish. In a reaction against impressionism, they rejected conventional prettiness.

Expressionist painters, such as Ernst Ludwig Kirchner, Emil Nolde, Edvard Munch, and Oskar Kokoschka, often used jarring colors and grotesque shapes. Expressionist art also tends to be fragmentary—for

(Jacques Lathion/Nasjonalgalleriet, Oslo)

The Scream (1893), by the Norwegian expressionist Edvard Munch. Expressionist painters reacted against French impressionism; they often used jarring colors and grotesquely distorted shapes to explore the subconscious.

example, the scenes of a play may be episodic and discontinuous. Expressionism was concerned with social protest: it movingly conveyed the anguish of the poor and oppressed and the horrors of war. There was close communication among expressionist writers, painters, and musicians, and many were creative in several areas. The painter Wassily Kandinsky wrote essays, poetry, and plays; the composer Arnold Schoenberg painted.

In Sections 7, 8, and 9, we'll study four expressionist compositions: Schoenberg's Five Pieces for Orchestra, Op. 16 (1909), and *A Survivor from Warsaw*; Alban Berg's opera *Wozzeck* (1917–1922); and Anton Webern's Five Pieces for Orchestra, Op. 10 (1911–1913). These works all avoid tonality and traditional chord progressions and stress harsh dissonance, fragmentation, extreme registers, and unusual instrumental effects. *A Survivor from Warsaw* and *Wozzeck* depict a nightmarish world and express a profound empathy with the poor and tormented.

ARNOLD SCHOENBERG

TWENTIETH CENTURY

7

Arnold Schoenberg (1874–1951), who was born in Vienna, was an almost entirely self-taught musician; he acquired his profound knowledge of music by studying scores, playing in amateur chamber groups, and going to concerts. After he lost his job as a bank clerk at age twenty-one, he devoted himself to music, earning a poor living conducting a choir of industrial workers and orchestrating popular operettas. Performances of his own early works met with hostility; but in 1904 he began to teach music theory and composition in Vienna, and he inspired love and loyalty in his students, two of whom—Alban Berg and Anton Webern—themselves became leading composers.

Around 1908 Schoenberg took the revolutionary step of abandoning the traditional tonal system. He was a man possessed ("I have a mission," he said; "I am but the loudspeaker of an idea"), and his productivity between 1908 and 1915 was incredible. For the next eight years, however, he searched for a way to organize his musical discoveries and published nothing. Then, in 1921, he told a student, "I have made a discovery which will ensure the supremacy of German music for the next hundred years," and shortly thereafter (1923–1925) he began publishing compositions using his new twelve-tone system. Although his music did not find a large audience, many important musicians respected it, and he received an important appointment at the Prussian Academy of Arts in Berlin.

After the Nazis seized power in Germany, Schoenberg, who was Jewish, was dismissed from his post; the same year—1933—he and his family came to the United States, where he joined the music faculty at the University of California in Los Angeles. Schoenberg felt neglected in America: his music was rarely performed and he was financially unsuccessful. But since his death, the twelve-tone system has been used increasingly by composers throughout the world.

SCHOENBERG'S MUSIC

Arnold Schoenberg.

"I claim the distinction of having written a truly new music which, based upon tradition as it is, is destined to become tradition." This proud assertion by Schoenberg contains a great deal of truth: his musical language was indeed new, but it had evolved from the past and was eventually widely adopted.

His early works, like the string sextet *Verklärte Nacht* (*Transfigured Night*, 1899), show many features of the late romantic style. Some of them—such as the immense cantata *Gurrelieder* (*Songs of Gurre*, 1901)—use very large orchestras; dissonances and angular melodies create a feeling of subjectivity; chromatic harmony is prominent; and the central tonality is weakened as the music moves through remote keys. But from 1903 to 1907, he moved further from romanticism, and in the *Chamber Symphony*, Op. 9 (1906), he uses whole-tone scales and fourth chords.

Atonality

Around 1908, Schoenberg began to write atonal music. *Atonality*—the absence of key—evolved from his earlier use of chromatic harmony and the chromatic scale; but in his atonal works, all twelve tones are used without regard for their traditional relationship to major and minor scales. Dissonances are "emancipated" from the necessity of resolving to consonances. Atonality does not imply a single system of composition: each atonal work has its own means of achieving unity, and a piece usually grows out of a few short motives that are transformed in many different ways.

Schoenberg's atonal compositions include Five Pieces for Orchestra, Op. 16 (1909), and *Pierrot lunaire*, Op. 21 (*Moonstruck Pierrot*, 1912); they are characterized by jagged melodies, novel instrumental effects, extreme contrasts of dynamics and register, and irregular phrases. *Pierrot lunaire* and some other works require an unusual style of vocal performance—*Sprechstimme* (literally, *speech-voice*)—halfway between speaking and singing. Schoenberg's atonal style was soon adopted by his students Berg and Webern; but their early atonal works tended to be short: without a musical system like tonality, extended compositions were possible only when there was a long text to serve as an organizing force.

The Twelve-Tone System

In the early 1920s, Schoenberg developed a more systematic method of organizing atonal music; he called it the "method of composing with twelve tones." It is partly applied in Five Piano Pieces, Op. 23, and Serenade, Op. 24, and fully elaborated in Suite for Piano, Op. 25 (all composed from 1920 to 1923); and it enabled him to write more extended compositions, such as the monumental Variations for Orchestra (1928) and the

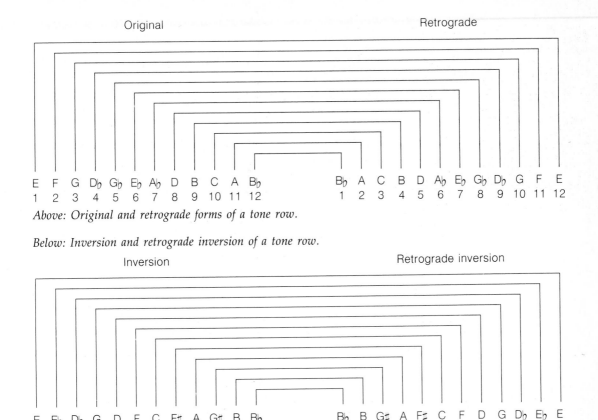

Original														Retrograde											
E	F	G	D♭	G♭	E♭	A♭	D	B	C	A	B♭			B♭	A	C	B	D	A♭	E♭	G♭	D♭	G	F	E
1	2	3	4	5	6	7	8	9	10	11	12			1	2	3	4	5	6	7	8	9	10	11	12

Above: Original and retrograde forms of a tone row.

Below: Inversion and retrograde inversion of a tone row.

Inversion														Retrograde inversion											
E	E♭	D♭	G	D	F	C	F♯	A	G♯	B	B♭			B♭	B	G♯	A	F♯	C	F	D	G	D♭	E♭	E
1	2	3	4	5	6	7	8	9	10	11	12			1	2	3	4	5	6	7	8	9	10	11	12

unfinished opera *Moses und Aron* (*Moses and Aaron*, 1930–1932). From 1933 to 1951, in the United States, he used it in many rich and varied works.

The **twelve-tone system** is a twentieth-century alternative to tonality, a new way of organizing pitch in a composition. It is a systematized form of atonality which gives equal importance to each of the twelve chromatic tones. In a twelve-tone composition, the ordering or unifying idea is called a **tone row, set,** or **series** (for this reason, the method is also referred to as *serial technique* or *serialism*). The composer creates a unique tone row for each piece (the choice of rows is practically limitless, since there are 479,001,600 possible arrangements of the twelve tones), and the row is the source of every melody and chord in it. No pitch occurs more than once in the row; this prevents any tone from receiving too much emphasis.

A composition is built by manipulating the tone row, which may be presented in four basic forms: (1) forward (original form), (2) backward (retrograde), (3) upside down (inversion), and (4) backward and upside down (retrograde inversion). (See the illustrations above, which show the row used in Suite for Piano, Op. 25.) Any of the four forms of a row may be shifted to any pitch level—that is, it can begin on any of the twelve

257

tones while keeping the original pattern of intervals. Thus there are forty-eight (twelve times four) possible versions of a row. Each tone of a row may also be placed in any register; this enhances the flexibility of the system and may partially explain why so many twelve-tone melodies have very wide leaps. Finally, the tones of a row may be presented one after another (as a melodic line) or simultaneously (as chords). Here is the row from the Suite for Piano treated in two different ways:

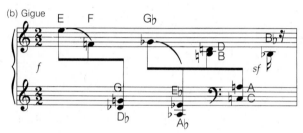

We'll now study Schoenberg's "freely" atonal Five Pieces for Orchestra, Op. 16 (1909), and the twelve-tone cantata *A Survivor from Warsaw*, Op. 46 (1947).

FIVE PIECES FOR ORCHESTRA, OP. 16 (1909)

"I can promise you something really colossal, especially in sound and mood," wrote Schoenberg to the composer and conductor Richard Strauss after completing his Five Pieces for Orchestra, Op. 16, in 1909. These revolutionary pieces were the first atonal works for full orchestra. Though Schoenberg calls for an especially large orchestra, he treats it as a group of soloists. (In 1949, Schoenberg rearranged the Five Pieces for a conventional orchestra.) Many novel orchestral effects are exploited, and instruments are often used at the top or bottom of their ranges. The pieces embody Schoenberg's concept of a **tone-color melody** (**Klangfarbenmelodie**, in German), a succession of varying tone colors used as a musical idea in a composition.

Schoenberg added descriptive titles after he composed the music. Each piece is quite brief; at the time, Schoenberg unconsciously felt the need to "counterbalance extreme emotionality with extraordinary shortness." We'll study the first piece, *Vorgefühle* (*Premonitions*).

Vorgefühle (Premonitions)

An amazing amount of musical activity takes place in the 2-minute span of *Premonitions*. It is "just an uninterrupted change of colors, rhythms, and moods," according to Schoenberg. The constant intensity and desperate energy of *Premonitions* are typically expressionistic.

The piece consists of two connected sections: an introductory part lasting about ½ minute, and a main part three times as long. The introduction sounds fragmentary and has a bewildering succession of musical ideas in different tempos, tone colors, dynamics, and registers. As though holding his full resources in reserve, Schoenberg uses only a few instruments at any one time. First, muted cellos introduce an abrupt upward motive (short-long-long, short-long-long):

[8-record/cassette set: Side 13, band 5]

The entire piece is built from rhythmic and melodic transformations of this idea.

The second part of *Premonitions* is rhythmically more continuous; it becomes increasingly complex in both texture and sound.

The cellos begin with a steady succession of rapid notes. They have a three-note figure that is repeated as a background ostinato throughout the piece.

The sound becomes increasingly loud and dense as more and more melodic fragments are piled on top of one another. After an earsplitting climax, the texture thins, and the volume decreases. *Premonitions* ends with a snarling chord played by trombones and tuba. (The effect results from flutter-tonguing; each brass player rapidly rolls the tongue as if pronouncing *d-r-r-r*.) This chord is sustained in the background throughout most of *Premonitions*, and it unifies the flow of free associations in the piece.

A SURVIVOR FROM WARSAW, OP. 46 (1947)

Side D, band 3

[8-record/cassette set: Side 13, band 6]

A Survivor from Warsaw, a dramatic cantata for narrator, male chorus, and orchestra, deals with a single episode in the murder of 6 million Jews by the Nazis during World War II. Schoenberg wrote the text himself, partly basing it on a direct report by one of the few survivors of the Warsaw ghetto. Over 400,000 Jews from this ghetto died in extermination camps or of starvation; many others perished during a heroic revolt against the Nazis in 1943. The narrator's text is spoken in English, except for some terrifying Nazi commands, which are shouted in German. The narrator's part is a kind of *Sprechstimme*, the novel speech-singing developed by Schoenberg. The rhythms of the spoken words are precisely notated, but their pitch fluctuations are indicated only approximately.

Besides English and German, the text includes Hebrew. These were the three languages of Schoenberg's life: German, his native tongue; English, his adopted language in the United States; and Hebrew, the language of the faith to which he returned. The 6-minute cantata builds to an overwhelming conclusion when the male chorus sings in unison the Hebrew words of the prayer *Shema Yisroel (Hear, O Israel)*. For centuries this has been the prayer of Jewish martyrs in their last agonized moments.

A Survivor from Warsaw is a twelve-tone composition written in 1947 when Schoenberg was seventy-two. Its tense, expressionistic style recalls the composer's orchestral piece *Premonitions*, written almost forty years earlier. The music vividly sets off every detail in the text.

A Survivor from Warsaw opens with a brief orchestral introduction that captures the nightmarish atmosphere that prevailed as Nazi soldiers awakened the Warsaw Jews for transport to death camps. We hear a weirdly shrill reveille in the trumpet and fragmentary sounds in the military drum and high xylophone.

During the narrator's opening lines, Schoenberg already prepares for the concluding Hebrew prayer. As the narrator speaks of "the old prayer they had neglected for so many years," a French horn softly intones the beginning of the melody that is later proclaimed by the chorus.

An especially vivid musical description comes when the narrator describes how the Nazis counted their victims: "They began again, first slowly: One, two, three, four, became faster and faster. . . ." The music itself becomes faster and louder, building to the powerful entrance of the chorus. The sung Hebrew contrasts dramatically with the spoken English and German that comes before, and it is the first extended melody in the work.

I cannot remember everything. I must have been unconscious most of the time; I remember only the grandiose moment when they all started to sing, as if prearranged, the old prayer they had neglected for so many years—the forgotten creed!

But I have no recollection how I got underground to live in the sewers of Warsaw so long a time.

The day began as usual. Reveille when it still was dark—get out whether you slept or whether worries kept you awake the whole night: you had been separated from your children, from your wife, from your parents, you don't know what happened to them; how could you sleep?

They shouted again: "Get out! The sergeant will be furious!" They came out; some very slow, the old ones, the sick men, some with nervous agility. They fear the sergeant. They hurry as much as they can. In vain! Much too much noise, much too much commotion and not fast enough!

The Feldwebel shouts: *"Achtung! Still gestanden! Na wird's mal, oder soll ich mit dem Gewehrkolben nachhelfen? Na jut; wenn Ihr's durchaus haben wollt!"* ("Attention! Stand still! How about it, or should I help you along with the butt of my rifle? All right, if you really want to have it!")

The sergeant and his subordinates hit everyone: young or old, strong or sick, guilty or innocent—it was painful to hear the groaning and moaning.

I heard it though I had been hit very hard, so hard that I could not help falling down. We all on the ground who could not stand up were then beaten over the head.

I must have been unconscious. The next thing I knew was a soldier saying, "They are all dead!" Whereupon the sergeant ordered to do away with us.

There I lay aside half conscious. It had become very still—fear and pain— Then I heard the sergeant shouting: *"Abzählen!"* ("Count Off!")

They started slowly, and irregularly: One, two, three, four, *"Achtung."* The sergeant shouted again: *"Rascher! Nochmals von vorn anfangen! In einer Minute will ich wissen wieviele ich zur Gaskammer abliefere! Abzählen!"* ("Faster! Once more, start from the beginning! In a minute I will know how many I am going to send off to the gas chamber! Count off!")

They began again, first slowly: one, two, three, four, became faster and faster, so fast that it finally sounded like a stampede of wild horses, and all of a sudden, in the middle of it, they began singing the *Shema Yisroel.*

Shema Yisroel Adonoy elohenoo Adonoy eḥod. Veohavto es Adonoy eloheḥo beḥol levoveḥo ooveḥol nafsheḥo ooveḥol meodeḥo. Vehoyoo haddevoreem hoelleh asher onoḥee metsavveḥo hayyom al levoveḥo. Veshinnantom levoneḥo vedibbarto bom beshivteḥo beveteḥo oovelehteḥo baddereḥ ooveshohbeḥo oovekoomeḥo. ("Hear, O Israel, the Lord our God, the Lord is One! And thou shalt love the Lord thy God with all thy heart, and with all thy soul, and with all thy might. And these words, which I command thee this day, shall be in thy heart. And thou shalt teach them diligently unto thy children, and speak of them when thou sittest in thy house, and when thou goest on the way, and when thou liest down, and when thou risest up.")

[8] ALBAN BERG

Alban Berg (1885–1935), a student of Schoenberg, wrote music that is a unique synthesis of traditional and twentieth-century elements. Berg, who was born in Vienna, first attracted international attention in 1925, when his opera *Wozzeck* was premiered in Berlin; its atonality baffled many critics, but it made a powerful impression on the public and was soon performed throughout Europe and in the United States. Perhaps because of chronic ill health, Berg did not perform or conduct, and he composed relatively few works— these include the *Chamber Concerto*, for piano, violin, and thirteen winds (1925); the *Lyric Suite*, for string quartet (1926); the opera *Lulu* (1929–1935, orchestration not completed); and the Violin Concerto (1935).

WOZZECK (1917–1922)

Wozzeck is the tragic story of a soldier who is driven to murder and madness by a hostile society. An antihero obsessed by strange visions, Wozzeck is persecuted by his sadistic captain, used as a guinea pig by a half-demented doctor, and betrayed by his mistress, Marie. Wozzeck stabs Marie to death and drowns while trying to wash her blood from his hands.

Berg's musical imagination was fired in 1914 when he saw *Woyzeck,* a play by the German dramatist and revolutionary Georg Büchner (1813–1837). Though written in the early 1830s, the play is amazingly modern in its starkly realistic dialogue and disconnected scenes. Berg adapted the play into an opera while in the Austrian army in World War I. His traumatic army experiences may well have deepened his sympathy for Wozzeck.

The opera's nightmarish atmosphere makes it a musical counterpart of expressionist painting and literature. Berg conveys the tensions and torments of the unconscious through harsh dissonances and grotesque distortions. The range of emotions and styles in the music is tremendous. Though most of *Wozzeck* is freely atonal—it does not use the twelve-tone system—major and minor keys occasionally add contrast. The vocal line includes speaking, shrieking, *Sprechstimme,* distorted folk songs, and melodies with wide leaps that are difficult to sing. The gigantic orchestra closely parallels the dialogue and stage action. Descriptive effects include vivid orchestral depiction of the moon rising, frogs croaking, and water engulfing the drowning Wozzeck. Berg's music rapidly shifts between very high and very low registers, between *ffff* and *pppp.*

Wozzeck has three acts, each with five scenes. Connecting the scenes are short orchestral interludes that comment musically on the preceding action and serve as preparation for what is to come. As in the music dramas of

Wagner, there is a continuous musical flow within each act, and characters are associated with specific musical ideas. A novel feature of *Wozzeck* is that the music for each scene is a self-contained composition with a particular form (passacaglia, sonata form, etc.) or of a definite type (military march, lullaby). The five scenes of the last act—we'll study Scenes 4 and 5—are organized as (1) variations on a theme, (2) variations on a single tone, (3) variations on a rhythmic pattern, (4) variations on a chord, and (5) variations on continuous running notes. But Berg did not intend for the listener to concentrate on or even be aware of these unifying techniques. He wanted the audience to be caught up in the opera's dramatic flow.

In Act II, Wozzeck has been driven to desperation by Marie's infidelity and by a savage beating from the man who has slept with her. Near the beginning of Act III, Wozzeck stabs Marie to death as they walk along a forest path near a pond.

Act III: Scenes 4 and 5

Scene 4: A path near a pond

Wozzeck returns to the scene of the crime to dispose of his knife. Berg's orchestra vividly evokes the dark forest scene as a background to Wozzeck's anguished shrieks. Rising harp tones suggest the blood-red moon coming up through the clouds. Wozzeck goes mad and drowns in the pond while trying to wash the blood from his hands. Soft chromatic slides depict the engulfing water as the Captain and the Doctor, Wozzeck's tormentors, indifferently comment that someone is drowning. As Wozzeck drowns, the slides become slower and narrower in range.

[*8-record/cassette set: Side 14, band 1*]

The long orchestral interlude that follows is a deeply moving expression of grief for Wozzeck's tragic fate. It recalls the musical themes associated with his life. Berg described it as "a confession of the author stepping outside the dramatic events of the theater and appealing to the public as representing mankind." For this outpouring of compassion, Berg returns to tonality (the interlude is in D minor) and the musical language of late romanticism.

Scene 5: A street before Marie's door

Children are playing in front of Marie's house; bright sunshine brings glaring contrast to the darkness of the preceding scenes. One of the children cruelly tells Wozzeck's son: "Hey! Your mother is dead." The boy rides off on his hobby horse with the other children to see the body. The orchestra is reduced in size to produce delicate sounds that match the children's high voices, and a continuous rhythm symbolizes their utter indifference. The opera does not end with a conclusive chord. It simply breaks off as though to suggest that the tragedy could begin again.

[*8-record/cassette set: Side 14, band 1 cont.*]

Scene 4

Winds, *p,* repeated chord.

(Forest path by the pond. Moonlit night as before. Wozzeck staggers on hastily, and then stops as he searches for something.)

Wozzeck

Spoken.

Das Messer? Wo ist das Messer? Ich hab's dagelassen . . . Näher, noch näher. Mir graut's! Da regt sich was.

Where is it? Where has the knife gone? Somewhere here I left it . . . Somewhere here, somewhere. Oh! Horror! There something moved!

Shouted.

Still! Alles still und tot . . . Mörder! Mörder! Ha! Da ruft's. Nein, ich selbst.

Still! All is still and dead! . . . Murder! Murder! Ah, who cried? No, 'twas me.

(Still searching, he staggers forward a few more steps, and comes on the corpse.)

Marie! Marie! Was hast Du für eine rote Schnur um den Hals? Hast Dir das rote Halsband verdient, wie die Ohrringlein, mit Deiner Sünde! Was hängen Dir die schwarzen Haare so wild? Mörder! Mörder! Sie werden nach mir suchen . . . Das Messer verrät mich! Da, da ist's. So! Da hinunter. Es taucht ins dunkle Wasser wie ein Stein.

Marie! Marie! What is that so like a crimson cord round your neck? And was that crimson necklace well earned, like the gold earrings: the price of sinning! Why hangs your fine black hair so wild on your head? Murder! Murder! For me they'll soon be searching . . . That knife will betray me! *(Seeks it feverishly.)* Ah! It's here! *(At the pond.)* Down to the bottom! *(Throws the knife in.)* It sinks through deep dark water like a stone.

Rising harp tones, *pp.*

(The moon comes up blood-red through the clouds.)

Aber der Mond verrät mich . . . der Mond ist blutig. Will denn die ganze Welt es ausplaudern?!—Das Messer, es liegt zu weit vorn, sie finden's beim Baden oder wenn sie nach Muscheln tauchen. Ich find's nicht . . . Aber ich muss mich waschen. Ich bin blutig. Da ein Fleck . . . und noch einer. Weh! Weh!

See how the moon betrays me . . . the moon is bloody! Must then the whole wide world be blabbing it?— The knife there, too near to the shore! They'll find it when bathing, maybe when they are mussel-gathering. *(He wades into the pond.)* It's gone now. I ought to wash my body. I am bloody. Here's a spot . . . and here . . . something. Woe! Woe!

Water music.

Ich wasche mich mit Blut! Das Wasser ist Blut . . . Blut . . .

I wash myself with blood! The water is blood . . . blood . . .

Upward orchestral slides, *pp.* Rhythm gradually slows.

(He drowns.)

(After a short time the Doctor enters, followed by the Captain.)

Captain

Spoken.

Halt!

Stop!

Doctor
(Stands still.)

Hören Sie? Dort! Do you hear? There!

Captain
(Stands still.)

Jesus! Das war ein Ton. Heavens! There was a sound.

Doctor
(Pointing to the pond.)

Ja, dort! Yes, there!

Captain

Es ist das Wasser im Teich. Das Wasser ruft. Es ist schon lange Niemand ertrunken. Kommen Sie, Doktor! Es ist nicht gut zu hören. It is the water in the pond. The water calls. It is a long time since anyone was drowned. Come, Doctor, this is not good to hear.

(He tries to drag off the Doctor.)

Doctor
(Stands still and listens.)

Das stöhnt . . . als stürbe ein Mensch. Da ertrinkt Jemand! It groans . . . like a dying man. There's someone drowning!

Captain

Unheimlich! Der Mond rot und die Nebel grau. Hören Sie? . . . Jetzt wieder das Ächzen. It's uncanny! The moon is red, and the mist is grey. Do you hear? . . . That groaning again. Celesta.

Doctor

Stiller, . . . jetzt ganz still. It's getting softer . . . and now quite gone.

Captain

Kommen Sie! Kommen Sie schnell. Come away! Quick!

(Drags the Doctor off with him.)

Extended orchestral interlude.

Scene 5
(Street before Marie's door. Bright morning. Sunshine. Children are playing and shouting. Marie's child is riding a hobby-horse.)

Children

Ringel, Ringel, Rosenkranz, Ringelreih'n! Ring-a-ring-a-roses, all fall down!

Ringel, Ringel, Rosenkranz, Rin . . . Ring-a-ring-a-roses, all . . .

(They stop, and other children come rushing on.)

One of them

Du Käthe! . . . Die Marie . . .　　　　Katie! . . . Marie . . .

Second Child

Was is?　　　　What is it?

First Child

Weisst' es nit? Sie sind schon Alle 'naus.　　Don't you know? They've all gone out there.

Third Child

(To Marie's child.)

Du! Dein Mutter ist tot!　　　　Hey! Your mother is dead.

Marie's Child

(Still riding his horse.)

Hopp, hopp! Hopp, hopp! Hopp, hopp!　　　　Hop, hop! Hop, hop! Hop, hop!

Second Child

Wo is sie denn?　　　　Where is she now?

First Child

Draus liegt sie, am Weg, neben dem Teich.　　Out there, on the path by the pond.

Third Child

Kommt, anschaun!　　　　Let's go and look!

(All the children run off.)

Marie's Child

(Continues to ride.)

Hopp, hopp! Hopp, hopp! Hopp, hopp!　　　　Hop, hop! Hop, hop! Hop, hop!

Music breaks off.　　(He hesitates a moment, and then rides off after the other children.)

TWENTIETH CENTURY

9

ANTON WEBERN

Anton Webern (1883–1945) was neglected during his lifetime, though his music influenced composers throughout the world during the 1950s and 1960s. He was born in Vienna; studied piano, cello, and music theory as a young man; and earned a doctorate in music history from the University of

Vienna. While at the university, he studied composition privately with Schoenberg. His career was solid but unspectacular: he made a modest income conducting various choruses and orchestras, though the rare performances of his own works were usually met with ridicule. He was a shy man, devoted to his family, and a Christian mystic who loved to commune with nature.

Although his life seems ordinary enough, his death was a bizarre tragedy—he was shot by mistake by an American soldier toward the end of World War II.

WEBERN'S MUSIC

Poetic lyricism pervades Webern's music, which is amazingly original in its brevity, quietness, and concentration. Most of his works are miniatures lasting only 2 or 3 minutes, and virtually all of his mature output fits onto four long-playing records—rarely has a composer achieved such world-wide influence on the basis of so little music.

About half of Webern's music is for solo voice or chorus; the rest is for chamber orchestra and small chamber groups. He wrote atonal works at about the same time as Schoenberg (starting in 1908–1909) and adopted the twelve-tone system soon after Schoenberg developed it. He also exploited Schoenberg's idea of a "melody built of tone colors." His melodic lines are "atomized" into two- or three-note fragments which may at first seem isolated but add up to a unified whole. He forces us to focus on the tone color, dynamic level, and register of each note. His textures are delicate and transparent; usually not more than a few solo instruments play at once. In his twelve-tone works, there is often strict polyphonic imitation.

Composers in the 1950s and 1960s were fascinated by Webern's techniques and often imitated his deceptively "cool" sound. Works that appealed to very few during his lifetime became a source of inspiration after his death.

FIVE PIECES FOR ORCHESTRA, OP. 10 (1911–1913)

Webern's unique style is fully revealed in his early, atonal Five Pieces for Orchestra, Op. 10, composed before he adopted the twelve-tone system. These five "expressions of musical lyricism," as Webern called them, are among the shortest orchestral compositions ever written. The fourth piece is only 6⅓ measures long and lasts less than 30 seconds. Webern's chamber orchestra of eighteen soloists includes unconventional instruments like the mandolin, guitar, cowbells, and harmonium (a small organ with metal reeds). Each piece (we'll consider the third) is scored for a different number and combination of instruments.

Melodic fragments are whispered by ever-changing solo instruments and framed by poetic silences. Tone-color melodies replace "tunes" in this music. There are few notes, but each is crucial. The tempo constantly fluctuates. Brasses and strings are usually muted.

Third Piece:

Very slow and extremely calm

Side D, band 4

[*8-record/cassette set:*
Side 13, band 7]

With its bell sounds coming as though from far off, the third piece has a feeling of solitude and eerie stillness. The dynamics never rise above *pp*. The sustained bell-like sounds—produced by mandolin, celesta, guitar, harp, glockenspiel, cowbells, chimes, and harmonium—are heard both at the beginning and at the ending. This creates a vague A B A' effect. Melodic fragments in ever-changing solo instruments are set apart from one another by brief moments of near silence.

Listening Outline   To be read while music is heard

THIRD PIECE (1913) FROM FIVE PIECES FOR ORCHESTRA,
OP. 10 (1911–1913), BY ANTON WEBERN

Clarinet, muted French horn, muted trombone, harmonium, mandolin, guitar, celesta, harp, bass drum, snare drum, chimes, cowbells, violin, muted viola, muted cello

Very slow and extremely calm

(About 1½ minutes)

1. *a.* Pulsating bell-like sounds, *ppp.*
    b. Violin, *pp*, pulsating bell-like sounds, *ppp.*
    c. Muted horn, *pp*, chimes, *ppp.*
2. Quicker notes in clarinet. Muted viola.
3. *a.* Pulsating bell-like sounds, *ppp.*
    b. Muted trombone, *ppp;* pulsating bell-like sounds, *ppp.* Snare-drum roll, extremely soft.

TWENTIETH
CENTURY

[10] BÉLA BARTÓK

Béla Bartók (1881–1945), whose music is infused with the spirit of east European folk song, was born in Hungary. His mother gave him his first lessons on the piano, an instrument which was important in his career; he

(© G. D. Hackett, New York)

Caught up in the nationalist movement that swept Hungary, Bartók spent most of his free time in tiny villages recording folk songs on a cylinder phonograph.

taught piano at his alma mater, the Budapest Academy of Music, from 1907 to 1934, and gave recitals throughout Europe. During the early 1900s, Bartók was influenced by the Hungarian nationalist movement and spent most of his free time in small villages recording peasant folk songs. He became an authority on peasant music, and his own music was profoundly influenced by it.

Though he was neglected in Hungary until the Budapest premiere of his ballet *The Wooden Prince* in 1917, Bartók was recognized early as an important composer abroad and had a successful career during the 1920s and 1930s. But he was violently anti-Nazi, and in 1940 he emigrated to the United States, where he was to spend the last five years of his life. This was a bleak period for him: he had little money, was in poor health, and felt isolated and neglected.

In 1943, while in a hospital in New York, he received an unexpected commission for the Concerto for Orchestra, now his best-known work; and its success resulted in a series of other commissions. Tragically, however, Bartók had only a year to live and could complete just two more compositions, the Sonata for Solo Violin (1944) and the Third Piano Concerto (1945). Soon after his death in New York in 1945, he became one of the most popular twentieth-century composers.

BARTÓK'S MUSIC

"I do not reject any influence," wrote Bartók, "provided it be pure, fresh, and healthy"; but he emphasized that the "Hungarian influence is the strongest." He evolved a completely individual style that fused folk elements, classical forms, and twentieth-century sounds. He did arrange many folk tunes (often with highly dissonant accompaniments), but in most of his works he does not quote folk melodies—he uses original themes that have a folk flavor.

Bartók's genius found its most characteristic expression in instrumental music; he wrote many works for piano solo, six string quartets (which are widely thought to be the finest since Beethoven's) and other chamber music, three piano concertos, one violin concerto, and several pieces for orchestra. His music embraces a wide range of emotions and is deeply expressive; and he revitalized and reinterpreted traditional forms such as the rondo, fugue, and sonata form.

He always organized his works around a tonal center; but within this framework he often used harsh dissonances, polychords, and tone clusters (though some of his late works have a more traditional, less dissonant vocabulary). Rhythmically, his music is characterized by a powerful beat, unexpected accents, and changing meters. He was imaginative in his use of tone colors, particularly of percussion instruments—in Music for Strings, Percussion, and Celesta (1936), for example, he drew unusual sounds from the xylophone and timpani. Like many other twentieth-century composers, he also drew percussive, drumlike sounds from the piano.

CONCERTO FOR ORCHESTRA (1943)

The commission which led to the Concerto for Orchestra was offered to Bartók in 1943, while he was hospitalized in New York City. Serge Koussevitzky, the conductor of the Boston Symphony Orchestra, offered him a $1,000 commission for a new work. While recuperating at Saranac Lake, New York, Bartók was able to work "practically day and night" on his new composition. He finished it in six weeks. The Concerto for Orchestra was an enormous success at its premiere in Boston in 1944 and has since become Bartók's most popular work.

"The general mood of the work," wrote Bartók, "represents, apart from the jesting second movement, a gradual transition from the sternness of the first movement and the lugubrious death-song of the third, to the life-assertion of the last one." Bartók explained that the unusual title *Concerto for Orchestra* reflects the work's "tendency to treat the single orchestral instruments in a *concertant* or soloistic manner."

Indeed, the Concerto for Orchestra is a showpiece for an orchestra of virtuosos. It is romantic in spirit because of its emotional intensity, memorable themes, and vivid contrasts of mood. Though its melodies were original with Bartók, they have a distinct folk flavor. The concerto is an example of Bartók's mellow "late" style, which is characterized by more frequent use of traditional chords. In all five movements, time-honored procedures like A B A form, sonata form, and fugue are fused with twentieth-century rhythms and tone colors. We'll study the second movement.

Second Movement: Game of Pairs
Allegretto scherzando

The jesting second movement, *Game of Pairs*, which is in A B A' form, is a "game" involving different pairs of woodwind and brass instruments. The instruments of each pair move in parallel motion and are separated by a distinctive pitch interval. In the opening section (A), a chain of five melodies is played consecutively by pairs of bassoons, oboes, clarinets, flutes, and muted trumpets. The contrasting middle section (B) is a hymnlike melody softly played by brass instruments. When the opening section returns (A'), it has a more active accompaniment. The incisive sound of a side drum (without snares) is prominent throughout the movement. It plays syncopated solos at both the beginning and the end, as well as in the hymnlike middle section.

Side D, band 5

[*8-record/cassette set:*
  Side 14, band 2]

Listening Outline   To be read while music is heard

CONCERTO FOR ORCHESTRA (1943), BY BÉLA BARTÓK

Second Movement: Game of Pairs (Allegretto scherzando)

A B A' form, duple meter ($\frac{2}{4}$)

2 flutes, 2 oboes, 2 clarinets, 3 bassoons, 4 French horns, 2 trumpets, 2 trombones, tuba, timpani, side drum, 2 harps, 1st violins, 2d violins, violas, cellos, double basses

(About 6½ minutes)

A
1. Solo side drum (without snares), *mf*.
2. Two bassoons, *p*, accompanied by pizzicato strings.
3. *a.* Two oboes, *p*, in higher register. Pizzicato strings accompany.
   b. Low strings, pizzicato, while oboes sustain tones.
4. *a.* Two clarinets.
   b. Low strings, accented notes.
5. *a.* Two flutes, *mf*, in higher register.
   b. Low strings, pizzicato, while flutes sustain tones.
6. Two muted trumpets, *p*. Muted string tremolos, *pp*, in background.

1. *a.* Brasses, *mf*, hymnlike legato melody. Side drum accompanies.
   b. French horns, *p*, conclude hymnlike melody and sustain chord.
2. Oboe, flute, and clarinet, *p*, lead to
1. Two bassoons, *p*, opening melody. Staccato third bassoon in background.
2. *a.* Two oboes, *p*, in higher register. Clarinets and strings in background.
   b. Low strings, pizzicato, while oboes sustain tones.
3. *a.* Two clarinets. Flutes and strings in background.
   b. Low strings, accented notes.
4. *a.* Two flutes, *mf*, in higher register. Woodwinds and strings in background.
   b. Low strings, pizzicato, while flutes sustain tones.
5. Two muted trumpets, *mf*. Harp glissandos and muted string tremolos in background.
6. Woodwinds, *p*, repeated chord; solo side drum, decrescendo, ends *Game of Pairs*.

11 CHARLES IVES

The American composer Charles Ives (1874–1954) wrote startlingly original music that was far ahead of its time. He was born in Danbury, Connecticut, the son of a bandmaster who loved to experiment with unusual sounds ("Pa taught me what I know," he later recalled), and he studied composition at Yale University. But when he graduated, he entered the insurance business, having decided that he could keep his music "stronger, cleaner, bigger, and freer" if he did not try to make a living out of it. (He also said that he did not want to raise a family who would "starve on his dissonances.") Eventually he founded a successful insurance agency and became very wealthy.

Ives composed furiously after business hours, on weekends, and on holidays, in isolation from the musical world; he was completely unknown, none of his major works was publicly performed, and his scores accumulated in the barn of his Connecticut farm. World War I dampened his creative urge, however, and in 1918 he had a heart attack from which he never completely recovered; after 1921 he composed almost nothing but instead began to make his work known to the public.

From 1920 to 1922, he privately printed and distributed his monumental *Concord* Sonata (1909–1915) for piano and his collection *114 Songs*; at first, they aroused little more than ridicule, but gradually a few young composers and performers recognized that Ives was enormously original. In 1939, the *Concord* Sonata received an ovation at its first complete New York performance; and by the 1940s, many considered Ives the first great composer from the United States. In 1947 he won a Pulitzer Prize for his Third Symphony (1904–1911), written some forty years earlier.

IVES'S MUSIC

Though experimental, Ives's compositions are rooted deeply in the folk and popular music he knew as a boy: revival hymns, ragtime, village bands, church choirs, patriotic songs, and barn dances. He was inspired by the "unconventional" features of the American tradition—the village fiddler playing slightly out of tune, the cornetist a fraction ahead of the rest of the band, the church organist accidentally holding one chord while the choir sings another. His polyrhythms, polytonality, and tone clusters grew out of the music he knew. One boyhood experience in particular seems to have had an important influence: two bands playing different music passed each other as they marched by him in opposite directions. In later works Ives simultaneously presents musical events that seem unrelated: two bands play in different keys; consonant chords are set against dissonant chords; conflicting meters and rhythmic patterns are intertwined. To evoke memories, he often quotes snatches of familiar tunes, develops them, and integrates them within his music. Even the titles of his works suggest his New England heritage—for example, the movements of the *Concord* Sonata are *Emerson*, *Hawthorne*, *The Alcotts*, and *Thoreau*; and we'll study one movement from a set of orchestral pieces called *Three Places in New England*.

Charles Ives.

(Omikron/Photo Researchers)

Ives's music has a wide range of emotions, styles, and musical techniques; it includes mild, consonant chords and earsplitting dissonances. (He scorned those who couldn't take dissonance: "Beauty in music," he wrote, "is too often confused with something that lets the ears lie back in an easy chair.") Much of his music is extraordinarily difficult to perform. His large and varied output includes five symphonies and other orchestral music; works for piano, chorus, and chamber ensembles; and over 200 songs.

PUTNAM'S CAMP, REDDING, CONNECTICUT (1903–1911), FROM THREE PLACES IN NEW ENGLAND (1903–1914)

Putnam's Camp, Redding, Connecticut, is part of *Three Places in New England,* a set of three movements for orchestra evoking American history, life, and landscape. Though completed in 1914, *Three Places in New England* was not performed until 1930, when it was booed and hissed at its premiere in Boston. Today, it is one of Ives's most popular works and a landmark in American music.

[8-record/cassette set: Side 14, band 3]

The daring and brilliant second movement, *Putnam's Camp,* is a child's impression of a Fourth of July picnic. Ives recaptures his boyhood memory of two marching bands clashing dissonantly as they play different tunes. He quotes many fragments from once well-known marches by John Philip Sousa (1854–1932), the American composer nicknamed the "march king."

273

Snatches of patriotic songs and folklike tunes written by Ives contribute to the piece's popular flavor.

In his preface to this score, Ives wrote, "Near Redding Center, Conn., is a small park preserved as a Revolutionary Memorial; for here General Israel Putnam's soldiers had their winter quarters in 1778–1779." One Fourth of July, "a child went there on a picnic held under the auspices of the First Church and the Village Cornet Band." The child wanders "away from the rest of the children past the camp ground into the woods. As he rests on the hillside of laurel and hickories, the tunes of the band and the songs of the children grow fainter. . . ." He falls asleep and dreams of the discouraged American soldiers breaking camp, marching out "with fife and drum to a popular tune of the day. Suddenly a new national note is heard. Putnam is coming over the hills from the center,—the soldiers turn back and cheer. The little boy awakes, he hears the children's songs and runs down past the monument to 'listen to the band' and join in the games and dances."

Putnam's Camp is in three sections (A B A') that parallel the descriptive program. The first, marked *quick step time*, captures the gaiety and confusion of a Fourth of July picnic in a nineteenth-century town. After a raucous, highly dissonant introduction, the strings play the main theme, a vigorous march that begins with conventional harmonies.

Such abrupt shifts between harsh dissonances and mild-sounding consonances are typical of Ives and are heard throughout *Putnam's Camp*. The piano, woodwinds, and brasses begin to compete for the listener's attention, and soon it sounds as though two bands are playing against each other. The mood becomes even more comic when a parody of the opening phrase of *Yankee Doodle* is quickly played by the trumpet, flute, and violins.

After more orchestral confusion, the music gradually becomes softer and slows to a halt, depicting the child as he falls asleep.

A mysterious high chord in the strings ushers in the middle section, which depicts the child's dream. Repeated piano and drum beats that seem out of phase with the rest of the orchestra begin one of the boldest parts of the score. Ives creates the impression of two bands playing at different tempos. (One band employs strings and woodwinds; the other has piano, drums, and trumpet.) Here the conductor must beat four bars with one hand against three bars in the other. The bands merge, and we hear a flute playing *The British Grenadiers*, a favorite tune of the Revolutionary army.

The riotous concluding section creates deliberate melodic and rhythmic confusion as the main march theme is combined with *The British Grenadiers* and other fragments. *Putnam's Camp* ends with an earsplitting dissonant chord. (In some recordings, the raucous sounds at the end drown out Ives's quotation from *The Star-Spangled Banner* in the last two bars.)

GEORGE GERSHWIN

TWENTIETH CENTURY

12

Popular songs and musical comedies as well as jazz-flavored orchestral works and opera won international fame for the American composer George Gershwin (1898–1937). His parents were Russian-Jewish immigrants, and he grew up on the lower east side of Manhattan. As a boy, he taught himself to play hit tunes on a neighbor's piano; when he was thirteen, he began studying with a teacher who recognized his talent and introduced him to piano works ranging from Bach to Liszt to Debussy.

At fifteen, he left school to become a pianist demonstrating new songs in the salesrooms of a music publisher; three years later, he started his own career as a songwriter, and in 1919 (at the age of twenty) he wrote *La, La, Lucille*, his first complete Broadway musical. The next year, his song *Swanee* was a tremendous hit; during the 1920s and 1930s he wrote one brilliant musical after another—including *Lady, Be Good* (1924), *Funny Face* (1927), and *Of Thee I Sing* (1931)—usually with his brother Ira as lyricist.

Gershwin was not only a creator of the golden age of American musical theater but also a successful composer of music for the concert hall, beginning with the triumphant premiere of *Rhapsody in Blue* in 1924. He gave the first performance of his Concerto in F at Carnegie Hall in 1925 and traveled to Europe in the 1920s (meeting Berg in Vienna and Ravel and Stravinsky in Paris); part of his symphonic poem *An American in Paris* (1928) was composed on one of these visits. His most extended work is the opera *Porgy and Bess* (1935), which deals with the lives of poor black people in Charleston, South Carolina, and has been performed all over the world.

Gershwin was outgoing, a sportsman, an art collector and amateur painter, and irresistible to women; he was also wealthy, from royalties,

(Bettmann Archive)

George Gershwin.

concert fees, and his weekly radio show. During the last year of his life, he lived in Hollywood, where he wrote the music for several movies (and played tennis with Arnold Schoenberg in his spare time). He died of a brain tumor at the age of thirty-eight.

RHAPSODY IN BLUE (1924)

[*Instructor's records:*
Side 3, band 3]

Rhapsody in Blue, Gershwin's most famous composition, is a one-movement work for piano and orchestra. The title reflects its free, rhapsodic form and blues flavor (see page 297 for a description of the blues). But it is not true jazz, though it employs jazzlike rhythms and melodies and the orchestration suggests the distinctive sounds of jazz. There are three main sections and a coda; the extended piano solos in the main sections reflect Gershwin's own dazzling pianism and his genius as an improviser.

The *Rhapsody* opens with a now-famous clarinet solo that starts from a low trill, climbs the scale, and then slides up to a high "wailing" tone. The blueslike opening theme, which grows out of the clarinet slide, is marked by the syncopations so typical of Gershwin's style. It is followed by a repeated-note theme, presented by French horns, which reappears many times. A new jazzlike theme, introduced in the low register, begins the lively second section, marked *con moto*. The moderately slow third section is based on a lyrical, romantic melody first presented by the violins. This memorable tune is combined with a countermelody played by the French horns. The rapid coda is ushered in by an accelerated transformation of the romantic melody. (In item 2*b* in the listening outline, several words are enclosed in brackets because the corresponding short passage for orchestra and piano is sometimes omitted in performance.)

Listening Outline   To be read while music is heard

RHAPSODY IN BLUE (1924), BY GEORGE GERSHWIN

B flat major

Solo piano, 2 flutes, 2 oboes, 2 clarinets, bass clarinet, 2 bassoons, 2 alto saxophones, tenor saxophone, 3 French horns, 3 trumpets, 3 trombones, tuba, timpani, bass drum, snare drum, cymbals, gong, triangle, 1st violins, 2d violins, violas, cellos, double basses

(About 15 minutes)

    1. a. Clarinet, *p*, trill, upward scale and slide (glissando) to blues theme, *mf*, moderate tempo.

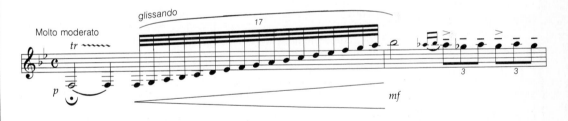

Repeated-note theme, faster tempo, French horns and woodwinds, *mf.*

Clarinet, *p*, trill, upward scale to blues theme in muted trumpet, *mf*, piano joins, crescendo to blues theme in full orchestra, *ff*, cymbal crashes.

b. Extended piano solo, begins *p*, fast repeated chords, *f*, upward scale to blues theme, low instruments join, piano alone, *p*, crescendo to brilliant rushing notes, fast repeated chords, *ff*.

c. Full orchestra, *ff*, blues theme in faster tempo, piano joins, strings, crescendo to blues theme in trombones, *f*, trumpets, *ff*.

d. Trumpet theme, marchlike beat in drums, piano.

Clarinet, *p*, repeated-note theme, piano, rushing notes, full orchestra, *ff*, repeated-note theme, piano chords, solo clarinet, "wha-wha" muted trumpet and trombone solos, orchestra, *ff*, cymbals, pause.

2. a. Orchestra, *f*, jazzlike theme in low register, steady beat in drums, piano chords.

Rising brass phrase, crescendo to full orchestra, *ff*, jazzlike theme in high register, piano joins, crescendo.

b. Extended piano solo, varied repeated-note theme, horn, *p*, accompanies piano,
[oboe, blues theme, piano running notes, faster tempo].
Extended piano solo, jazzlike theme in low register, steady beat, jazzlike theme in high register, *ff*, brilliant ascending running notes, descending octaves, *ff*, sudden *pp*, ascending phrases, pause.

3. a. Strings, *p*, romantic theme, horns, *p*, moderate tempo, high violin solo.

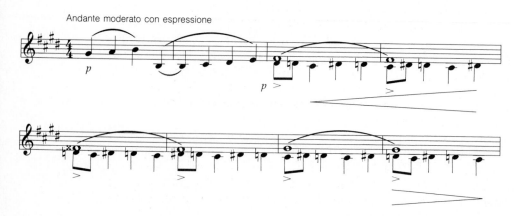

b. Full orchestra, *ff,* romantic theme, drumrolls, cymbals, piano joins, bells.
c. Extended piano solo, romantic theme, very fast repeated notes, brilliant ascending scale to
4. *a.* Brasses and piano, accelerated romantic theme, brass swells and sustained chord, *fff.*

b. Piano and orchestra, rising chromatic scale, crescendo, ritardando.
c. Piano and orchestra, *ff,* repeated-note theme, ritardando.
d. Full orchestra, *fff,* blues theme, cymbal crashes, piano chords, crescendo to final orchestral chord, *ff.*

AARON COPLAND

Aaron Copland (b. 1900), a leading American composer, was born in Brooklyn; his parents (like Gershwin's) were Russian-Jewish immigrants. "No one ever talked music to me or took me to a concert," he recalled; but he discovered music on his own and at fifteen decided to become a composer. He was drawn to "modern" music, although his first teacher discouraged it; and in 1921 he went to France to study with Nadia Boulanger, an extraordinary woman who taught several generations of American composers and was sympathetic to contemporary trends.

Copland's music went through several phases. When he first returned to New York, he wanted to write works that would be "American in character"—and to him, *American* meant jazz. An example is his *Music for the Theater* (1925), a piece for small orchestra with elements of blues and ragtime; but this "jazz period" lasted only a few years. During the early 1930s he composed serious, very dissonant, sophisticated works (such as the highly regarded *Piano Variations,* 1930) that convey starkness, power, percussiveness, and intense concentration.

In the late 1930s, he modified his style again, writing more accessible works for a larger audience. These were the depression years, when many composers rejected the idea of writing for an elite, and Copland now drew on American folklore—as in his ballets *Billy the Kid* (1938), *Rodeo* (1942), and *Appalachian Spring* (1944)—and on jazz, revival hymns, cowboy

279

(Marianne Barcellona)

Aaron Copland.

songs, and other folk tunes. His scores for films and his patriotic works (such as *A Lincoln Portrait*, 1942) also reached a mass public, and his name became synonymous with American music.

Copland accomplished the difficult feat of writing simple yet highly professional music. His textures are clear; his slow-moving harmonies—often almost motionless—seem to evoke the openness of the American landscape; and, though strongly tonal, his works embody twentieth-century techniques such as polychords, polyrhythms, changing meters, and percussive orchestration. He has also used serial technique (the manipulation of a tone row, or series) in such works as *Connotations* for orchestra (1962).

Aside from his numerous compositions, Copland has made many other contributions to American music by directing composers' groups, organizing concerts, lecturing, writing books and articles, teaching, and conducting.

APPALACHIAN SPRING (1943–1944)

Appalachian Spring originated as a ballet score for Martha Graham, the great modern dancer and choreographer. It took Copland about a year to finish the music. While composing *Appalachian Spring*, he thought, "How foolhardy it is to be spending all this time writing a thirty-five-minute score for a modern-dance company, knowing how short-lived most ballets *and* their scores are." But Copland arranged parts of the ballet as a suite for full orchestra (originally, the ballet used only thirteen instrumentalists) that won important prizes and brought his name to a large public. Today, *Appalachian Spring* is widely performed both as a ballet and as a concert piece.

The ballet concerns a "pioneer celebration in spring around a newly built farmhouse in the Pennsylvania hills" in the early 1800s. The rhythms and melodies are American-sounding and suggest barn dances, fiddle tunes, and revival hymns. But Copland uses only one actual folk tune in the score—a Shaker melody entitled *Simple Gifts*. (The Shakers were a religious sect established in America around the time of the Revolution. They expressed religious fervor through shaking, leaping, dancing, and singing.) *Appalachian Spring* is bright and transparent, has a clear tonality, and is basically tender and calm in mood. The score's rhythmic excitement comes from delightful syncopations and rapid changes of meter. As in many twentieth-century works, the orchestra contains a piano and a large percussion section, including xylophone, snare drum, wood block, and glockenspiel. The eight sections of the suite follow one another without pause; we'll examine section 7.

Copland composed the music for Martha Graham's ballet Appalachian Spring.

(Arnold Eagle)

Side C, band 6

[*8-record/cassette set:*
  Side 14, band 4]

Section 7: Variations on Simple Gifts

In his synopsis of the score, Copland describes section 7 as "Calm and flowing. Scenes of daily activity for the Bride and her Farmer-husband." There are five variations on the Shaker melody *Simple Gifts*. The theme is introduced by a clarinet.

Variation 1: An oboe presents the theme "a trifle faster" and in a higher register.

Variation 2: Against high sounds in the piano and harp, the violas play the theme at half its previous speed. Then the violins and cellos in turn imitate the theme, creating a polyphonic texture. A brief transition leads to

Variation 3: Trumpets and trombones proclaim the theme at twice the speed of variation 2, against rapid notes in the strings.

Variation 4: Woodwinds quietly play the second part of the theme at a tempo "a trifle slower" than the preceding variation.

Variation 5: The first part of the theme is majestically played *fff* by the full orchestra.

[TWENTIETH
CENTURY
14]

MUSICAL STYLES SINCE 1950

Since World War II, we have lived with instant communication—television, computers, and space satellites provide access to a virtually unlimited flow of information. Not only have we been bombarded by an incredible variety of stimuli, but there has also been a constant demand for novelty. New styles in fashion and the visual arts spread rapidly and then disappear.

In music as well, emphasis has been on novelty and change. Musical innovations since 1950 have been even more far-reaching than those of the earlier 1900s. There have been many new directions, and the range of musical styles and systems is wider than ever. As the American composer Hugo Weisgall has observed, "Many composers today change their musical points of view with astonishing rapidity, composing this way and that, moving easily from complete traditionalism into the 'avant' *avant garde*."

CHARACTERISTICS OF MUSIC SINCE 1950

Accurately describing the recent past is a difficult task. Yet any overview of music since 1950 must include the following major developments:

1. Increased use of the twelve-tone system
2. Composition of music in which the techniques of the twelve-tone system are used to organize rhythm, dynamics, and tone color (*serialism*)
3. Spread of *chance music,* in which a composer chooses pitches, tone colors, and rhythms by random methods, or allows a performer to choose much of the musical material
4. Composition of *minimalist music,* characterized by a steady pulse, clear tonality, and insistent repetition of short melodic patterns
5. Composition of works containing deliberate quotations from earlier music; and a return to tonality by some composers
6. Development of electronic music
7. Greater exploitation of noiselike sounds ("liberation of sound")
8. Use of mixed media
9. New concepts of rhythm and form

Since 1950, long-playing records and audiotape have spread these new musical ideas far and wide.

Increased Use of the Twelve-Tone System

A striking development after World War II (1945) was the gradual abandonment of tonality in favor of the twelve-tone system. From the early 1920s—when Schoenberg invented the system—to about 1950, most composers still wrote music with a tonal center. Few were attracted to the new method, because it was associated with Schoenberg's expressionist style, which had gone out of fashion. During the 1950s, however, the twelve-tone system was adopted by many composers, including Stravinsky, who had been the leading composer of tonal music.

The most important reason for this dramatic shift was probably composers' discovery that the system was a compositional technique rather than a special musical style, and that diversity and individuality were possible within it. The system also had the advantage of stimulating unconventional approaches to melody, harmony, and form: Aaron Copland said once, "I began to hear chords that I wouldn't have heard otherwise."

Many composers of the 1950s and 1960s wrote music that was stylistically reminiscent of Webern, whose lean, "modern" sound appealed to the postwar generation. (Schoenberg's works, by contrast, were considered too "romantic" and traditional in form.)

Extensions of the Twelve-Tone System: Serialism

The twelve-tone system was originally used to organize pitch; but during the later 1940s and 1950s, its techniques were also used to organize rhythm, dynamics, tone color, and other dimensions of music. For example, a rhythmic or dynamic series might be manipulated like a twelve-tone row. Use of a series—an ordered group of musical elements—to organize several dimensions of a composition is called *serialism*. Proponents of serialism include Milton Babbitt (American, b. 1919), Karlheinz Stockhausen (German, b. 1928), and Pierre Boulez (French, b. 1925). Their methods produce totally controlled and organized music; but the complex relationships in it are often difficult to perceive, and the actual sound may seem random and chaotic.

Chance Music

Chance, or *aleatory, music* (from the Latin *alea*, or *game of dice*) is the opposite of serialism. In chance music, composers choose pitches, tone colors, and rhythms by random methods, such as flipping a coin or having the performers choose the ordering of the musical material or even much of the material itself. For example, performers might be told to play certain passages in any order they like, or to invent rhythmic patterns for a given group of pitches.

The most famous and influential creator of chance music is the American John Cage (b. 1912), who has said, "I try to arrange my composing means so that I won't have any knowledge of what might happen. . . . My purpose is to eliminate purpose." Cage's approach is illustrated by his *Imaginary Landscape No. 4* (1951) for twelve radios. The score gives precise instructions to the performers—two at each radio—for turning the dials to affect wavelength and volume, but these instructions disregard local station frequencies and the time of performance, and Cage chose them by throwing dice. With Cage's work as an example, some serial composers (including Boulez and Stockhausen) introduced elements of chance into their compositions during the mid-1950s.

Chance music makes a complete break from traditional values in music—it asserts, in effect, that one sound or ordering of sounds is as meaningful as another.

Minimalist Music

Minimalism—an artistic movement of the mid-1960s—was partly a reaction against the complexity of serialism and the randomness of chance music. *Minimalist music* is characterized by steady pulse, clear tonality, and insistent repetition of short melodic patterns. Its dynamics, textures, and harmony stay constant for long stretches of time, creating a trancelike or hypnotic effect. Leading minimalist composers, such as Terry Riley (b. 1935), Steve Reich (b. 1936), and Philip Glass (b. 1937), have been profoundly influenced by nonwestern thought and music. Their work grew out of the same intellectual climate as minimalist art, which features simple forms, clarity, and understatement.

Minimalist composers have generally tried to reach the widest possible audience; Reich and Glass, for example, have ensembles which perform in both auditoriums and rock clubs. After the early 1970s, minimalist music became progressively richer in harmony, tone color, and texture; and an important turning point in public acceptance came in New York in 1976, when Reich's *Music for 18 Musicians* received an ovation in Town Hall and Glass's opera *Einstein on the Beach* sold out the Metropolitan Opera House.

Musical Quotation and the Return to Tonality

Since the mid-1960s, many composers have made extensive use of quotations from earlier music, usually fairly familiar works of the eighteenth, nineteenth, and twentieth centuries. "Quotation music" often represents a conscious break with serialism as well as an attempt to improve the communication between composer and listener. The quoted material usually conveys a symbolic meaning or is varied, transformed, and juxtaposed with other music. For example, one section of *Sinfonia* (1968), a composition for voices and orchestra by Luciano Berio (Italian, b. 1925), is based on the scherzo of Mahler's Second Symphony, with fragments of music by Bach, Debussy, Ravel, Berlioz, Schoenberg, and others superimposed. Often, composers juxtapose heterogeneous material; George Crumb (American, b. 1929) has said that in writing his song cycle *Ancient Voices of Children* (1970), he "was conscious of an urge to fuse various unrelated stylistic elements, . . . Flamenco with a Baroque quotation . . . or Mahler with a breath of the orient."

[*8-record/cassette set:*
Side 15, band 3]

Occasionally, modern composers also imitate earlier styles. In the String Quartet No. 3 (1972) by George Rochberg (American, b. 1918), there are atonal sections but also passages in the styles of Beethoven and Mahler.

Paralleling the use of musical quotation is the return to tonality in some recent music. Some works are entirely tonal; others, although basically atonal, contain traditional chord progressions that give a fleeting sense of stability. Tonality could be a fascinating "new" option for composers trained in the twelve-tone system.

Electronic Music

Since the development of tape studios, synthesizers, and computers in the 1950s and 1960s (see page 24 in Part I), composers have had potentially unlimited resources for the production and control of sound. Electronic music is as diverse as nonelectronic music; it includes rock, chance music, and serial compositions.

For the first time, composers no longer need intermediaries—that is, performers—since the audiotape of a composition *is* the composition. But many composers "humanize" their electronic music by combining taped sounds with live performers in various ways, and there are works for traditional instruments and electronic synthesizers that are played "live." Traditional instruments (such as pianos and violins) may also be "electrified" through amplification.

Electronic music is important not only in itself, but in its influence on musical thought in general. Electronic instruments have suggested new sounds and new forms of rhythmic organization—and have also indicated new boundaries and limits. Milton Babbitt has observed, "Very often we will specify something and discover that the ear can't take [it] in, . . . cannot perceive and differentiate [it] as rapidly and precisely as the synthesizer can produce it and as the loudspeaker can reproduce it."

"Liberation of Sound"

Composers today use a wider variety of sounds than ever before, including many that were once considered undesirable noises. Edgard Varèse (whose *Poème électronique* we'll study) calls this the "liberation of sound . . . the right to make music with any and all sounds."

Electronic music may include environmental sounds, such as thunder, and electronically generated hisses and blips. But composers also draw novel sounds from voices and nonelectronic instruments. Singers may be asked to scream, whisper, laugh, groan, sneeze, etc., or to sing phonetic sounds rather than words. Wind and string players may tap, scrape, and rub the bodies of their instruments. A brass or woodwind player may hum while playing, to produce two pitches at once; a pianist may reach inside the piano to pluck a string and then run a chisel along it. The greatest expansion and experimentation have involved percussion instruments, which outnumber strings and winds in many recent compositions. Traditional percussion instruments are struck with new types of beaters, and unconventional instruments—tom-toms, bongos, slapsticks, maracas, and so on—are widely used.

In the search for novel sounds, increased use has been made of *microtones*, intervals smaller than the half step. (Microtones have long been used in nonwestern music but have only recently become important in western music.) Composers such as Krzysztof Penderecki (Polish, b. 1933) create sounds bordering on electronic noise through tone clusters—

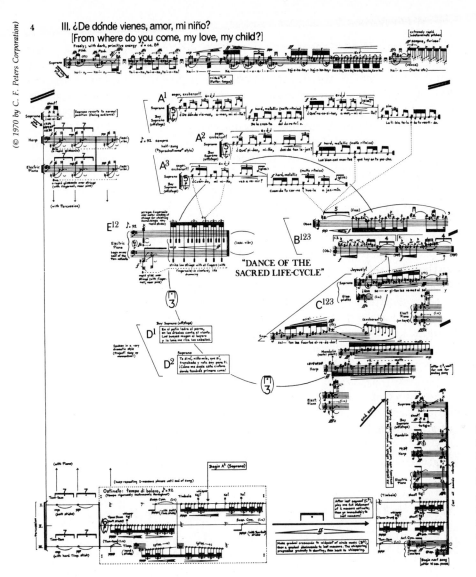

(© 1970 by C. F. Peters Corporation)

Scores for recent music often contain notes in new shapes, or new symbols, as well as novel ways of arranging notation on the page. Here is a page from the score of Ancient Voices of Children, by George Crumb.

closely spaced tones played together and heard as a mass, block, or band of sound. The directional aspect of sound has taken on new importance; loudspeakers or groups of instruments may be placed at opposite ends of the stage, in the balcony, or at the back and sides of the auditorium.

Because standard notation makes no provision for many of these innovations, such as noiselike sounds, recent music scores may contain graphlike diagrams, new note shapes and symbols, and novel ways of arranging notation on the page (see the illustration above, from George Crumb's *Ancient Voices of Children*).

[8-record/cassette set: Side 15, band 3]

Mixed Media

Electronic music is often presented with visual counterparts such as slide projections, films, light shows, gestures, and theatrical actions; Varèse's *Poème électronique*, for instance, combined electronic sounds with images projected on walls. But multimedia works are not confined to electronic music. Other types of recent music sometimes require performers to be actors as well as sound producers, as in *Ancient Voices of Children* (1970) by George Crumb (b. 1929). Mixed-media presentations are generally intended to break down the ritual surrounding traditional concerts and increase communication between composer and audience.

Rhythm and Form

Rhythm and form have undergone some of the most striking changes in music since 1950. Earlier in the century, composers often changed meters or used unconventional ones such as $\frac{7}{8}$ and $\frac{5}{8}$. Today, some composers abandon the concepts of beat and meter altogether. This is a natural outcome of electronic music, which needs no beat to keep performers together. In nonelectronic music, too, the composer may specify duration in absolute units such as seconds rather than in beats, which are relative units. In some recent music, there may be several different speeds at the same time.

More than ever, each piece of music follows its own laws, and its form grows out of its material. Many composers no longer write music in the traditional forms, such as A B A, sonata form, or rondo. Indeed, form may unfold with little or no obvious repetition of material.

TWENTIETH CENTURY

15 MUSIC SINCE 1950: THREE REPRESENTATIVE PIECES

SONATA FOR FLUTE, OBOE, CELLO, AND HARPSICHORD (1952), BY ELLIOTT CARTER

Elliott Carter (b. 1908) is an American composer who is recognized as a major figure in contemporary music. He first attracted international attention when his String Quartet No. 1 (1951) won first prize at a composition contest held by the city of Liège in Belgium in 1953. Since then, he has produced an imposing series of instrumental works, including two other string quartets (1959, 1972), the Variations for Orchestra (1955), the Double Concerto (1961), the Piano Concerto (1966), the Concerto for Orchestra (1969), the *Symphony of Three Orchestras* (1977), and the *Night Fantasies* for solo piano (1980). In Carter's works, several highly contrasting ideas are often presented simultaneously. These superimposed ideas may differ in melodic character, rhythm, meter, and even tempo. Carter's music has many tempo changes that are precisely regulated. He developed a technique called *metrical modulation*, which has been defined as "a means of going smoothly, but with complete accuracy, from one absolute metronomic speed to another, by lengthening or shortening the value of the basic note unit." Carter does not belong to any compositional "school" but has evolved a personal style; that style is illustrated in his Sonata for Flute, Oboe, Cello, and Harpsichord (1952).

"The *Sonata*," explains Carter, "was commissioned by the Harpsichord Quartet of New York. My idea was to stress as much as possible the vast and wonderful array of tone-colors available on the modern harpsichord. . . . This aim of using the wide variety of the harpsichord involved many tone colors which can only be produced very softly and therefore conditioned very drastically the type and range of musical expression, all the details of shape, phrasing, rhythm, texture, as well as the large form." Carter has said that at the time he was composing the sonata in 1952, "it seemed very important to have the harpsichord speak in a new voice, expressing characters unfamiliar to its extensive Baroque repertory."

Each of the four instrumental parts has a separate, highly individual identity, like a character in a drama. As Carter put it, "I regard my scores as scenarios, auditory scenarios, for performers to act out with their instruments, dramatizing the players as individuals and participants in the ensemble. . . ." The three movements of the sonata are not in traditional forms; they have a feeling of purposeful improvisation. We'll focus on the first movement.

First Movement:

Risoluto (determined)

"The music starts, *Risoluto*," writes Carter, "with a splashing dramatic gesture whose subsiding ripples form the rest of the movement." This 3-minute movement consists of a furiously energetic opening half and a calmer second half that contains a gradual decrescendo. The opening is mostly loud, with complex rhythms and polyphonic texture; several different, apparently unrelated things go on at once. Each of the simultaneous instrumental parts has individualized rhythms and melodic gestures, the flute and cello playing in their highest registers. Near the beginning of the first section comes a brief moment of relative calm when the harpsichord plays a succession of even eighth notes while the other instruments comment with short phrases.

[8-record/cassette set:
Side 15, band 1]

This contrast between a steady mechanical pulse in the harpsichord and more fluid, impulsive rhythms in the other instruments becomes the basis of the second part of the movement, which is marked *tempo giusto (moderate tempo)*. This part begins with a harpsichord phrase in even quarter notes.

The harpsichord phrase returns several times, each time varied, expanded, and with different responses from the other instruments. Usually only one other instrument is heard with the harpsichord, so that the texture is less dense than that of the opening section. The movement's last "subsiding ripples" result from the soft dynamic level and the ever-widening distance between low and high harpsichord tones.

POÈME ÉLECTRONIQUE (ELECTRONIC POEM), BY EDGARD VARÈSE

[8-record/cassette set: Side 15, band 2]

Edgard Varèse (1883–1965), one of the great innovators of twentieth-century music, was born in France but spent most of his life in the United States. As early as 1916, he dreamed of freeing music from the limitations of traditional instruments and expanding the vocabulary of sounds. During the 1920s and 1930s, Varèse pioneered in the exploration of percussive and noiselike sounds, and he wrote the first important work for percussion ensemble *(Ionisation,* 1931).

But it was the new electronic developments of the 1950s that enabled Varèse to realize his vision of the "liberation of sound." In 1958, at the age of seventy-five, he composed *Poème électronique,* one of the earliest masterpieces of electronic music created in a tape studio. The 8-minute work was designed to be heard within the pavilion of the Philips Radio Corporation at the 1958 Brussels World Fair. Varèse obtained unique spatial effects by projecting sound from 425 loudspeakers placed all over the interior surfaces of the pavilion. The composer worked in collaboration with the architect Le Corbusier, who selected the series of images—photographs, paintings, and writing—that were projected on the walls as the music was heard. But there was no attempt to synchronize the sounds with the images, which included "birds and beasts, fish and reptiles, . . . masks and skeletons, idols, girls clad and unclad, cities in normal appearance and then suddenly askew," as well as atomic mushroom clouds.

Varèse's raw sound material—tones and noises—came from a wide variety of sources, including electronic generators, church bells, sirens, organs, human voices, and machines. The sounds are often electronically processed in such a way that they cannot be precisely identified. In the listening outline, the effect of such sounds is conveyed by words placed in quotation marks; for example, "wood blocks" or "animal noises." Varèse organized his sounds into an electronic poem that seems weird, yet is amazingly logical and compelling.

Poème électronique is subdivided into two main sections, the first lasting 2 minutes and 36 seconds and the second 5 minutes and 29 seconds. Each section begins with low bell tolls and ends with sirens. Heard several times during the *Poème* is a distinctive group of three rising tones. Human voices and recognizable organ tones appear only during the second section. Varèse once remarked about the female voice heard toward the end of the *Poème:* "I wanted it to express tragedy—and inquisition."

Because it was created in a tape studio, *Poème électronique* exists in only a single "performance" whose duration is fixed on audiotape. Thus the listening outline can indicate the precise moment at which a sound occurs.

Listening Outline To be read while music is heard

POÈME ÉLECTRONIQUE (ELECTRONIC POEM; 1958),
BY EDGARD VARÈSE (1883–1965)

Tape studio

(8 minutes, 5 seconds)

0 s	1. *a.* Low bell tolls. "Wood blocks." Sirens. Fast taps lead into high, piercing sounds. 2-second pause.
43 s	*b.* "Bongo" tones and higher grating noises. Short "squawks." Three-tone group stated three times.
1 min 11 s	*c.* Low sustained tones with grating noises. Sirens. Short "squawks." Three-tone group. 2-second pause.
1 min 40 s	*d.* Short "squawks." High "chirps." Variety of "shots," "honks," "machine noises." Sirens. Taps lead to
2 min 36 s	2. *a.* Low bell tolls. Sustained electronic tones. Repeated "bongo" tones. High and sustained electronic tones. Low tone, crescendo. Rhythmic noises lead to
3 min 41 s	*b.* Voice, "Oh-gah." 4-second pause. Voice continues softly.
4 min 17 s	*c.* Suddenly loud. Rhythmic percussive sounds joined by voice. Low "animal noises," scraping, shuffling, hollow vocal sounds. Decrescendo into 7-second pause.
5 min 47 s	*d.* Sustained electronic tones, crescendo and decrescendo. Rhythmic percussive sounds. Higher sustained electronic tones, crescendo. "Airplane rumble," "chimes," jangling.
6 min 47 s	*e.* Female voice. Male chorus. Electronic noises, organ. High taps. Swooping organ sound. Three-note group stated twice. Rumble, sirens, crescendo (8 minutes and 5 seconds).

(NYT Pictures)

Ellen Taaffe Zwilich.

PASSAGES (1981), BY ELLEN TAAFFE ZWILICH

The American composer Ellen Taaffe Zwilich (b. 1939) won the 1983 Pulitzer Prize for Music for her Symphony No. 1. Zwilich was born in Miami, Florida, the daughter of an airline pilot. She studied at Florida State University and at the Juilliard School and played for several years as a professional violinist in the American Symphony Orchestra under the direction of Leopold Stokowski. She has composed an impressive series of widely performed instrumental works, including the String Quartet (1974), Chamber Symphony (1979), String Trio (1982), Double Quartet for Strings (1984), Symphony No. 2 (1985), and Concerto for Piano and Orchestra (1986).

    Passages is a cycle of six songs for soprano, piccolo, flute, alto flute, clarinet, bass clarinet, violin, viola, cello, piano, and a large group of percussion instruments. (It is also available in a version for soprano and orchestra.) "*Passages* is based on poems by A. R. Ammons, the 1981 recipient of the National Book Critics' Circle Award for poetry," writes Zwilich. It "was conceived as a dramatic whole, consisting of poem settings and 'interludes' in which the voice is used like an instrument." The whole cycle "is a kind of existential encounter among poet, singer, and musician, confronting various forms of the passage of time and the passage of life." We'll focus on the second song of the cycle, *Reversal*.

Reversal

8-record/cassette set:
Side 15, band 4

Ammons's poem presents a dramatic antagonism between the human imagination and the nature that inspires it. In *Reversal*, Zwilich creates an angry atmosphere with music that is characterized by percussive sounds, assertive rhythms, and a rapid tempo. The song opens with an instrumental introduction in which the alto flute and bass clarinet—supported by piano and percussion—present a repeated-note figure that serves as a kind of refrain.

The figure anticipates the repeated notes of the soprano's opening phrase, *The mountain in my head*, which returns toward the end of the song. The instrumentalists play an important role in this work. "They deal not only with what the singer is saying at the moment," Zwilich explains, "but with what has been said, and with what is coming. In this way, they are almost like a Greek chorus." A striking moment of instrumental tone painting comes when the word *mist* is reflected by rapid rising scales played in a high register by the piccolo and violin. The vocal melody usually has only one note to each syllable, except for the climactic setting of *far*, which is extended over five tones. For greater emphasis, the soprano is directed to speak—not sing—the key word *arrogance*. (The bracketed words in the text were supplied by the composer, who has substituted *rising* for *opening*.)

The mt in my head surpasses you

I said

becomes at the base

more nearly incalculable with

bush

more divisive with suckers and roots

and at the peak

far less visible

plumed and misty

[rising] from unfinal rock to air

[The mt in my head surpasses you

I said]

arrogance arrogance

the mt said

the wind in your days

accounts for this arrogance

[16] JAZZ

About the time Schoenberg and Stravinsky were changing the language of music in Europe, a new musical style called *jazz* was being developed in America.* It was created by musicians—predominantly black Americans—performing in the streets, bars, brothels, and dance halls of New Orleans and other southern cities. *Jazz* can be described generally as music rooted in improvisation and characterized by syncopated rhythm, a steady beat, and distinctive tone colors and techniques of performance. Although the term *jazz* became current in 1917, the music itself was probably heard as early as 1900. We do not know exactly when jazz started or how it sounded at first, because this new music existed only in performance, not musical notation. Moreover, very little jazz was captured on recordings before 1923, and none at all before the Original Dixieland Jazz Band recorded in 1917.

Since its beginnings, jazz has developed a rich variety of substyles such as New Orleans style (or Dixieland), swing, bebop, cool, free jazz, and jazz rock. It has produced such outstanding figures as Louis Armstrong, Duke Ellington, Benny Goodman, Charlie Parker, and John Coltrane. Its impact has been enormous and worldwide, affecting not only many kinds of popular music, but the music of such composers as Maurice Ravel, Darius Milhaud, and Aaron Copland. For a long time, jazz was basically music for dancing; but since the 1940s, many jazz styles have been intended for listening.

ROOTS OF JAZZ

Early jazz blended elements from many musical cultures, particularly west African, American, and European. West African influences included an emphasis on improvisation, drumming, percussive sounds, and complex

*An excellent recorded anthology of jazz is the *Smithsonian Collection of Classic Jazz*, available from Smithsonian Books and Recordings (P.O. Box 10229, Des Moines, Iowa 50381-0229) as a set of seven records (no. 2500), five cassettes (no. 2501), or five compact disks (no. 2502).

rhythms, as well as a feature known as *call and response*. In much west African vocal music, a soloist's phrases are repeatedly answered by a chorus; similarly, in jazz, **call and response** occurs when a voice is answered by an instrument, or when one instrument or group of instruments is answered by another instrument or group.

Actually, the call-and-response pattern of jazz was derived more directly from black American church services in which the congregation vocally responds to the preacher's "call." Other American influences on jazz were the rich body of music that blacks developed here—including work songs, spirituals, gospel hymns, and dances like the cakewalk—and the music of white America. Nineteenth-century American and European musical traditions became elements in the background of jazz. In addition to hymns, popular songs, folk tunes, dances, and piano pieces, the American band tradition was a major influence. Many marching band instruments were used in early jazz bands, and band music helped shape the forms and rhythms of early jazz.

Along with band music, the immediate sources of jazz were ragtime and the blues, discussed below.

ELEMENTS OF JAZZ

Tone Color

Jazz is generally played by a small group (or *combo*) of three to eight players, or by a "big band" of ten to fifteen. The backbone of a jazz ensemble is its rhythm section, which is comparable to the basso continuo in baroque music. The **rhythm section,** usually made up of piano, plucked double bass (bass), percussion, and—sometimes—banjo or guitar, maintains the beat, adds rhythmic interest, and provides supporting harmonies.

The main solo instruments of jazz include the cornet, trumpet, saxophone (soprano, alto, tenor, baritone), piano, clarinet, vibraphone, and trombone. Jazz emphasizes brasses, woodwinds, and percussion rather than the bowed strings that dominate symphonic music. A jazz performance usually involves both solo and ensemble sections. For example, a full ensemble might be followed by a trumpet solo and then by a clarinet solo or a duet for saxophone and trumpet.

The distinctive sounds of jazz are easy to recognize but hard to describe. They result from the particular way tones are attacked, "bent," and released; from the type of vibrato employed; and from a variety of pitch inflections that might be described as "smears," "scoops," "falloffs," and "shakes."

Improvisation

At the heart of jazz lies improvisation. Jazz musicians create a special electricity as they simultaneously create and perform, making decisions at lightning speed. The fertility of great improvisers is staggering. Their recorded performances represent only a tiny fraction of the music they create almost nightly. Of course, not all jazz is improvised, and most contains both improvised and composed sections. Yet it is improvisation that contributes most to the freshness and spontaneity of jazz.

A jazz improvisation is usually in theme-and-variations form. The theme is often a popular song melody in A A B A form made up of 32 **bars,** or measures. The improviser varies this original melody by adding embellishments and changing its pitches and rhythms. Some jazz improvisations are based on a harmonic pattern, or series of chords. This harmonic pattern will be repeated over and over while the improviser creates melodies above it. In jazz, each statement of the basic harmonic pattern or melody is called a **chorus.**

A jazz performance usually includes improvised solos by various members of the ensemble. In addition, there may be sections of *collective* improvisation, during which several musicians make up different melodies simultaneously. Their music is held together by the underlying chords.

Rhythm, Melody, and Harmony

Syncopation and rhythmic swing are two of the most distinctive features of jazz. We say jazz performers "swing" when they combine a steady beat with a feeling of lilt, precision, and relaxed vitality. In most jazz styles, the beat is provided by the percussionist (on drums or cymbals) and by the bass player. There are usually four beats to the bar. Accents often come on the weak beats: 1–**2**–3–**4.** Many kinds of syncopated rhythms result when accented notes come *between* the beats. Jazz musicians also create a swing feeling by playing a series of notes slightly unevenly. For example, the second note of a pair of eighth notes will be shorter than the first:

But the rhythms of jazz are so irregular that it is difficult to notate them accurately. A performer must deviate from the notated rhythms to get a true jazz feeling. And as jazz has evolved, rhythms have become ever more irregular and complex.

Jazz melodies are as flexible in pitch as in rhythm. They employ a major scale in which the third, fifth, and seventh notes are often lowered, or flatted. These "bent," or "blue," notes came into jazz through the vocal blues. Jazz uses chord progressions like those of the traditional tonal system. But over the years, the harmonic vocabulary of jazz—like its rhythm—has become increasingly complex and sophisticated.

JAZZ STYLES

Ragtime

Ragtime (1890s to about 1915) is a style of composed piano music developed primarily by black pianists who played in southern and midwestern saloons and dance halls. It is generally in duple meter ($\frac{2}{4}$) and performed at a moderate march tempo; the pianist's right hand plays a highly syncopated melody while the left hand steadily maintains the beat with an "oom-pah" accompaniment. The "king of ragtime" was Scott Joplin (1868–1917), whose most famous pieces include *Maple Leaf Rag* and *The Entertainer*.

Scott Joplin.

(Granger Collection)

The Blues

The *blues* (developed in the 1890s) is a style of vocal music, originating among blacks, that involves "bent" notes and slides of pitch; "blue" notes are produced by slightly lowering, or flatting, the third, fifth, and seventh notes of the major scale. The intensely personal lyrics of vocal blues consist of several 3-line stanzas, each set to a harmonic framework that is usually

(CBS Records)

Bessie Smith, the "empress of the blues."

297

12 bars long and is thus known as the *12-bar blues*. This pattern involves only three basic chords: tonic (I), *subdominant* (IV, based on the fourth note of the scale, *fa*), and dominant (V). These are ordered: tonic (4 bars)–subdominant (2 bars)–tonic (2 bars)–dominant (2 bars)–tonic (2 bars). Each stanza is sung to the same series of chords, although other chords may be inserted. The music is in quadruple meter ($\frac{4}{4}$).

Jazz instrumentalists imitate the performing style of blues singers and use the harmonic pattern of 12-bar blues as a basis for improvisation. This 12-bar pattern is repeated over and over while new melodies are improvised above it.

Notable blues figures include W. C. Handy (1873–1958), who wrote *Memphis Blues* (1912) and *St. Louis Blues* (1914); and the singer Bessie Smith (1894–1937), known as the "empress of the blues."

New Orleans Style

Jazz in *New Orleans style* (or *Dixieland*), as its name suggests, was developed in New Orleans, which was the major center of jazz from 1900 to 1917. It was typically played by five to eight performers: a *front line* of melodic instruments (cornet or trumpet; clarinet; and trombone) and a supporting rhythm section (drums; chordal instruments such as piano, banjo,

New Orleans style (or Dixieland) was typically played by five to eight performers. King Oliver (standing, at left rear) is shown here with his Creole Jazz Band in 1923. The band included Louis Armstrong (seated, center) and Lil Hardin (at the piano).

(Frank Driggs Collection)

(UPI/Bettmann Newsphotos)

Duke Ellington and his orchestra in 1943. Ellington was perhaps the most important swing composer, arranger, and conductor.

and guitar; and a single-line low instrument such as a tuba or plucked bass). The front-line players would improvise several contrasting melodic lines at once, producing a kind of polyphonic texture; and their syncopations and rhythmic independence created a marvelous sense of excitement. This collective improvisation, in which each instrument had a special role, was the most distinctive feature of New Orleans jazz, though as the style evolved during the 1920s (mainly in Chicago), solo playing came to be more emphasized. New Orleans jazz was usually based on a march, a church melody, a ragtime piece, a popular song, or 12-bar blues.

Notable figures of New Orleans jazz include Ferdinand "Jelly Roll" Morton, Joseph "King" Oliver, and especially Louis "Satchmo" Armstrong (1900–1971). *Hotter Than That*, in a rendition by Louis Armstrong and His Hot Five, was studied in Part I, Section 1 (see the discussion and listening outline on pages 6–7); since the emphasis is on improvisatory solos, it shows how New Orleans style developed in Chicago in the 1920s. Listen for the exciting vocal and instrumental solos (items 2, 3, 4, 5, and 6*a*), the syncopations of Armstrong's vocal melody (item 4), and the dissonant guitar chord at the end.

Side D, band 6
[*8-record/cassette set:*
Side 15, band 8]

Swing

A new jazz style called *swing* developed in the 1920s and flourished from 1935 to 1945 (the "swing era"). It was played mostly by big bands; the typical **swing band** had about fifteen players in three sections— saxophones, brasses (trumpet and trombone), and rhythm (piano, percussion, guitar, and bass). A band of that size needed music which was more

299

composed than improvised and also *arranged*, that is, notated in written-out parts for the musicians. With swing, the arranger became an important figure in jazz.

Melodies were often performed by entire sections of a swing band, either in unison or in harmony. The main melody was frequently accompanied by saxophones and brasses playing short, repeated phrases called *riffs*. The saxophone became one of the most important solo instruments, and percussionists also had a more prominent and spectacular role.

The swing era produced hundreds of "name" bands—both black and white—like those of Count Basie, Glenn Miller, Tommy Dorsey, and Benny Goodman (the "king of swing"). Duke Ellington (1899–1974) was perhaps the most important composer, arranger, and conductor. Some bands included leading musicians like the saxophonists Coleman Hawkins and Lester Young and featured singers like Billie Holiday, Ella Fitzgerald, and Frank Sinatra.

Bebop

Bebop, or *bop* (developed in the early 1940s), was a complex style, usually for small jazz groups, and meant for attentive listening rather than dancing. It had sophisticated harmonies and unpredictable rhythms, and its performers were a special "in" group. A typical bebop ensemble might have a saxophone and a trumpet supported by a rhythm section of piano, bass, and percussion. The role of the rhythm instruments was different from that in earlier jazz—the beat was marked mainly by a pizzicato bass, with the drum supplying occasional irregular accents (*bombs*) and the pianist's left hand supplying chords at irregular intervals. Melodic phrases were often varied in length, and chords might have six or seven notes rather than the four or five characteristic of earlier jazz. A bop performance generally began and ended with a statement of the main theme (often derived from a popular song or 12-bar blues) by a soloist, or two soloists in unison; the remainder of the piece was made up of solo improvisations based on the melody or harmonic structure.

Notable bebop performers included the trumpeter Dizzy Gillespie and the pianist Thelonious Monk. The alto saxophonist Charlie "Bird" Parker (1920–1955) was a towering figure among bebop musicians and an important influence on instrumentalists.

Cool Jazz

Cool jazz (which emerged in the late 1940s and early 1950s) was related to bop, but far calmer and more relaxed. Cool jazz pieces also tended to be longer than bebop and relied more on arrangements; and they sometimes used instruments new to jazz, including the French horn, flute, and cello. The tenor saxophonists Lester Young (1909–1959) and Stan Getz (b. 1927), the pianist Lennie Tristano (1919–1978), and the trumpeter and bandleader Miles Davis (b. 1926) were important figures.

Free Jazz

Until about 1960, improvised jazz variations tended to keep the length and chord structure of the original theme, if not its melody. But during the 1960s, some musicians created *free jazz*, a style that was not based on regular forms and established chord patterns. *Free Jazz*, recorded in 1960 by Ornette Coleman (b. 1930) with several other musicians improvising individually and collectively, is an example: it can be compared to the chance music of John Cage and his followers. Another free-jazz musician was John Coltrane (1926–1967), who was influential as an improviser, tenor and soprano saxophonist, and composer.

Jazz Rock (Fusion)

Rock music became a potent influence on jazz during the later 1960s, the 1970s, and the 1980s. This influence led to *jazz rock*, or *fusion*, a new style combining the jazz musician's improvisatory approach with rock rhythms and tone colors. A jazz rock group typically has acoustic instruments (which may have electric attachments) along with sythesizers and electric piano, guitar, and bass (which takes a melodic role). The percussion section is larger than that in earlier jazz groups and often includes instruments from Africa, Latin America, or India. A distinctive feature is the insistent repetition of rhythmic figures.

Miles Davis, a leading musician in cool jazz, has also been important in jazz rock; Herbie Hancock, Chick Corea, Joe Zawinul, and Wayne Shorter—who made recordings with Davis—became pacesetters of jazz rock in the 1970s and 1980s.

ROCK $\left[\begin{array}{c} \text{TWENTIETH} \\ \text{CENTURY} \\ \textbf{17} \end{array}\right]$

The mid-1950s saw the growth of a new kind of popular music that was first called *rock and roll* and then simply *rock*. Though it includes diverse styles, **rock** tends to be vocal music with a hard, driving beat, often featuring electric guitar accompaniment and heavily amplified sound. Early rock grew mainly out of *rhythm and blues,* a dance music of American blacks that fused blues, jazz, and gospel styles. Rock also drew upon *country and western,* a folklike, guitar-based style associated with rural white Americans. In little more than a decade, rock evolved from a simple, dance-oriented style to music that was highly varied in its tone colors, lyrics, and electronic technology.

DEVELOPMENT OF ROCK

In the late 1940s, rhythm and blues became the dominant style among American blacks. The rhythm and blues of the 1950s differed from earlier blues in its more powerful beat and its use of the saxophone and electric guitar. Among the leading performers were Little Richard, Chuck Berry, and vocal groups such as the Platters. During the 1950s many rhythm-and-blues hits were issued by white performers in versions with less sexually explicit lyrics.

The earliest of the important rock and roll groups was Bill Haley and His Comets, whose *Rock Around the Clock* (1954) was the first big hit of the new style. To many people, the new music seemed rebellious in its loudness, pounding beat, and sexual directness; and the image of youthful rebellion was also projected by Elvis Presley, who reigned as "king" of rock and roll.

During the 1960s, much of the rock music by black performers was called *soul*, a term that emphasized its emotionality, its gospel roots, and its relationship to the black community. Soul musicians included James Brown, Ray Charles, and Aretha Franklin. *Motown* (after the name of a record company) was a type of soul music that blended rhythm and blues with popular music; among its stars were Diana Ross and the Supremes, and Stevie Wonder.

A new era began in 1964 with the American tour of the Beatles, an English rock group who were the most influential performers in the history of rock. The Beatles—the singer-guitarists Paul McCartney, John Lennon, and George Harrison, and the drummer Ringo Starr (all born in the early 1940s)—came to dominate the popular music scene in the United States, along with the Rolling Stones (also English). Under their influence, rock musicians explored a wider range of musical sources and sounds, including electronic effects, "classical" and nonwestern instruments, and unconventional chord progressions. Rock in the 1960s also absorbed elements of folk music and expressed contemporary social issues; *Blowin' in the Wind*, by the songwriter and singer Bob Dylan, is a well-known example. The diversity of rock styles in this period—which produced the first rock musical (*Hair*) and the first rock opera (*Tommy*)—is reflected in the terms *folk rock*, *jazz rock*, *classical rock*, *psychedelic rock*, and *acid rock*.

The 1970s saw a continuation of many 1960s styles, the revival of early rock and roll, and the rise of a dance music called *disco*. In addition to veteran performers, new stars emerged, such as Linda Ronstadt, Billy Joel, Bruce Springsteen, and Donna Summer. A blend of country music and rock called *country rock* became popular; other musical styles included *reg-*

(Michael Putland/Retna)

Police.

gae (from the West Indies), *funk* (featuring electrification and jazzlike rhythms), and *punk*, or *new wave* (a primitive form of rock and roll). Some groups performed *classical rock* (rock arrangements of earlier serious music), and jazz rock reached a wider audience than ever before through groups like Chicago; Weather Report; and Blood, Sweat, and Tears.

In the early 1980s, new wave bands from Britain such as Police, Culture Club, and Eurhythmics were popular in America—a "second British invasion" comparable to that of the Beatles. Though their styles varied, most of these groups used electronic technology (synthesizers and computers) and featured outlandish-looking performers. *Heavy metal* bands such as Quiet Riot, Iron Maiden, and Black Sabbath played a type of basic rock with sexually explicit lyrics, bizarre costumes, and tremendous volume. *Rapping (rap music)*—a kind of rhythmic talking accompanied by a disk jockey who alternates between recordings on two turntables—developed among young urban blacks. Groups such as the Talking Heads and Police drew inspiration from "exotic" sources like African music and Jamaican reggae.

ELEMENTS OF ROCK

Tone Color

The electric-guitar sound of rock is very different from the brass-reed sound of the "big band" heard in earlier popular music. Rock music is amplified powerfully, and the guitar is often manipulated electronically to produce a wide range of tone colors. Along with singers (who also play instruments), a rock group typically includes two electric guitars (lead and rhythm), electric bass, percussion, and keyboard instruments such as piano, electric piano, and synthesizer. Some groups also include one or more trumpets, trombones, or saxophones.

As rock evolved during the 1960s, a wide range of instruments—from the harpsichord to the Indian sitar—were occasionally added to the basic rock group, particularly for recording sessions. Rock recordings use such diverse sounds as electronic blips, crowd noises, and a fifty-piece orchestra. During the 1970s and 1980s, rock musicians exploited the ever-expanding capacities of synthesizers and computers. Sophisticated electronic technology made it possible for a few performers to sound like a large ensemble.

The singing style of rock is drawn largely from black, folk, and country-and-western music. Although singing styles vary, they all are different from the crooning sound cultivated by earlier popular vocalists. Rock singers shout, cry, wail, growl, and use guttural sounds, as well as *falsetto*, a method of singing used by males to reach notes higher than their normal range. Nonsense syllables and repeated chants (such as *Yeah! Yeah! Yeah!*) are also featured.

Rhythm

Rock is based on a very powerful beat in quadruple ($\frac{4}{4}$) meter with strong accents on the second and fourth beats of the bar. The rhythmic excitement is heightened because each beat is subdivided into 2 equal notes. This produces 8 faster pulses, which are superimposed on the 4 basic beats. To get the effect, count out the following: 1-and-**2**-and-3-and-**4**-and. Rock of the 1960s and 1970s often combined complicated rhythms with this basic pattern; for example, the bass player might emphasize the offbeats—the *ands*. During the late 1970s and 1980s, some rock music became more rhythmically complex, as performers drew inspiration from the poly-rhythms of African music.

Form, Melody, and Harmony

Rock music is usually in 12-bar blues form (see Section 16), in 32-bar A A B A form, or in variants of these forms. Earlier popular songs usually consisted of 4- or 8-bar phrases, but rock melodies sometimes contain phrases that are irregular in length. Rock songs tend to have short melodic patterns that are repeated several times. They are occasionally built on modes, rather than on traditional major or minor scales.

The harmonic progressions of rock are usually quite simple, often consisting of just three or four basic chords. Sometimes, the harmony can be restricted deliberately to only two chords, as in *Eleanor Rigby*, by John

(Don McCullin/Magnum)

The Beatles.

Lennon and Paul McCartney. Rock often uses chord progressions that are rare in earlier popular music.

LUCY IN THE SKY WITH DIAMONDS, FROM SGT. PEPPER'S LONELY HEARTS CLUB BAND (1967), BY THE BEATLES

Sgt. Pepper's Lonely Hearts Club Band, a landmark of rock music, was one of the first rock recordings to be presented as a unified song cycle: its thirteen songs are linked by the device of a music hall show with a dazzling succession of acts. The impact of this record comes largely from its tremendous range of sounds and electronic effects—audience noises, barnyard sounds, weird orchestral tone colors, and instruments such as the harpsichord, harp, and sitar. There is also a wide range of musical styles, including traditional rock and roll, a parody of a 1920s music-hall tune, an old-fashioned melodramatic ballad, and the exotic sounds of Indian music.

    Lucy in the Sky with Diamonds, the third song of the cycle, evokes a world of daydream and fantasy. But the dreamlike mood is shattered by a brusque refrain. Apart from its introduction, the song is made up of three sections that are repeated: A, B, and C. Sections A and B are relatively soft, gently pulsating, and in triple meter. In contrast, section C (the refrain *Lucy in the sky*) is loud, heavily accented, and in quadruple meter.

Listening Outline <small>To be read while music is heard</small>

LUCY IN THE SKY WITH DIAMONDS,
FROM SGT. PEPPER'S LONELY HEARTS CLUB BAND (1967), BY THE BEATLES

A B C A B C A CC form
(About 3½ minutes)

Introduction	1. *a.* Unaccompanied melody, synthesized sound suggests "electric harpsichord."
A	*b.* Soft, triple meter, stepwise vocal melody repeats 3-note idea in narrow range, "electric harpsichord," electric bass; lightly stroked cymbals join.
B *(Cellophane flowers)*	2. Moderately soft, triple meter, repeated-note melody, voice doubled by guitar and electronically manipulated to sound slightly "unreal," fuller accompaniment, electric bass more active, marks beat.
C (refrain)	3. Loud, quadruple meter, single phrase sung three times (during some repetitions, phrase doubled at higher pitch), higher range than in sections A and B, driving rhythm, drummer accents second and fourth beats of each bar.
A	4. Soft, triple meter, stepwise vocal melody.
B *(Newspaper taxis)*	5. Moderately soft, triple meter, repeated-note melody.
C (refrain)	6. Loud, quadruple meter.
A	7. Soft, triple meter, stepwise vocal melody.
CC (refrain)	8. Loud, quadruple meter; fade-out at end.

GLOSSARY

A B form See *two-part form.*

A B A form See *three-part form.*

absolute music Instrumental music having *no* intended association with a story, poem, idea, or scene; nonprogram music.

accent Emphasis of a note, which may result from its being louder (dynamic accent), longer, or higher in pitch than the notes near it.

accompanied recitative Speechlike melody that is sung by a solo voice accompanied by strings as well as basso continuo.

aerophone Any instrument—such as flute or trumpet—whose sound is generated by a vibrating column of air.

aleatory music See *chance music.*

answer Second presentation of the subject in a fugue, usually in the dominant scale.

aria Song for solo voice with orchestral accompaniment, usually expressing an emotional state through its outpouring of melody; found in opera.

arpeggio See *broken chord.*

art song Setting of a poem for solo voice and piano, translating the poem's mood and imagery into music, common in the romantic period.

atonality Absence of tonality, or key, characteristic of much twentieth-century music.

augmentation Variation of a fugue subject in which the original time values of the subject are lengthened.

bar Another term for *measure,* often used in jazz.

bass clef Symbol on the staff indicating relatively low pitch ranges, such as those played by a pianist's left hand.

basso continuo (figured bass) Baroque accompaniment made up of a bass part together with numbers (figures) indicating the chords to be played above it. Usually the basso continuo is played by two instruments, a keyboard plus a low melodic instrument.

basso ostinato See *ground bass*.

beam Horizontal line connecting the flags of several eighth or sixteenth notes in succession to facilitate reading these notes.

beat Regular, recurrent pulsation that divides music into equal units of time.

bebop (bop) Complex jazz style, usually for small groups, developed in the 1940s and meant for attentive listening rather than dancing.

bitonality Approach to pitch organization using two keys at one time, often found in twentieth-century music.

blues Term referring both to a style of performance and to a form; an early source of jazz, characterized by flatted, or "blue," notes in the scale; vocal blues consist of 3-line stanzas in the form a a' b.

bop See *bebop*.

brass instrument Instrument, made of brass or silver, whose sound is produced by the vibrations of the player's lips as he or she blows into a cup- or funnel-shaped mouthpiece. The vibrations are amplified and colored in a tube that is flared at the end.

bridge (transition) In the exposition of the sonata form, a section which leads from the first theme in the tonic, or home, key to the second theme, which is in a new key.

broken chord (arpeggio) Sounding of the individual tones of a chord in sequence rather than simultaneously.

cadence (1) Resting place at the end of a phrase in a melody. (2) Progression giving a sense of conclusion, often from the dominant chord to the tonic chord.

cadenza Unaccompanied section of virtuoso display for the soloist in a concerto, usually appearing near the end of the first movement, and sometimes in the last movement.

call and response (1) In jazz, a pattern wherein one voice or instrument is answered by another voice, instrument, or group of instruments. (2) Performance style in which the phrases of a soloist are repeatedly answered by those of a chorus, often found in African and other nonwestern music.

Camerata In Italian, *fellowship* or *society*; a group of nobles, poets, and composers who began to meet regularly in Florence around 1575 and whose musical discussions prepared the way for the beginning of opera.

cantata Composition in several movements, usually written for chorus, one or more vocal soloists, and orchestra. The church cantata for the Lutheran service in Germany during the baroque period often includes chorales.

cantus firmus Melody—often a Gregorian chant—used as the basis of a polyphonic composition.

castrato Male singer castrated before puberty to retain a high voice range; the most important vocal soloist in opera during the baroque period.

chamber music Music employing a small group of musicians, with one player to a part.

chance (aleatory) music Music composed by the random selection of pitches, tone colors, and rhythms; developed in the 1950s by John Cage and others.

chorale Hymn tune sung to a German religious text.

chorale prelude Short composition for organ, based on a hymn tune and often used to remind the congregation of the melody before the hymn is sung.

chord Combination of three or more tones sounded at once.

chordophone Instrument—such as a harp or lute—whose sound is generated by a stretched string.

chorus In jazz, a statement of the basic harmonic pattern or melody.

chromatic harmony Use of chords containing tones not found in the prevailing major or minor scale but included in the chromatic scale (which has twelve tones); often found in romantic music.

chromatic scale Scale including all twelve tones of the octave; each tone is a half step away from the next one.

church modes Scales containing seven tones with an eighth tone duplicating the first an octave higher, but with different patterns of whole and half steps from major and minor scales; used in medieval, Renaissance, and twentieth-century music and in folk music.

clef Symbol placed at the beginning of the staff to show the exact pitch of each line and space.

climax Highest tone or emotional focus in a melody or a larger composition.

coda In a sonata-form movement, a concluding section following the recapitulation and rounding off the movement by repeating themes or developing them further.

complete cadence Definite resting place, giving a sense of finality, at the end of a phrase in a melody.

concert overture Independent composition for orchestra in one movement, usually in sonata form, often found in the romantic period.

concerto Extended composition for instrumental soloist and orchestra, usually in three movements: (1) fast, (2) slow, (3) fast.

concerto grosso Composition for several instrumental soloists and small orchestra; common in late baroque music.

consonance Tone combination that is stable and restful.

contrast Striking differences of pitch, dynamics, rhythm, and tempo that provide variety and change of mood.

cool jazz Jazz style related to bebop, but more relaxed in character and relying more heavily on arrangements; developed around 1950.

counterpoint Technique of combining two or more melodic lines into a meaningful whole.

countersubject In a fugue, a melodic idea that accompanies the subject fairly constantly.

da capo aria Aria in A B A form; after the B section, the term *da capo* is written; this means *from the beginning* and indicates a repetition of the opening A section.

development Second section of a sonata-form movement, in which themes from the exposition are developed and the music moves through several different keys.

diminution Variation of a fugue subject in which the original time values of the subject are shortened.

dissonance Tone combination that is unstable and tense.

Dixieland See *New Orleans jazz*.

dominant chord Triad built on the fifth note of the scale, which sets up tension that is resolved by the tonic chord.

dotted note   Note with a dot to the right of it. This dot increases the note's un-dotted duration by half.

dotted rhythm   Long-short rhythmic pattern in which a dotted note is followed by a note that is much shorter.

double-reed woodwinds   Instruments whose sound is produced by two narrow pieces of cane held between the player's lips, which vibrate when the player blows between them.

double stop   See *stop.*

downbeat   First, or stressed, beat of a measure.

duple meter   Pattern of 2 beats to the measure.

dynamic accent   Emphasis that a note receives when it is played more loudly than the surrounding notes.

dynamics   Degrees of loudness or softness in music.

electronic instrument   Instrument whose sound is produced, modified, or amplified by electronic means.

embellishments   Ornamental tones that are either improvised by the performer or indicated in the music by signs or notes in small print.

ensemble   In opera, a piece sung by three or more solo singers.

episode   Transitional section in a fugue between presentations of the subject, which offers either new material or fragments of the subject or countersubject.

étude   In French, *study;* a piece designed to help a performer master specific techni-cal difficulties.

exoticism   Use of melodies, rhythms, or instruments that suggest foreign lands; common in romantic music.

exposition   First section of a sonata-form movement, which sets up a strong con-flict between the tonic key and the new key, between the first theme (or group of themes) and the second theme (or group of themes).

expressionism   Musical style stressing intense, subjective emotion and harsh disso-nance, typical of German and Austrian music of the early twentieth century.

figured bass   See *basso continuo.*

flag   Wavy line attached to the stem on a note, indicating how long that note is to be held relative to the notes around it.

flat sign   Symbol for a pitch one half step lower than the pitch that would other-wise be indicated—for example, the next lower black key on the piano.

form   Organization of musical ideas in time.

fourth chord   Chord in which the tones are a fourth apart, instead of a third; used in twentieth-century music.

free jazz   Jazz style which departs from traditional jazz by not being based on regular forms and established chord patterns; developed during the 1960s.

French overture   Common opening piece in baroque suites, oratorios, and operas; usually in two parts: the first a slow section with characteristic dotted rhythms, full of dignity and grandeur; the second quick and lighter in mood, often begin-ning like a fugue.

front line   In Dixieland or New Orleans jazz, the group of melodic instruments which improvise on a melody, supported by the rhythm section.

fugue   Polyphonic composition based on one main theme, or subject.

fusion   See *jazz rock.*

glissando   Rapid slide up or down a scale.

grand staff Combination of the treble and bass staves, used in keyboard music to encompass the wide range of pitches produced by both hands.

Gregorian chant Melodies set to sacred Latin texts, sung without accompaniment; the official music of the Roman Catholic church.

ground bass (basso ostinato) Variation form in which a musical idea in the bass is repeated over and over while the melodies above it constantly change; common in baroque music.

half step Smallest interval traditionally used in western music; for example, the interval between *ti* and *do*.

harmonics Very high-pitched tones, like a whistle's, produced in bowed string instruments by lightly touching the string at certain points while bowing.

harmony How chords are constructed and how they follow each other.

home key See *tonic key*.

homophonic texture Term describing music in which one main melody is accompanied by chords.

idiophone Instrument—such as bells, a gong, a scraper, a rattle, or a xylophone—whose sound is generated by the instrument's own material with no applied tension.

imitation Presentation of a melodic idea by one voice or instrument that is immediately followed by its restatement by another voice or instrument, as in a round.

impressionism Musical style which stresses tone color, atmosphere, and fluidity (flourished 1890–1920), exemplified by Debussy.

improvisation Creation of music at the same time as it is performed.

incidental music Music intended to be performed before and during a play, setting the mood for the drama.

incomplete cadence Inconclusive resting point at the end of a phrase which sets up expectations for phrases to follow.

interval "Distance" in pitch between any two tones.

inversion Variation of a fugue subject in which each interval of the subject is reversed in direction.

jazz Music rooted in improvisation and characterized by syncopated rhythm, a steady beat, and distinctive tone colors and performance techniques. Jazz was developed in the United States predominantly by black musicians and gained popularity in the early twentieth century.

jazz rock (fusion) Style which combines the jazz musician's improvisatory approach with rock rhythms and tone colors; developed in the 1960s.

key (tonality) Central note, scale, and chord within a piece, in relationship to which all other tones in the composition are heard.

key signature Sharp or flat signs immediately following the clef sign at the beginning of a piece of music, indicating the key in which the music is to be played.

keyboard instrument Instrument—such as the piano, organ, or harpsichord—played by pressing a series of keys with the fingers.

keynote (tonic) Central tone of a melody or larger piece of music. When a piece is in the key of C major, for example, C is the keynote.

Klangfarbenmelodie See *tone-color melody*.

leap Interval larger than that between two adjacent tones in the scale.

ledger lines Short, horizontal lines above or below the staff, used to indicate a pitch that falls above or below the range indicated by the staff.

legato Smooth, connected manner of performing a melody.

leitmotif Short musical idea associated with a person, object, or thought, characteristic of the operas of Wagner.

librettist Dramatist who writes the *libretto,* or text, of an opera.

libretto Text of an opera.

madrigal Composition for several voices set to a short secular poem, usually about love, combining homophonic and polyphonic textures and often using word painting; common in Renaissance music.

major scale Series of seven different tones within an octave, with an eighth tone repeating the first an octave higher, composed of a specific pattern of whole and half steps; the whole step between the second and third tones is characteristic.

mass Sacred choral composition made up of five sections: Kyrie, Gloria, Credo, Sanctus, and Agnus Dei.

mass ordinary Roman Catholic church texts which remain the same from day to day throughout most of the year: Kyrie, Gloria, Credo, Sanctus, and Agnus Dei.

measure Rhythmic group, set off by bar lines, containing a fixed number of beats.

melody Series of single tones that add up to a recognizable whole.

membranophone Instrument—basically, a drum—whose sound is generated by a stretched skin or other membrane.

meter Organization of beats into regular groups.

meter signature See *time signature.*

metronome Apparatus which produces ticking sounds or flashes of light at any desired constant speed.

microtone Interval smaller than a half step.

middle C The note C nearest to the center of the piano keyboard, notated as the pitch on the ledger line below the treble clef and above the bass clef.

minimalist music Music characterized by steady pulse, clear tonality, and insistent repetition of short melodic patterns; its dynamic level, texture, and harmony tend to stay constant for fairly long stretches of time, creating a trancelike or hypnotic effect; developed in the 1960s.

minor scale Series of seven tones within an octave, with an eighth tone repeating the first tone an octave higher, composed of a specific pattern of whole and half steps; the half step between the second and third tones is characteristic.

minuet See *minuet and trio.*

minuet and trio (minuet) Compositional form—derived from a dance—in three parts: minuet (A) trio (B) minuet (A). Often employed as the third movement of classical symphonies, string quartets, and other works, it is in triple meter ($\frac{3}{4}$ time) and usually in a moderate tempo.

modified strophic form Form in which two or more stanzas of poetry are set to the same music while other stanzas have new music; found in art songs of the romantic period.

modulation Shift from one key to another within the same piece.

monophonic texture Single melodic line without accompaniment.

motet Polyphonic choral work set to a sacred Latin text other than that of the mass; one of the two main forms of sacred Renaissance music.

motive Fragment of a theme, or short musical idea which is developed within a composition.

movement Piece that sounds fairly complete and independent but is part of a larger composition.

musical texture Number of layers of sound that are heard at once, what kinds of layers they are, and how they are related to each other.

mute Device used to veil or muffle the tone of an instrument. In string instruments, the mute is a clamp which fits onto the bridge; in brass instruments, it is a funnel-shaped piece of wood, metal, or plastic which fits into the bell.

nationalism Inclusion of folk songs, dances, legends, and other national material in a composition to associate it with the composer's homeland; characteristic of romantic music.

natural sign Symbol used in notation of pitch to cancel a previous sharp or flat sign.

neoclassicism Musical style marked by emotional restraint, balance, and clarity, inspired by the forms and stylistic features of eighteenth-century music, found in many works from 1920 to 1950.

New Orleans (Dixieland) jazz Jazz style in which the front line, or melodic instruments, improvise several contrasting melodic lines at once, supported by a rhythm section that clearly marks the beat and provides a background of chords; usually based on a march or church melody, a ragtime piece, a popular song, or the 12-bar blues.

nocturne In French, *night piece;* a composition, usually slow, lyrical, and intimate in character, often for piano solo.

notation System of writing down music so that specific pitches and rhythms can be communicated.

note In notation, a black or white oval to which a stem and flags can be added.

octave Interval between two tones in which the higher tone has twice the frequency of the lower tone.

opera Drama that is sung to orchestral accompaniment, usually a large-scale composition employing vocal soloists, chorus, orchestra, and costumes and scenery.

oratorio Large-scale composition for chorus, vocal soloists, and orchestra, usually set to a narrative text, but without acting, scenery, or costumes; often based on biblical stories.

organ point See *pedal point.*

organum Medieval polyphony that consists of Gregorian chant and one or more additional melodic lines.

ostinato Motive or phrase that is repeated persistently at the same pitch, used in twentieth-century music to stabilize a group of pitches.

overture (prelude) Short musical composition, purely orchestral, which opens an opera and sets the overall dramatic mood. Orchestral introductions to later acts of an opera are called *preludes.*

pedal point (organ point) Single tone, usually in the bass, which is held while the other voices produce a series of changing harmonies against it; often found in fugues.

pentatonic scale Five-tone scale, such as that produced by the five black keys of the piano in succession, starting on any one of them (e.g., F♯–G♯–A♯–C♯–D♯); used in nonwestern music and impressionistic music.

percussion instrument Instrument of definite or indefinite pitch whose sound is produced by striking by hand, or with a stick or hammer, or by shaking or rubbing.

phrase Part of a melody.

pitch Relative highness or lowness of a sound.

pitch range Distance between the highest and lowest tones that a given voice or instrument can produce.

pizzicato Means of playing a string instrument by which the strings are plucked, usually with a finger of the right hand.

polonaise Composition in triple meter with a stately character, often for piano solo; originally a Polish court dance.

polychord Combination of two chords sounded at the same time, used in twentieth-century music.

polyphonic texture Performance of two or more melodic lines of relatively equal interest at the same time.

polyrhythm Use of two or more contrasting and independent rhythms at the same time, often found in twentieth-century music.

polytonality Approach to pitch organization using two or more keys at one time, often found in twentieth-century music.

postlude Concluding section; the section at the end of an art song which sums up its mood, played by the piano alone.

prelude (1) Short piece usually serving to introduce a fugue or other composition; a short piece for piano. (2) See *overture*.

primitivism Evocation of primitive power through insistent rhythms and percussive sounds, most notable in Stravinsky's *Rite of Spring* (1913).

program Explanatory comments specifying the story, scene, or idea associated with program music.

program music Instrumental music associated with a story, poem, idea, or scene, often found in romantic music.

program symphony Symphony (a composition for orchestra in several movements) related to a story, idea, or scene, in which each movement usually has a descriptive title; often found in romantic music.

progression Series of chords.

quadruple meter Pattern of 4 beats to the measure.

quadruple stop See *stop*.

quintuple meter Pattern of 5 beats to the measure.

ragtime Style of composed piano music, generally in duple meter with a moderate march tempo, in which the pianist's right hand plays a highly syncopated melody while the left hand maintains the beat with an "oom-pah" accompaniment. Ragtime was developed primarily by black American pianists and flourished from the 1890s to about 1915.

range See *pitch range*.

recapitulation Third section of a sonata-form movement, in which the first theme, bridge, second theme, and concluding section are presented more or less as they were in the exposition, with one crucial difference: all the principal material is now in the tonic key.

recitative Vocal line in an opera, oratorio, or cantata that imitates the rhythms and pitch fluctuations of speech, often serving to lead into an aria.

reed Very thin piece of cane, used in woodwind instruments to produce sound as it is set into vibration by a stream of air.

register Part of the total range of an instrument or voice. The tone color of the instrument or voice may vary with the register in which it is played or sung.

repetition Reiteration of a phrase, melody, or section, often used to create a sense of unity.

resolution   Progression from a dissonance to a consonance.

rest   In notation of rhythm, a symbol to indicate the duration of silence in the music.

retrograde   Variation of a fugue subject in which the subject is presented by beginning with its last note and proceeding backward to the first.

rhythm   Ordered flow of music through time; the pattern of durations of sounds and silences in music.

rhythm section   Instruments in a jazz ensemble which maintain the beat, add rhythmic interest, and provide supporting harmonies. The rhythm section is usually made up of piano, plucked double bass, percussion, and sometimes banjo or guitar.

ricercar   Polyphonic instrumental composition which makes extensive use of imitation, often found in Renaissance music.

riff   In jazz, a short repeated phrase that may be an accompaniment or a melody.

ritornello   In Italian, *refrain;* a repeated section of music usually played by the full orchestra, or tutti, in baroque compositions.

ritornello form   Compositional form usually employed in the baroque concerto grosso, in which the tutti plays a ritornello, or refrain, alternating with one or more soloists playing new material.

rock   First called *rock and roll,* a style of popular vocal music which developed in the 1950s, characterized by a hard, driving beat; featuring electric-guitar accompaniment and heavily amplified sound.

rondo   Compositional form featuring a main theme (A) which returns several times in alternation with other themes, such as A B A C A and A B A C A B A. Rondo is often the form of the last movement in classical symphonies, string quartets, and sonatas.

rubato   Slight holding back or pressing forward of tempo to intensify the expression of the music, often used in romantic music.

scale   Series of pitches arranged in order from low to high or high to low.

scherzo   Compositional form in three parts (A B A), sometimes used as the third movement in classical and romantic symphonies, string quartets, and other works. A scherzo is usually in triple meter, having a faster tempo than a minuet.

score   Notation showing all the parts of a musical ensemble, with a separate staff for each part, and with simultaneously sounded notes aligned vertically, used by the conductor.

secco recitative   Speechlike melody that is sung by a solo voice accompanied only by a basso continuo.

septuple meter   Pattern of 7 beats to the measure.

sequence   In a melody, the immediate repetition of a melodic pattern on a higher or lower pitch.

serenade   Instrumental composition, light in mood, usually meant for evening entertainment.

serialism   Method of composing which uses an ordered group of musical elements to organize rhythm, dynamics, and tone color, as well as pitch; developed in the mid-twentieth century.

series   See *tone row.*

set   See *tone row.*

sextuple meter   Pattern of 6 beats to the measure.

sharp sign   Symbol which notates a pitch one half step higher than the pitch that would otherwise be indicated—for example, the next higher black key on the piano.

single-reed woodwinds Instruments whose sound is produced by a single piece of cane, or reed, fastened over a hole in the mouthpiece, which vibrates when the player blows into it.

sonata In baroque music, an instrumental composition in several movements for one to eight players. In music after the baroque period, an instrumental composition usually in several movements for one or two players.

sonata form Form of a single movement, consisting of three main sections: the exposition, where the themes are presented; the development, where themes are treated in new ways; and the recapitulation, where the themes return. A concluding section, the coda, often follows the recapitulation.

sonata-rondo Compositional form that combines the repeating theme of rondo form with a development section similar to that in sonata form, outlined A B A–development–A B A.

song cycle Group of art songs unified by a story line that runs through their poems, or by musical ideas linking the songs; often found in romantic music.

sound Vibrations which are transmitted, usually through air, to the eardrum, which sends impulses to the brain.

Sprechstimme In German, *speech-voice;* a style of vocal performance halfway between speaking and singing, typical of Schoenberg and his followers.

staccato Short, detached manner of performing a melody.

staff In notation, a set of five horizontal lines between or on which notes are positioned.

stem Vertical line on a note indicating how long that note is to be held relative to the notes around it.

step Interval between two adjacent tones in the scale.

stop (double, triple, quadruple) Means of playing a string instrument by which the bow is drawn across two, three, or four strings at the same, or almost the same, time.

stretto Compositional procedure used in fugues, in which a subject is imitated before it is completed; one voice tries to catch the other.

string instrument Instrument whose sound is produced by the vibration of strings.

string quartet Composition employing two violins, a viola, and a cello; usually consisting of four movements. (*Also,* the four instrumentalists.)

strophic form Vocal form in which the same music is repeated for each stanza of a poem.

style Characteristic way of using melody, rhythm, tone, color, dynamics, harmony, texture, and form in music.

subdominant Fourth note (*fa*) of the scale, or the triad (chord) based on this note.

subject Theme of a fugue.

suite In baroque music, a set of dance-inspired movements that are all written in the same key but differ in tempo, meter, and character.

swing band Typically, a large band made up of fourteen or fifteen musicians grouped in three sections: saxophones, brasses, and rhythm. They play swing, a jazz style which was developed in the 1920s and flourished between 1935 and 1945.

symphonic poem (tone poem) Programmatic composition for orchestra in one movement, which may have a traditional form (such as sonata or rondo) or an original, irregular form.

symphony   Orchestral composition, usually in four movements, typically lasting between 20 and 45 minutes, exploiting the expanded range of tone color and dynamics of the orchestra.

syncopation   Accenting of a note at an unexpected time, as between two beats or on a weak beat. Syncopation is a major characteristic of jazz.

tempo   Basic pace of the music.

tempo indication   Words, usually at the beginning of a piece of music, often in Italian, which specify the pace at which the music should be played.

terraced dynamics   Abrupt alternation between loud and soft dynamic levels; characteristic of baroque music.

thematic transformation   Alteration of the character of a theme by means of changes in dynamics, orchestration, or rhythm, when it returns in a later movement or section; often found in romantic music.

theme   Melody which serves as the starting point for an extended piece of music.

theme and variations   Form in which a basic musical idea (the theme) is repeated over and over and is changed each time in melody, rhythm, harmony, dynamics, or tone color. Used as an independent piece or as one movement of a larger work.

three-part form (A B A)   Form that can be represented as statement (A); contrast (B); return of statement (A).

through-composed form   Vocal form in which there is new music for each stanza of a poem.

tie   In notation of rhythm, an arc between two notes of the same pitch indicating that the second note should be added to the duration of the first (the first note is not repeated).

timbre   See *tone color*.

time signature (meter signature)   Two numbers, one above the other, appearing at the beginning of the staff at the start of a piece, indicating the meter of the piece.

tonality   See *key*.

tone   Sound that has a definite pitch, or frequency.

tone cluster   Chord made up of tones only a half step or a whole step apart, used in twentieth-century music.

tone color (timbre)   Quality of sound that distinguishes one instrument or voice from another.

tone-color melody   Succession of varying tone colors serving as a musical idea in a composition, used by Schoenberg and his followers.

tone poem   See *symphonic poem*.

tone row (set, series)   Particular ordering of the twelve chromatic tones, from which all pitches in a twelve-tone composition are derived.

tonic   See *keynote*.

tonic chord   Triad built on the first, or tonic, note of the scale, serving as the main chord of a piece and usually beginning and ending it.

tonic key (home key)   Central key of a piece of music, usually both beginning and ending the piece, regardless of how many other keys are included.

transition   See *bridge*.

treble clef   Notation on a staff to indicate relatively high pitch ranges, such as those played by a pianist's right hand.

tremolo   Rapid repetition of a tone, produced in string instruments by quick up-and-down strokes of the bow.

triad   Most basic of chords, consisting of three alternate tones of the scale, such as *do, mi, sol.*

trill   Musical ornament consisting of the rapid alternation of two tones that are a whole or half step apart.

trio sonata   Baroque composition which has three melodic lines: two high ones, each played by one instrument; and a basso continuo, played by two instruments.

triple meter   Pattern of 3 beats to the measure.

triple stop   See *stop.*

triplet   In notation of rhythm, three notes of equal duration grouped within a curved line with the numeral 3, lasting only as long as two notes of this same length normally would last.

tutti   In Italian, *all;* the full orchestra, or a large group of musicians contrasted with a smaller group, often heard in baroque music.

12-bar blues   In vocal blues and jazz, a harmonic framework that is 12 bars in length, usually involving only three basic chords: tonic (I), subdominant, (IV), and dominant (V).

twelve-tone system   Method of composing in which all pitches of a composition are derived from a special ordering of the twelve chromatic tones (tone row or set); developed by Schoenberg in the early 1920s.

two-part form (A B)   Form that can be represented as statement (A) and counterstatement (B).

unison   Performance of a single melodic line by more than one instrument or voice.

upbeat   Unaccented pulse preceding the downbeat.

variation   Changing some features of a musical idea while retaining others.

vibrato   Small fluctuations of pitch which make the tone warmer, produced in string instruments by rocking the left hand while it presses the string down.

virtuoso   Artist of extraordinary technical mastery.

voice categories of opera   Voice ranges which include coloratura soprano, lyric soprano, dramatic soprano, lyric tenor, dramatic tenor, basso buffo, and basso profundo, among others.

whole step   Interval twice as large as the half step; for example, the interval between *do* and *re.*

whole-tone scale   Scale made up of six different tones, each a whole step away from the next, which conveys no definite sense of tonality; often found in the music of Debussy and his followers.

woodwind instrument   Instrument whose sound is produced by vibrations of air in a tube; holes along the length of tube are opened and closed by the fingers, or by pads, to control the pitch.

word painting   Musical representation of specific poetic images—for example, a falling melodic line to accompany the word *descending*—often found in Renaissance and baroque music.

CHRONOLOGY

MIDDLE AGES (450–1450)

Musicians	Artists and Writers	Historical and Cultural Events
		Sack of Rome by Vandals (455)
		Reign of Pope Gregory I (590–604)
		First Crusade (1096–1099)
Perotin (late twelfth century)		Beginning of Notre Dame Cathedral in Paris (1163)
		King John signs Magna Carta (1215)
	Dante (1265–1321)	
	Giotto (1266–1337)	
Guillaume de Machaut (c. 1300–1377)		
	Boccaccio (1313–1375)	
	Chaucer (c. 1343–1400)	Hundred Years' War (1337–1453)
		Black death (1348–1350)

RENAISSANCE (1450–1600)

Musicians	Artists and Writers	Historical and Cultural Events
Guillaume Dufay (c. 1400–1474)		Fall of Constantinople (1453)
Josquin Desprez (c. 1440–1521)	Leonardo da Vinci (1452–1519)	Gutenberg Bible (1456)
		Columbus discovers America (1492)
	Michelangelo (1475–1564)	
	Raphael (1483–1520)	Martin Luther's ninety-five theses (1517)
	Titian (c. 1477–1576)	
	François Rabelais (c. 1494–c. 1553)	

319

Musicians	Artists and Writers	Historical and Cultural Events
Andrea Gabrieli (c. 1520–1586)		
Giovanni Pierluigi da Palestrina (c. 1525–1594)		Council of Trent (1545–1563)
Roland de Lassus (1532–1594)	Michel de Montaigne (1533–1592)	
William Byrd (1543–1623)		
Giovanni Gabrieli (c. 1555–1612)		
Thomas Morley (1557–1603)	Cervantes (1547–1616)	Elizabeth I, queen of England (1558–1603)
	William Shakespeare (1564–1616)	
		Spanish Armada defeated (1588)
Thomas Weelkes (1575–1623)		

BAROQUE (1600–1750)

Musicians	Artists and Writers	Historical and Cultural Events
		Jamestown founded (1607)
Claudio Monteverdi (1567–1643)		
	Peter Paul Rubens (1577–1640)	
Heinrich Schütz (1585–1672)		Thirty Years' War (1618–1648)
	Gian Lorenzo Bernini (1598–1680)	
	Rembrandt (1606–1669)	
	John Milton (1608–1674)	
Jean-Baptiste Lully (1632–1687)	Molière (1622–1673)	Louis XIV reigns in France (1643–1715)
	Baruch Spinoza (1632–1677)	
Arcangelo Corelli (1653–1713)		
Henry Purcell (c. 1659–1695)	Jonathan Swift (1667–1745)	Newton, *Principia Mathematica* (1687)
François Couperin (1668–1733)		
Antonio Vivaldi (1678–1741)		Louis XV reigns in France (1715–1774)
Johann Sebastian Bach (1685–1750)	Jean Antoine Watteau (1684–1721)	
George Frideric Handel (1685–1759)		

CLASSICAL (1750–1820)

Musicians	Artists and Writers	Historical and Cultural Events
	Voltaire (1694–1778)	Maria Theresa reigns in Austria (1740–1780)
		Frederick the Great reigns in Prussia (1740–1786)
	Benjamin Franklin (1706–1790)	Publication of the French *Encyclopedia* begins (1751)
Christoph Gluck (1714–1787)	Jean Jacques Rousseau (1712–1778)	
		Seven Years' War (1756–1763)
Carl Philipp Emanuel Bach (1714–1788)		Winckelmann's *History of the Art of Antiquity* (1764)
	Immanuel Kant (1724–1804)	
Joseph Haydn (1732–1809)		
	Goya (1746–1828)	
	Jacques Louis David (1748–1825)	
	Johann Wolfgang von Goethe (1749–1832)	Louis XVI reigns in France (1774–1792)
Wolfgang Amadeus Mozart (1756–1791)		American Declaration of Independence (1776)
Ludwig van Beethoven (1770–1827)		French Revolution begins (1789)
		Eli Whitney invents cotton gin (1792)
		Napoleon becomes first consul of France (1799)
		Battle of Waterloo (1815)

ROMANTIC (1820–1900)

Musicians	Artists and Writers	Historical and Cultural Events
	William Wordsworth (1770–1850)	
	J. M. W. Turner (1775–1851)	
Carl Maria von Weber (1786–1826)		
Gioacchino Rossini (1792–1868)		
Franz Schubert (1797–1828)	Heinrich Heine (1797–1856)	
	Eugène Delacroix (1798–1863)	

321

Musicians	Artists and Writers	Historical and Cultural Events
	Honoré de Balzac (1799–1850)	Revolutions in France, Belgium, Poland (1830)
Hector Berlioz (1803–1869)	Victor Hugo (1802–1885)	
	George Sand (1804–1876)	First Reform Bill in Britain (1832)
Felix Mendelssohn (1809–1847)	Edgar Allan Poe (1809–1849)	
Frédéric Chopin (1810–1849)		Revolutions of 1848; Marx and Engels, *The Communist Manifesto* (1848)
Robert Schumann (1810–1856)		
Franz Liszt (1811–1886)		Darwin's *Origin of Species* (1859)
		American Civil War (1861–1865)
	Charles Dickens (1812–1870)	
Richard Wagner (1813–1883)		Franco-Prussian War (1870)
Giuseppe Verdi (1813–1901)		
César Franck (1822–1890)	Fëdor Dostoevsky (1821–1881)	
Anton Bruckner (1824–1896)		
Bedřich Smetana (1824–1884)	Leo Tolstoy (1828–1910)	
	Emily Dickinson (1830–1886)	
Johannes Brahms (1833–1897)	Edouard Manet (1832–1883)	
Georges Bizet (1838–1875)	Paul Cézanne (1839–1906)	
Modest Mussorgsky (1839–1881)		
Peter Ilyich Tchaikovsky (1840–1893)	Claude Monet (1840–1926)	First group exhibition of impressionists in Paris (1874)
Antonin Dvořák (1841–1904)	Stéphane Mallarmé (1842–1898)	
John Philip Sousa (1854–1932)		
Giacomo Puccini (1858–1924)	Friedrich Nietzsche (1844–1900)	Bell invents telephone (1876)
Gustav Mahler (1860–1911)		
	Vincent Van Gogh (1853–1890)	
Richard Strauss (1864–1949)		Spanish-American War (1898)

TWENTIETH CENTURY

Musicians	Artists and Writers	Historical and Cultural Events
		Freud, *The Psychopathology of Everyday Life* (1904)
Claude Debussy (1862–1918)	Wassily Kandinsky (1866–1944)	Einstein, special theory of relativity (1905)
Scott Joplin (1868–1917)		

Musicians	Artists and Writers	Historical and Cultural Events
	Henri Matisse (1869–1954)	
	Marcel Proust (1871–1922)	
Arnold Schoenberg (1874–1951)	Gertrude Stein (1874–1946)	
		World War I (1914–1918)
Charles Ives (1874–1954)		Russian Revolution begins (1917)
Maurice Ravel (1875–1937)		
Béla Bartók (1881–1945)	Pablo Picasso (1881–1973)	
	James Joyce (1882–1941)	Beginning of Great Depression (1929)
	Virginia Woolf (1882–1945)	
Igor Stravinsky (1882–1971)		
	Franz Kafka (1883–1924)	Franklin D. Roosevelt inaugurated (1933)
Anton Webern (1883–1945)		Hitler Chancellor of Germany (1933)
Edgard Varèse (1883–1965)		
Alban Berg (1885–1935)		
	T. S. Eliot (1888–1965)	World War II (1939–1945)
Sergei Prokofiev (1891–1953)		
Bessie Smith (1894–1937)		
Paul Hindemith (1895–1963)		
Roger Sessions (b. 1896)		
George Gershwin (1898–1937)	William Faulkner (1897–1962)	
E. K. ("Duke") Ellington (1899–1974)	Henry Moore (b. 1898)	
	Ernest Hemingway (1899–1961)	
Louis Armstrong (1900–1971)	Louise Nevelson (b. 1900)	
Aaron Copland (b. 1900)	Isaac Bashevis Singer (b. 1904)	
Ruth Crawford-Seeger (1901–1953)		
Miriam Gideon (b. 1906)	Willem de Kooning (b. 1904)	
Dmitri Shostakovich (1906–1975)	Jean Paul Sartre (1905–1980)	
Elliott Carter (b. 1908)	David Smith (1906–1965)	
Olivier Messiaen (b. 1908)		Atomic bomb destroys Hiroshima (1945)
John Cage (b. 1912)		Korean war begins (1950)
Benjamin Britten (1913–1976)	Jackson Pollock (1912–1956)	

Musicians	Artists and Writers	Historical and Cultural Events
Billie Holiday (1915–1959)	Albert Camus (1913–1960)	
	Saul Bellow (b. 1915)	
	Robert Motherwell (b. 1915)	
Milton Babbitt (b. 1916)	Andrew Wyeth (b. 1917)	
Leonard Bernstein (b. 1918)		
Charlie Parker (1920–1955)	Alexander Solzhenitsyn (b. 1918)	
Pierre Boulez (b. 1925)	Roy Lichtenstein (b. 1923)	
John Coltrane (1926–1967)	Norman Mailer (b. 1923)	
Karlheinz Stockhausen (b. 1928)	James Baldwin (b. 1924)	American involvement in Vietnam increases dramatically (1965)
	Allen Ginsberg (b. 1926)	
	John Hollander (b. 1928)	
	Helen Frankenthaler (b. 1928)	
George Crumb (b. 1929)	Andy Warhol (1931–1987)	
Joe Zawinul (b. 1932)		
Krzysztof Penderecki (b. 1933)		American astronauts land on moon (1969)
Mario Davidovsky (b. 1934)		
Steve Reich (b. 1936)		
Charles Wuorinen (b. 1938)		Resignation of President Nixon (1974)
Philip Glass (b. 1937)		
Ellen Taaffe Zwilich (b. 1939)		
John Lennon (1940–1980)		End of American involvement in Vietnam (1975)
		United States and China establish diplomatic relations (1979)
		Revolution in Iran (1979)
		Ronald Reagan inaugurated (1981)
		Wars in Lebanon and the Falkland Islands (1982)
		Ronald Reagan inaugurated for second term (1985)
		Nuclear accident at Chernobyl, Soviet Union (1986)

RECORDINGS

6. Desprez: *Ave Maria . . . virgo serena*
7. A. Gabrieli: *Ricercar in the Twelfth Mode*
8. Weelkes: *As Vesta Was Descending*
9. Morley: *Now Is the Month of Maying*
10. G. Gabrieli: *Plaudite*, Motet in Twelve Parts for Three Choirs

Side 2
1. Praetorius: *La Bourée*
2. Monteverdi: *Tu se' morta* from *Orfeo*, Act II
3. Purcell: *Dido's Lament* from *Dido and Aeneas*
4. Vivaldi: *La Primavera*, Concerto for Violin and String Orchestra, Op. 8, No. 1, from *The Four Seasons*, first movement
5. Bach: *Brandenburg* concerto No. 5 in D Major, first movement
6. Bach: Organ Fugue in G Minor *(Little Fugue)*
7. Bach: *Badinerie* from Suite No. 2 in B Minor, S. 1067.

Side 3
1. Bach: Air from Suite No. 3 in D Major, S. 1068
2. Bach: Gigue from Suite No. 3 in D Major, S. 1068
3. Bach: Cantata No. 140: *Wachet auf, ruft uns die Stimme*, first movement
4. Bach: Cantata No. 140: *Wachet auf, ruft uns die Stimme*, fourth movement
5. Bach: Contata No. 140: *Wachet auf, ruft uns die Stimme*, seventh movement
6. Handel: *Comfort ye, my people*, from *Messiah*
7. Handel: *Ev'ry valley shall be exalted*, from *Messiah*

Side 4
1. Handel: *For unto us a Child is born*, from *Messiah*
2. Handel: *Hallelujah* chorus from *Messiah*
3. Haydn: Symphony No. 94 in G Major *(Suprise)*, second movement
4. Haydn: Trumpet Concerto in E Flat Major, third movement
5. Mozart: *Eine kleine Nachtmusik* K. 525, third movement

6. Mozart, Symphony No. 40 in G Minor, K. 550, first movement

Side 5
1. Mozart: Symphony No. 40 in G Minor, K. 550, third movement
2. Mozart: Symphony No. 40 in G Minor, K. 550, fourth movement
3. Mozart: *Don Giovanni*, K. 527, Act I: Introduction (opening scene)
4. Mozart: *Don Giovanni*, K. 527, Act I: Catalog aria *(Madamina)*
5. Mozart: *Don Giovanni*, K. 527, Act I: *Là ci darem la mano*
6. Beethoven: String Quartet in C Minor, Op. 18, No. 4, fourth movement

Side 6
1. Beethoven: Symphony No. 5 in C Minor, Op. 67, first movement
2. Beethoven: Symphony No. 5 in C Minor, Op. 67, second movement
3. Beethoven: Symphony No. 5 in C Minor, Op. 67, third and fourth movements

Side 7
1. Beethoven: Piano Sonata in C Minor, Op. 13 *(Pathétique)*, first movement
2. Beethoven: Piano Sonata in C Minor, Op. 13 *(Pathétique)*, second movement
3. Beethoven: Piano Sonata in C Minor, Op. 13 *(Pathétique)*, third movement
4. Schubert: Piano Quintet in A Major, D. 667 *(Trout)*, fourth movement
5. Schubert: *Erlkönig*
6. Schubert: *Heidenröslein*

Side 8
1. Schumann: *Aufschwung* from *Fantasiestücke*, Op. 12
2. Chopin: Prelude in E Minor, Op. 28, No. 4
3. Chopin: Prelude in C Minor for Piano, Op. 28, No. 20
4. Chopin: Nocturne in E Flat Major, Op. 9, No. 2
5. Chopin: Étude in C Minor, Op. 10, No. 12 *(Revolutionary)*
6. Mendelssohn: Concerto for

Violin and Orchestra in E Minor, Op. 64, first movement
7. Bizet: *Farandole* from *L'Arlésienne* Suite No. 2

Side 9
1. Liszt: *Les Préludes*
2. Smetana: *The Moldau* from *Má Vlast*

Side 10
1. Berlioz: *Symphonie fantastique*, fourth movement *(March to the Scaffold)*
2. Tchaikovsky: *Romeo and Juliet*, Overture-Fantasy
3. Tchaikovsky: *Dance of the Reed Pipes* from *Nutcracker* Suite, Op. 71a
4. Sousa: *The Stars and Stripes Forever*

Side 11
1. Verdi: *La donna è mobile* and Quartet from *Rigoletto*, Act III
2. Puccini: *La Bohème*, Act I: excerpt (Mimi's entrance through conclusion of act)
3. Wagner: *Lohengrin*, Prelude to Act III

Side 12
1. Wagner: *Götterdämmerung*, Act III: *Immolation* Scene (conclusion)
2. Brahms: Symphony No. 4 in E Minor, Op. 98, fourth movement
3. Debussy: *Prélude à "L'Après-midi d'un Faune"*
4. Stravinsky: *Firebird* Suite, Finale

Side 13
1. Stravinsky: *Russian Dance* from *Petrushka*
2. Stravinsky: *Introduction, Omens of Spring—Dances of the Youths and Maidens, Ritual of Abduction*, from *Le Sacre du Printemps*, Part I
3. Stravinsky: *Sacrificial Dance* from *Le Sacre du Printemps*, Part II
4. Stravinsky: *Symphony of Psalms*, first movement
5. Schoenberg: Five Pieces for Orchestra, Op. 16, 1: *Vorgefühle*
6. Schoenberg: *A Survivor from Warsaw*, Op. 46

7. Webern: Five Pieces for Orchestra, Op. 10, 3: Very slow and extremely calm

Side 14
1. Berg: Wozzark, Act III, Scenes 4 and 5
2. Bartók: Concerto for Orchestra, first movement
3. Ives: *Putnam's Camp, Redding, Connecticut,* from *Three Places in New England*
4. Copland: *Appalachian Spring,* section 7: theme and variations on *Simple Gifts*
5. Babbitt: *Composition for Synthesizer,* excerpt

Side 15
1. Carter: Sonata for Flute, Oboe, Cello, and Harpsichord, first movement
2. Varèse: *Poème électronique*
3. Crumb: *From Where Do You Come, My Love, My Child?* from *Ancient Voices of Children*
4. Zwilich: *Reversal,* from *Passages* for Soprano and Instrumental Ensemble
5. Joplin: *Maple Leaf Rag*
6. Smith: *Lost Your Head Blues*
7. Oliver: *Dippermouth Blues*

8. Lillian Hardin Armstrong: *Hotter Than That*

Side 16
1. Berlin: *Blue Skies*
2. Ellington: *Concerto for Cootie*
3. Parker: *KoKo*
4. Brubeck: *Unsquare Dance*
5. Zawinul: *Birdland,* excerpt
6. Song from Angola (Gangele Song)
7. *Mitamba Yalagala Kumchuzi*
8. *Hinganyengisa Masingita*
9. *Maru-Bihag,* excerpt
10. Mitsuzaki Kengyo: *Godan Ginuta*

INSTRUCTOR'S RECORD SET FOR MUSIC: AN APPRECIATION FOURTH EDITION

Side 1
1. Palestrina: Kyrie from *Pope Marcellus Mass*
2. Corelli: Trio Sonata in E Minor, Op. 3, No. 7, first movement
3. Corelli: Trio Sonata in E Minor, Op. 3, No. 7, second movement
4. Mozart: Piano Concerto in D Minor, K. 466, first movement

5. Beethoven: String Quartet in F Major, Op. 18, No. 1, first movement

Side 2
1. Berlioz: *Symphonie fantastique,* fifth movement (*Dream of a Witches' Sabbath*)
2. Mussorgsky: Coronation Scene from *Boris Gudonov*
3. Mahler: Symphony No. 1 in D Major, third movement

Side 3
1. Dvořák: Symphony No. 9 in E Minor, Op. 95 (*From the New World*), first movement
2. Schoenberg: Five Pieces for Orchestra, Op. 16, 2: *Vergangenes*
3. Gershwin: *Rhapsody in Blue*

Side 4
1. Debussy: *Fêtes,* from *Nocturnes*
2. Bartók: Concerto for Orchestra, second movement (*Game of Pairs*)
3. Britten: *The Young Person's Guide to the Orchestra* (Variations and Fugue on a Theme of Purcell)

ACKNOWLEDGEMENTS

PART-OPENING PHOTOGRAPHS

I. Burton McNeely/Image Bank
II. Glasgow University Library
III. Dick Davis/Photo Researchers
IV. National Gallery, London
V. Deutsche Fotothek Dresden
VI. Henri Matisse. *Piano Lesson.* 1916. Oil on canvas, 8½" × 6' 11¾". Collection, The Museum of Modern Art, New York. Mrs. Simon Guggenheim Fund.

MUSIC AND MUSICAL TEXTS

Bach, Johann Sebastian: Cantata No. 140. Translated by Gerhard Herz. In Roger Kamien (ed.): *The Norton Scores,* Norton, New York, 1970. Copyright 1970, W. W. Norton.

Bartók, Béla: *Six Dances in Bulgarian Rhythm* from *Mikrokosmos,* vol. 6, nos. 148–153. Copyright © 1940 by Hawkes & Son (London) Ltd. Renewed 1967. Reprinted by permission of Boosey & Hawkes, Inc.

Berg, Alban: *Wozzeck,* Act III, scenes 4 and 5. Translation by Eric Blackall and Vida Harford. © 1923, 1931 by Universal Edition, A. G., Wien.

English translation © 1952 by Alfred A. Kalmus, London. Copyright renewed. All rights reserved. Reprinted by permission of European American Music Distributors Corporation, sole U.S. agent for Universal Edition.

Carter, Elliott: Sonata for Flute, Oboe, Cello, and Harpsichord. Copyright © 1962 by Associated Music Publishers. Reprinted by permission of Associated Music Publishers.

Copland, Aaron: *Appalachian Spring.* Copyright © 1945 by Aaron Copland. Renewed 1972. Reprinted by permission of Aaron Copland, copyright owner, and Boosey & Hawkes, Inc., sole licensees.

Crumb, George: *Dance of the Sacred Life Cycle* from *Ancient Voices of Children.* Copyright © 1970 by C. F. Peters Corporation. Reprint permission granted by the publisher. Texts by Federico García Lorca, translations by J. L. Gili and Edwin Honig. Copyright © 1955 by New Directions Publishing Corp. Reprinted by permission of New Directions.

Gershwin, George: *Rhapsody in Blue.* © 1924 (renewed) W B Music Corp. All rights reserved. Re-

printed by permission of Warner Bros. Music Corp.

Ives, Charles: *Three Places in New England.* © 1935 Mercury Music Corporation. Reprinted by permission of Mercury Music Corporation.

Ives, Charles: *Three Places in New England.* © 1935 Mercury Music Corporation. Reprinted by permission of Mercury Music Corporation.

Mozart, Wolfgang Amadeus: *Don Giovanni.* Translation of libretto by William Murray. Copyright © 1961 Capitol Records, Inc. Reprinted by permission of Angel Records.

Puccini, Giacomo: *La Bohème.* Translation of libretto by William Weaver. Copyright © 1952 Capitol Records, Inc. Reprinted by permission of Angel Records.

Schoenberg, Arnold: *Five Pieces for Orchestra.* Copyright © 1952 by Henmar Press, Inc., New York. Reprinted by permission of C. F. Peters Corporation, publisher.

Schoenberg, Arnold: *A Survivor from Warsaw.* Copyright © 1949 by Boelke-Bomart, Inc. Reprinted by permission of Associated Music Publishers.

Schubert, Franz: *Der Erlkönig.* Translation from Philip L. Miller (ed.): *The Ring of Words.* Reprinted by permission of Doubleday & Company, Inc., and Philip L. Miller.

Stravinsky, Igor: *The Rite of Spring.* © 1913. Reprinted by permission of Boosey & Hawkes, Inc.

Verdi, Giuseppe: *Rigoletto.* Translation of libretto by William Weaver. © 1963 by William Weaver. Reprinted by permission of Doubleday & Company, Inc., and William Weaver.

Wagner, Richard: *Götterdämmerung.* Translation of libretto by Stewart Robb. Copyright © 1960 by Stewart Robb. All rights reserved. Reprinted by permission of G. Schirmer.

Zwilich, Ellen Taaffe: *Reversal* from *Passages.* © 1983 Margun Music, Inc., Newton Center, Massachusetts. Text by A. R. Ammons from *Collected Poems 1951–1971.* Copyright © 1972 by A. R. Ammons. Reprinted by permission of W. W. Norton and Company, Inc.

QUOTATIONS

Large, Brian. *Smetana.* Copyright 1970. Reprinted by permission of Henry Holt and Company, Inc.

Schwartz, Charles: *Gershwin, His Life and Music.* Copyright 1973 by Charles Schwartz. Reprinted by permission of the author.

Shapiro, Nat, and Nat Hentoff. *Hear Me Talkin' to Ya.* © 1955 by Nat Shapiro and Nat Hentoff. Reprinted by permission of Henry Holt and Company, Inc.

REPRODUCTIONS FROM THE MUSEUM OF MODERN ART

In Part VI:

Henri Matisse. *Piano Lesson.* 1916. Oil on canvas, 8½" × 6' 11¾". Collection, The Museum of Modern Art, New York. Mrs. Simon Guggenheim Fund.

Pablo Picasso. *Girl Before a Mirror.* 1932, March 14. Oil on canvas, 64" × 51¼". Collection, The Museum of Modern Art, New York. Gift of Mrs. Simon Guggenheim.

Pablo Picasso. *Les Demoiselles d'Avignon.* 1907. Oil on canvas, 8' × 7'8". Collection, The Museum of Modern Art. Acquired through the Lillie P. Bliss bequest.

Color Plates:

Ernst Ludwig Kirchner. *Street Scene Dresden.* 1908; dated on painting 1907. Oil on canvas, 59¼" × 6' ⅞".

Collection, The Museum of Modern Art, New York. Purchase.

Wassily Kandinsky. *Painting No. 198.* 1914. Oil on canvas, 64 × 31½". Collection, The Museum of Modern Art, New York. Mrs. Simon Guggenheim Fund.

Wassily Kandinsky. *Painting No. 200.* 1914. Oil on canvas, 64 × 31½". Collection, The Museum of Modern Art, New York. Mrs. Simon Guggenheim Fund.

Pablo Picasso. *Three Musicians.* 1921 (summer). Oil on canvas, 6'7" × 7'3¾". Collection, The Museum of Modern Art, New York. Mrs. Simon Guggenheim Fund.

Andy Warhol. Untitled, from the portfolio *Marilyn.* 1967. Serigraph, printed in color, 36 × 36". Collection, The Museum of Modern Art, New York. Gift of David Whitney.

INDEX

Note: Page references in *italic* indicate illustrations; the notation (LO) indicates a Listening Outline; *n.* indicates a footnote.

331

335

338

341

342